MASKS OF LOVE
AND DEATH

Yeats as Dramatist

MASKS OF LOVE
AND DEATH

Yeats as Dramatist

JOHN REES MOORE

Cornell University Press

ITHACA AND LONDON

International Standard Book Number 0-8014-0608-0
Library of Congress Catalog Card Number 70-137012

PRINTED IN THE UNITED STATES OF AMERICA
BY VAIL-BALLOU PRESS, INC.

To my mother,
    Florence Rees Moore

Contents

Contents

Preface

Yeats's plays span almost his entire writing career and represent a notable effort on the part of a great poet to restore poetry to the theater. My study of Yeats the playwright and my interpretive readings of his plays are not intended to be "definitive"—we are still too close to Yeats for that. But I do hope to gain more readers for the plays, and to help those already familiar with them to understand them better. They can, I think, stand on their own without inordinate claims being made for them.

In Part I of the book, I explore the reasons why Yeats felt compelled to become a dramatist. His imagination was self-centered, but he could conceive of the self only in terms of conflict. Moreover, he was aware of the temptation and danger of reverie; the antidote was to bring his art directly into the world so that he could see and hear its immediate effect on others. Fortunately, what he wanted to do for himself and what he wanted to do for his country came together. I try to show how his literary patriotism and his poetic ideals interact in his experiments in playwriting. His doctrine of the mask can be viewed as both a means and an end; it is a strategy for carrying on the quarrel he had with himself and others, but it is also a plan for comprehending the final goals of human achievement and their cosmic significance.

Yeats's strong sense of the ritual substructure of art appears in both his theory and practice. To emphasize the ritual was to de-emphasize the surface of life, to restore a lost ideal of community based on admiration for the heroic virtues: devotion to a precious racial heritage and the courage to die for one's convictions. The Yeatsian hero (or heroine) is always identified with a kind of divine principle that far transcends personal ambition; in fact, heroic strength shows itself less in the assertion of individual will than in a triumphant surrender to impersonal, supernatural law. The moment Yeats wanted to capture in his plays is that still point where the most fundamental human passions merge into a timeless gesture of dispassionate acceptance. He was not interested (as a dramatist) in creating an imitation of the busy contemporary life around him, and yet, since he believed that *permanent* truth is embodied in ritual and myth, he would never have been willing (except ironically) to grant that his plays were antiquarian or irrelevant to modernity. But it is drama he was after. One cannot imagine him wanting to devote close study to the rituals of a truly primitive society. He required the sophisticated richness of occult symbolism as well as the fierce simplicity of a life unencumbered by the complications of urban existence.

I describe how Yeats developed his conception of Cuchulain from the figure that emerges (in English translation) from the early saga material. It is fascinating to see how Yeats strives to keep some of the primitive roughness of this archetypal Irish hero while reshaping him into an aristocratic culture hero who will be a fit vehicle to express Yeats's deepest convictions about the problem of being a superman among more ordinary mortals. A central irony of this predicament is that, though the hero is caught in a situation where he rebels against the authority of the society in which he finds himself, he is asserting values on behalf of the very people he opposes. The tragedy of being a hero is that every good he struggles for brings suffering on himself and others. For Yeats this suffering took the particular form of an ever-increasing distance between the hero and the everyday world of common sense. Finally, to be a hero is hardly distinguishable from being insane—with the very important reservation that in the fantasy world that the hero inhabits he is still a champion, in however perverted or ineffective a way, of true value.

Part II of the book consists of commentaries on individual plays. In looking at the plays up to 1910, I emphasize Yeats's developing conception of the dramatic hero, but I also try to convey some sense of contemporary attitudes toward the plays and of later critical opinion. Because *The King's Threshold, On Baile's Strand,* and *Deirdre* are the major dramatic achievements of this period, I give each of them a chapter, attempting to show how theme, structure, and language contribute to a unified dramatic effect. I also devote a full chapter to *The Player Queen,* because it seems to me of crucial interest as an example of Yeats's art; and it represents a kind of summing up of what Yeats had learned as a dramatist, although simultaneously it points the direction his future efforts would take. The later plays, more esoteric than the earlier ones, nevertheless are as much a continuation of the dramatic themes and techniques of the younger Yeats as they are a new departure. Because of their greater complexity, they demand (and repay) a somewhat fuller analysis in proportion to their length than the earlier plays require. My contention is that their symbolic richness never destroys the basically simple, ritualistic pattern underneath. Yeats's sophistication was always in the service of a profound, and essentially dramatic, simplicity.

Yeats's efforts to create a theater both popular and distinguished, to provide a focus for truly national aspirations founded on both an emotional and intellectual attachment to a great tradition lost sight of for many centuries, are often regarded as misplaced. If his achievement failed to match his dream—and of course it did—the degree of his success is nevertheless astonishing. Frank O'Connor says: "Sometimes one gets the impression that all the vital political issues of the time were unimportant compared with the task of bringing the name of Cu Chulainn into English literature. This was finally achieved by a combination of great Celtic scholars and the literary genius of Yeats and his circle, and by the year 1910 it could be said that Irish literature again existed in something like the way in which it had existed about the year 800." [1] Though Yeats himself became discouraged with the Abbey Theatre and turned his attention to a less "popular" kind of drama, it may take some time before we are able to disentangle what failed from what succeeded.

My work has been made possible by a Danforth grant to the first Yeats Summer School in Sligo in 1960 and by a sabbatical leave to study in Ireland in 1962–1963. Miss Dorothy Doerr of the Hollins College Library and Mr. Alf MacLochlainn of the National Library in Dublin have been particularly helpful. To David Krause for his critical reading and practical suggestions I owe much; the book is more shapely than it might have been because of his keen eye for

[1] *A Short History of Irish Literature* (New York, 1967), p. 6.

what should stay in and what should go out. For what isn't there but should be, however, he cannot be blamed. I am also grateful to Mrs. Elizabeth Riley for typing the manuscript. Parts of the book appeared in a slightly different form in *Modern Drama* for December, 1964, and in the *Sewanee Review* for Autumn, 1968, copyright by the University of the South.

During the years in which Yeats has seldom been far from my thoughts my wife, Betty, has contributed vital encouragement, fertile ideas, and practical assistance. Without her help the book could not have come into being.

For permission to quote from copyrighted materials, acknowledgment is gratefully made to the following: To A. P. Watt & Son, London, on behalf of M. B. Yeats, Anne Butler Yeats, and the Macmillan Companies of London and Canada, and to the Macmillan Company, New York, for quotations from *The Variorum Edition of the Poems of W. B. Yeats*, edited by Peter Allt and Russell K. Alspach, copyright 1903, 1906, 1907, 1912, 1916, 1918, 1919, 1924, 1928, 1931, 1933, 1934, 1935, 1940, 1944, 1945, 1946, 1950, 1956, 1957, by the Macmillan Company, copyright 1940, by Georgie Yeats, published by the Macmillan Company, the Macmillan Company of Canada, and Macmillan & Company, Limited; from *Explorations*, by W. B. Yeats, copyright Mrs. W. B. Yeats 1962, published by the Macmillan Company, the Macmillan Company of Canada, and Macmillan & Company, Limited; from *Essays and Introductions*, by W. B. Yeats, copyright Mrs. W. B. Yeats 1961, published by the Macmillan Company, the Macmillan Company of Canada, and Macmillan & Company, Limited; from *The Autobiography of William Butler Yeats*, by W. B. Yeats, copyright 1916, 1936, by the

JOHN REES MOORE

Hollins College
November 1970

[PART I]

THE USES OF DRAMA

[1]

The Making of the Mask

In one sense, people were less important to Yeats than the truths they embodied; the accidents of character were as nothing compared to the substance of immutable passions and motives. In poetic tragedy—for Yeats the greatest form of drama—the supreme moments come when character gives way to "tragic reverie" and "all is lyricism, unmixed passion, 'the integrity of fire.'" The busyness of individual existence fades away to disclose the eternal gestures of the fundamental Man or Woman, and no matter how uncommonly well language may express the heart's desire or aversion, it speaks of common things. Nor, says Yeats, would we think of saying in these moments

"How well that man is realised! I should know him were I to meet him in the street," for it is always ourselves that we see upon the stage, and should it be a tragedy of love, we renew, it may be, some loyalty of our youth, and go from the theatre with our eyes dim for an old love's sake.[1]

This sounds middle-aged, and in fact "The Tragic Theatre" was written in 1910—and Synge's *Deirdre of the Sorrows* was fresh in Yeats's memory. A young man or woman would undoubtedly put his or her reaction differently. But

[1] *Essays and Introductions* (London, 1961), pp. 240–241.

the process of identification Yeats is describing clearly differentiates pleasure in mimesis from the ecstasy of a communion. The ideal spectator is enabled to recollect his own moments of most intense life and, by sharing his emotion with the rest of the audience (even though silently), to enlarge his capacity for exalted experience. It is as though all those gathered together become a fellowship of kings and queens in full possession of a language adequate to express the pity, terror, and wonder of loving and dying with appropriate grandeur. Compared to this tragic joy, the undeniable satisfaction we take from a spirited and convincing display of human diversity is a lesser thing.

As we grow older, Yeats thought, we develop those individual idiosyncrasies that give us character; unspoiled youth has much passion but little character. "[Character] grows," he says paraphrasing Congreve, "with time like the ash of a burning stick, and strengthens towards middle life till there is little else at seventy years." [2] The prospect of strengthening into ash is not a cheerful one, but the figure accurately represents Yeats's bias in favor of "the integrity of fire." The pressure of circumstance reduces us to creatures of habit and the wrong sort of eccentricity unless we can devise some way to make our desires the shaping force of our personalities. The mask became for Yeats a means of combatting the erosion of exterior fate. More than an ideal of character, the mask was that anti-self reminding the poet that *his* reality was not the comings and goings outside his window in the street, but the comings and goings in his own mind. But, as we have seen, Yeats did not (at least in theory) regard what was peculiar to him as the most interesting part of his mind. What came to him from the space-

[2] *Ibid.*, p. 241.

and-time-free region associated with revery and dream made possible his art, and sometimes this art itself he sees as mask. So he says, "If we are painters, we shall express personal emotion through ideal form, a symbolism handled by the generations, a mask from whose eyes the disembodied looks." [3] (He speaks of painters but his thought equally applies to poets.) The mask is both an end and a means. As the expression of a great life attitude it urges a man on to remake himself in order to be worthy of it; as the image of a certain philosophy of life it serves to link nature and supernature, the visible and the invisible. And this was what Yeats intended his art to do.

He came to realize that energetic pursuit of the mask, involving great intensification of the will, was not the proper task for all men. Some, like AE, must empty their hearts and wills, "become the lamp for another's wick and oil," the vehicle for a creative energy not their own. This is the way of the saint and the scientist, the moralist and the politician.[4] But for all those "who must spin a web out of their own bowels," daily existence is a continual battle against fate, a recapturing of the vital essence time would snatch away. For they are divided against themselves and have no choice but to struggle unceasingly for a lost unity of being. It is their (and his own) predicament Yeats has in mind in his famous statement, "We begin to live when we have conceived life as tragedy." [5]

Whether or not Yeats would have approved of the later fashionable primitivism, with its cult of native wood-carving and its sophisticated rejection of European inhibitions (a movement he largely anticipated), his idea of the mask has

[3] *Ibid.*, p. 243.   [4] *Autobiography* (New York, 1938), p. 150.
[5] *Ibid.*, p. 116.

something in common with its primitive tradition in those cultures brought to light by anthropologists in the later nineteenth century and since. In rites of initiation, for instance, the mask can represent the longed for future state of the wearer. More than that, it can help the wearer transform himself from one state to another. Frazer noted its metamorphic use among Oceanian peoples. In this magical aspect, "the mask is equivalent to the chrysalis." [6] It always retains a certain ambiguity because it both reveals and conceals. It offers a way of exploring possibilities, of practicing the willing suspension of disbelief, in order to penetrate that area of experience where the logical distinctions of the secular world yield to the entirely different rules of a divine game. And because this is a realm of metaphor and analogy, "whenever a myth has been taken literally the sense has been perverted; but also . . . whenever it has been dismissed as a mere priestly fraud or sign of inferior intelligence, truth has slipped out the other door." [7] Yeats's ability to believe many things (in contrast to the type of mind that finds it difficult to believe anything) made it possible for him to play the divine game with a confidence that was shocking to some and a source of amusement to others.

As a student of myth, Yeats examined claims with a sharp eye and was a connoisseur of comparative mythology; but as a practicing mythologist himself, he interpreted the world as a vast arena in which conflicting human purposes were forever engaged in realizing and unrealizing themselves at each other's expense. In the long view, everything was con-

[6] See J. E. Cirlot, *A Dictionary of Symbols* (New York, 1962), pp. 195–196.

[7] Joseph Campbell, *The Masks of God: Primitive Mythology* (New York, 1959), p. 27. For a lucid rationale of the psychology of myth, see pp. 21–29.

nected with everything else in one great continuum; nothing was ever lost. In the shorter view of the individual life or historical epoch, however, the pain of loss was a conspicuous and unavoidable condition, and the more painful in proportion to one's awareness of incompatible alternatives. Yeats's mythological approach may have blinded him to certain qualities of human character and unduly limited his sympathies—his basis for rejecting Wilfred Owen from *The Oxford Book of Modern Verse* and his attack on O'Casey's *The Silver Tassie* are cases in point—but it helped him to focus life's meanings and to disengage the significant from the trivial. How central to all his work the aspiring will and the effort to understand, if not answer, the great questions!

The way to rise above the more or less violent unpleasantness of conflicting desires and aversions, Yeats discovered, was to find joy in the struggle itself. So in Balzac what is so admirable "is the intensity of the struggle—an intensity beyond that of real life—which makes his common soldiers, his valets, his commercial travellers, all men of genius." [8] To be a man of genius it was not necessary to be an aristocrat, only to have an energy proceeding from unity of character. This unity—where all a man's varied interests become expressions of a single dominating conviction—was for Yeats an obsessive but difficult attainment. Instinct and reason do not easily come together in the modern cultivated man. In a long, frank letter to Robert Gregory (which Richard Ellmann says was probably never sent) Yeats explained that he had reasoned away his personal instincts, and therefore could never act on natural impulse except in impersonal and public affairs where self-distrust did not enter in.

[8] *Explorations* (London, 1962), p. 272.

I want you to understand that once one makes a thing subject to reason, as distinguished from impulse, one plays with it, even if it is a very serious thing. I am more ashamed because of the things I have played with in life than of any other thing.

All my moral endeavor for many years [Yeats is writing in 1910] has been an attempt to recreate practical instinct in myself. I can only conceive of it as a kind of acting.[9]

The mask was, among other things, Yeats's way of attempting to restore the lost unity between artifice and sincerity, art and nature. And his doctrine itself was an example of the wholeness he sought to achieve: a bringing together of his moral, aesthetic, and philosophic interests.

His plays can be regarded both as masks concealing and revealing the internal conflicts of the poet and as structures in which the dialectic of his doctrine is acted out. They are moral in their intense concern for the right relationship between character and action, aesthetic in their insistence on the decorum of a proper life style, and philosophic in their conviction that individual attitudes and behavior can best be understood as manifestations of cosmic forces. Lyric in their incantatory evocation of an underlying bond between the particular occasion of the play and a life beyond, they are dramatic in their unfolding of an action in which the clash of human passions leads to a sudden transformation of the immediate situation. The epiphany unites the lyric and dramatic, being at once a kind of tableau emblematic of some deep-rooted, permanent life attitude and the culmination of the action. In its different aspects, the mask is the

[9] Richard Ellmann, *Yeats: The Man and the Masks* (New York, 1948), p. 175.

motive of the action, the form created by the action, and the final meaning of the action.

Yeats's conception of character is crucial to an understanding of his drama. He is not primarily interested, we know, in those little touches of nature which make the individual vivid, but he is very interested in the master images of desire which give coherence and definition to a man's life. What a man does if his activity is not directed by a strong inner necessity will lack character, in the sense of the word that applies to Yeats's dramatic practice. And character defines itself in the act of identifying that purpose for the sake of which all lesser satisfactions are expendable. To put it paradoxically, a man discovers, or creates, his character by the process of shedding it. In Balzac's novels we may see the gradual development of character, but in a Yeats play the chief characters have already attained definition except for the final stage. They are confronted with a fateful choice between possible masks, and by their decision they "fix," or complete their characters. They themselves become masks for the contemplation of choral commentators in the play and for us.

Of course the depth of character revealed is a matter of degree. In general the younger and more informal the person is the less character matters, and the emphasis falls on a way of life. In *The Land of Heart's Desire*, to put it a little crudely, joyless puritanism is rejected for a "life" of happy impulse; in *Cathleen ni Houlihan*, a narrow domesticity is vanquished by commitment to the cause of national independence. The young people transformed in these plays seem hardly to possess any wills that matter; they are acted upon as by a kind of hypnosis, and circumstance places the moral significance of their acts outside themselves. But the

Seanchan of *The King's Threshold* acts out of a sense of vocation built up over a lifetime, and the Cuchulain of *On Baile's Strand* tests his action by standards he himself has helped create. Character and action have a necessary, even inevitable, unity. It is still true, in one sense, that Seanchan and Cuchulain cannot help themselves; they are obeying a higher law. But this law, in turn, derives its ultimate sanction from their example. By their moral integrity they demonstrate to the community the value of an absolute standard that outlives, and deserves to outlive, the lesser laws whose authority derives from the expediency of the moment. And how can we tell the higher law from the lower? Not from a study of metaphysical jurisprudence but from the nobility of character that obedience to the law produces. Thus it would be a mistake to say that character, properly defined, is not an essential ingredient of the Yeatsian dramatic formula.

But if by being true to his mask the Yeatsian superman inspires his less morally gifted countrymen to develop a more exalted sense of honor—and his success in this respect is at best ambiguous—his virtue elevates him to an uncomfortable distance from ordinary humanity. He must appeal to a vision of reality that seems quite unreal to blind men and fools. The very sense of community that he struggles to maintain or restore seems ironically to be threatened by his insistence on being a law unto himself. It is difficult for the small-minded egotist to imagine a conception of self not based on simple self-interest. That is why death or its moral equivalent is so often required to complete the tragic effect —nothing less would offer convincing proof of the hero's sincerity.

As the hero surrenders the lesser self—those traits that

link him by comradeship and affection to ordinary mortals
—in order to assert his higher self—that lonely, impersonal,
and inflexible loyalty to an ageless ideal—an odd thing happens: suddenly his suffering restores him to humanity. Yeats
dramatized this pattern most directly and beautifully in
The Only Jealousy of Emer, but it is evident in many of
the plays. In *Emer* Cuchulain's mask is personified in the
gorgeous but inhuman Fand. Though in terms of literal
narrative Bricriu, the god of discord, is presiding over the
disposal of Cuchulain, who is suspended uncertainly between the living and the dead, the play is a phantasmagoric
projection of the by now familiar heroic predicament.
Cuchulain has gone so far in his pursuit of a disembodied
ideal that he has almost irretrievably cut his ties with humanity. Fand has something of the vampire in her—she
would like to be an abstraction blooded by her human
worshipper. But this would mean that Cuchulain must give
up his substance and become a shade, which he is almost
prepared to do. Should not the hero die to prove his faith?
The intricate subtlety of this play demands something different. Being "dead" already, Cuchulain cannot undergo
the martyrdom of dying—he is past that. Instead he must
bear the martyrdom of returning to all the aches and pains
of life. Under the circumstances Fand is a false mask, and
to yield to her would not be a fulfillment of the higher
self but, paradoxically enough, an indulgence of the lesser
self. That is why the physical mask the figure of Cuchulain
wears when he is under the domination of Fand is deformed;
the hero can only assume his true mask again when he has
rejected the temptation to rest on his well-earned laurels
and forget his obligation to mankind. It is not for the hero
to enjoy the private felicity of a perfect but "useless"

beauty. Passion belongs to the world of flesh and blood, and without passion the hero is only a shadow of himself. In *At the Hawk's Well* Cuchulain successfully (in fact with an ironically naive ease) resisted the temptation to give up the pursuit of an ideal in order to enjoy the comforts of ordinary humanity; in *Emer* he is faced with the opposite temptation—to give up the devastating strain of harrowing human emotions for the tranquillity of mystic oblivion. The heroic choice is always the difficult one—so difficult here that Emer must make it for him. Humanity loves its heroes at least partly because of their immense capacity for suffering—they suffer for us and thereby confer dignity on our lesser sufferings. In *Emer* Cuchulain is tragically saved for his heroic vocation.

It takes the discipline of style to make suffering beautiful. Yeats was not afraid of the flowers of evil, but he didn't want their stench in his nostrils. He preferred distance. Legends taught him what to leave out and the poets what to put in. His practice as a dramatist was a continual exercise in austerity; whatever did not contribute to heighten the mood or forward the action was expendable. Everything must be judged by its effectiveness in making the climax toward which the action tended as resonant in its multiple implications as it was brief and decisive in its narrative impact. Ideally, Yeats would combine the simplicity of earth with the grandeur of heaven in a wedding of passion and perfection.

Unfortunately, the theater is a place where the collaboration of many people is necessary, and not least of all the audience. It is instructive to look at the occasion that probably marks Yeats's greatest success in this collaboration—the performance of *Cathleen ni Houlihan* with Maud

Gonne in the title role, presented on April 2, 3, and 4 of
1902. Stephen Gwynn has memorably described the impact
of this performance.

I went home asking myself if such plays should be produced
unless one was prepared for people to go out to shoot and be
shot. Yeats was not alone responsible; no doubt that Lady
Gregory helped him to get the peasant speech so perfect; but
above all, Miss Gonne's impersonation had stirred the audience
as I have never seen another audience stirred. At the height of
her beauty, she transformed herself there into one of the half-
mad old crones whom we were accustomed to see by Irish
roadsides, and she spoke, as they spoke, in a half-crazy chant.
But the voice in which she spoke, a voice that matched her
superb stature and carriage, had rich flexibility and power to
stir and to stimulate; and the words which she spoke were the
words of a masterpiece. Yeats has said somewhere that his de-
fect as a dramatist is that normal men do not interest him; but
here in one brief theme he had expressed what a hundred
others have tried to do, the very spirit of a race for ever defeated and for ever insurgent against defeat. He had linked
this expression with the picture of a perfectly normal Irish
household group; the small farmer, greedy for more land, his
wife even more set on gain than he, their son who is about to
marry, and the girl who is to bring her portion with herself.

Into this group comes the Old Woman, stirring ancient
memories. As she arouses Michael Gillane she simultaneously arouses the audience. She speaks of the young men
who have given their life blood for her sake.

As she speaks, a far-off noise of cheering is heard; the old
woman rises, still bent and weighed down with years or centuries; but for one instant, before she went out at the half-door,
she drew herself up to her superb height; change was manifest;
patuit dea. Then in an instant the younger son of the house

rushes in crying out: "The French are in the bay! They are landing at Killala!" and such a thrill went through the audience as I have never known in any other theatre.[10]

This experience of "total theater" was possible because *Cathleeen ni Houlihan* could represent so many things to so many people: for Maud Gonne and her followers a symbol of their aspirations for Ireland, for Yeats a more complex compound of his love for a beautiful woman and his yearning for identification with the "popular" mind of his country, for many Irishmen like Stephen Gwynn a superbly eloquent statement of Irish indomitability, and even for non-Irishmen an unforgettable parable of how love of country can raise men above self-interest and ennoble their aggressions. The little play hinted at the sorrow but showed none of the pain of self-sacrifice, and it demanded neither effort of intellect nor comprehension of poetry. Patriotism was invested with all the excitement of a sexual seduction so safely decent that not even the most respectable guardian of the Irish image could impute sinister or scandalous motives to it. Such a happy conjunction of sentiments is rare in any theater and doubly rare in the Irish theater.

Yeats could not be content with it. It met all his specifications for theater, yet it lacked true poetic distinction. Its very popularity was gratifying but suspicious. Did it not appeal more to mob instinct than to a traditional understanding of community? In the future Yeats kept his distance and refused to offer incitements to action. His aesthetic insisted on the primacy of spiritual conversion over the release of pent-up emotional energy. Just as he valued

[10] Stephen Gwynn, *Irish Literature and Drama* (New York, 1936), pp. 158–160.

courtesy because it showed a respect for the privacy of others while protecting one's own, so he felt that the proper decorum of a play demanded a diction in which the chaos of the passions was subdued to intellectual order. And economy of means was an aesthetic merit in itself. As he wrote to Mrs. Patrick Campbell (in 1901), his artistic ideal was "to be impassioned and yet to have a perfect self-possession, to have a precision so absolute that the slightest inflection of voice, the slightest rhythm of sound or emotion plucks the heart strings." [11] To this delicate yet powerful simplicity he devoted his best efforts.

What changed after he gave up writing for the Abbey audience in 1910 was not his ideal of theater nor his theory of drama—these were essentially formed before Synge died —but his strategy of attack. He moved his drama inward. No longer are his heroes or heroines allowed an unequivocal moral victory over their less enlightened opponents (if they are allowed victory at all), and there are no more great public scenes in which a character is allowed the romantic indulgence of dying with a magnificent gesture like Deirdre's. All beauty becomes more costly, and love exacts not only the old tragic price of isolation and death but the more bitter penalty of a self-mutilating kind of horror. Yeats's sense of metaphysical destiny is more imperative, which is not at all to say that the plays become overtly philosophical, except where (as in *The Resurrection*) ideas are the dramatic substance of the action.

In *The Death of Cuchulain*, Yeats's final play, Cuchulain is able to say, "I make the truth!" He has earned the right to say this because he is utterly unself-seeking; his will has become indifferent to all but his mask; he has no identity

[11] *Letters* (London, 1954), p. 360.

separate from the completed image of a desire become impersonal because beyond mortality. Yet this pageant of man becoming a god-principle is intensely moving. Single-handed, surrounded by people in fact drawn from myth but who in the play have no more idea of the "timeless" event they are witnessing than the Blind Man and Fool of many years earlier, Cuchulain bequeaths himself to their descendants by an act of will is simultaneously a complete surrender of will. He has come through. But his heaven is to be remembered in the songs of beggar-man and harlot centuries later—which is as he would have it. He now belongs to the people as he never could while he was alive.

In Yeats's philosophy all things come round again, but passions spin the plot. Life is violent, excessive, savage, but Yeats takes no sadistic pleasure in its cruelty. Rather he has an admiring eye for that spiritual magnanimity possessed of such faith in the beauty of human possibility that, despite all evidence to the contrary, it not only believes but wills the immortality of the song of itself.

Yeats wrote Ethel Mannin (in 1938) that he was writing a play about Cuchulain's death that contained his philosophy but that "there must be no sign of it; all must be like an old faery tale." Then he goes on to say, "To me all things are made of the conflict of two states of consciousness, beings or persons which die each other's life, live each other's death. That is true of life and death themselves." [12] A man toils for love toward his own stillness, and out of his death life is renewed. Yeats's plays are masks of love and death.

[12] *Ibid.*, pp. 917–918.

[2]

Toward Defining
the Yeatsian Drama

The average man, Yeats thought, is not a fit subject for
drama at all, because he has not the freedom to express his
own soul. "Habit, routine, fear of public opinion, fear of
punishment here or hereafter, a myriad of things that are
'something other than human life,' something less than
flame, work their will upon his soul and trundle his body
here and there." [1] Consequently when he saw Ibsen's *Ghosts*
he had the impression, as he mockingly puts it, of a huge
stage and tiny characters. "Little whimpering puppets
moved here and there in the middle of that great abyss.
Why did they not speak out with louder voices or move
with freer gestures? What was it that weighed upon their
souls perpetually? Certainly they were all in prison, and
yet there was no prison." [2] The trouble was that this was
an art for people who lived in cities and never developed
the strength that comes from solitude. And Yeats asked,
"Will not our next art be rather of the country, of great
open spaces, of the soul rejoicing in itself?" [3]

Though we may disagree with Yeats's estimates of his
two greatest dramatic adversaries, Ibsen and Shaw, it is easy

[1] *Plays and Controversies* (London, 1923), pp. 121–122.
[2] *Ibid.*, p. 122.   [3] *Ibid.*, p. 123.

to understand what annoyed him. He felt they were trapped in the very world they were rebelling against. As he saw them, they were moralists, critics, reformers. Shaw's kind of energy both frightened and fascinated him. He had occasion to watch the rehearsals of *Arms and the Man* when it was being prepared for a double bill with his own *Land of Heart's Desire*, and he listened "with admiration and hatred." Shaw's play seemed to him "inorganic, logical straightness and not the crooked road of life." [4] Yeats was convinced that religion, not morality, was the true basis for drama. Not, of course, the religion represented by any existing church (his father had made that impossible for him), but the faith in an order of things that gave a man's destiny more mystery and significance than the isolated events of any single human lifetime by themselves ever could. Compared to the interest of man viewed from the aspect of eternity, his "moral" career in the world, however admirable, distressing, or puzzling it might be, was little more than a curiosity. The dramatic conflict most moving to Yeats was that between man-made law, suited to upholding the rights and guaranteeing the security of ordinary man, and the divine law, capable of upsetting man's most cherished rational preconceptions, which governed the actions of heroes, and the feelings of all other men at their best and deepest moments. [5] Yeats looked in vain for this sort of exhilaration in the English-speaking theater at the turn of the century.

The ideal kind of theater Yeats imagined underwent con-

[4] *Autobiography* (New York, 1938), p. 169.

[5] "First Principles," from *Samhain* of 1904, gives an eloquent summary of Yeats's conception of drama. See *Plays and Controversies*, pp. 87–115.

siderable changes during his fifty years of experience with writing and staging plays, but the guiding principles of his experimentation were as constant as his interest in the occult. Underlying his many speculations about the forms of tragedy and comedy was his conviction that, whether written in prose or verse, drama must essentially be the creation of a poet. It cannot be concerned with the eccentric, the accidental, the incoherent, as the novel may be; it must go below the surface of life, with all its animation and variety, to the comparative simplicity and stillness to be found at the center of experience. Rather than a conversation between one man and another, it is a dialogue between generations imitating those actions that make *all* men laugh or cry. In this sense originality is a curse. "Talk to me of originality," says Yeats in a 1937 introduction to a never published complete edition of his works, "talk to me of originality and I will turn on you with rage. I am a crowd, I am a lonely man, I am nothing. Ancient salt [a symbol of eternity] is best packing." [6] The ecstasy of Shakespeare's heroes as death approaches makes of them impersonal avatars of sudden visionary truth. Their tragedy is joyous because, lifted out of the confusion of external circumstance, they have shed the accidents of individual personality and become part of the eternal design.

They have become God or Mother Goddess, the pelican, "My baby at my breast," but all must be cold; no actress has ever sobbed when she played Cleopatra, even the shallow brain of a producer has never thought of such a thing. The supernatural is present, cold winds blow across our hands, upon our faces, the thermometer falls, and because of that cold we are hated by journalists and groundlings. There may be in this or

[6] *Essays and Introductions* (London, 1961), p. 522.

that detail painful tragedy, but in the whole work none. I have heard Lady Gregory say, rejecting some play in the modern manner sent to the Abbey Theatre, "Tragedy must be a joy to the man who dies." Nor is it any different with lyrics, songs, narrative poems; neither scholars nor the populace have sung or read anything generation after generation because of its pain. The maid of honour whose tragedy they sing must be lifted out of history with timeless pattern, she is one of the four Maries, the rhythm is old and familiar, imagination must dance, must be carried beyond feeling into the aboriginal ice.[7]

In the Yeatsian theater there is little room for the excited feelings of the propagandist who wants to send us out of the theater to improve the world. In fact the great problem for the dramatist is to so loosen us from our normal worldly preoccupations that we lie open to the marvels otherwise vouchsafed only in myths and dreams.

To find a proper language for such a theater was enough work for a lifetime. At first Yeats tried for a concentrated language full of emotional tension; gradually he worked to bring his poetry closer to "passionate, normal speech." From the perspective of 1937, he says he did not begin to be satisfied until he had learned that he "must seek, not as Wordsworth thought, words in common use, but a powerful and passionate syntax, and a complete coincidence between period and stanza." Free verse was not available to him because it would have seemed too personal; he needed the distance imposed by traditional forms. "If I wrote of personal love or sorrow in free verse, or in any rhythm that left it unchanged, amid all its accidence, I would be full of self-contempt because of my egotism and indiscre-

[7] *Ibid.*, p. 523.

tion, and foresee the boredom of my reader." [8] As for his plays, where a certain impersonality was demanded by the form, his dissatisfaction with blank verse led him to try ballad meter in *The Green Helmet* and later, in the dance plays, to vary the blank verse with lyric meters. Blank verse seemed already too modern a form to express Ireland's Heroic Age, the stories of Deirdre and Cuchulain. "When I speak blank verse and analyse my feelings, I stand at a moment of history when instinct, its traditional songs and dances, its general agreement, is of the past. I have been cast up out of the whale's belly though I still remember the sound and sway that came from beyond its ribs, and . . . I smell the fish of the sea." [9]

Yeats's early interest in experimenting with the speaking of verse to the psaltery in order to bring into prominence the underlying metrical norm was an attempt to keep alive in the hearer's mind the folk song origins of verse. The very sound of the words was a way of linking past and present, as Yeats illustrates by scanning the first line of *Paradise Lost*, first to emphasize the metrical pattern and then to demonstrate the rhythms of passionate prose. Cross the two and "the folk song is still there, but a ghostly voice, an unvariable possibility, an unconscious norm." The two voices must combine in contrapuntal style if the precise and delicate state of mind, attentive and yet receptive, necessary for Yeats's purpose was to be evoked. "What moves me and my hearer is a vivid speech that has no laws except that it must not exorcise the ghostly voice. I am awake and asleep, at my moment of revelation, self-possessed in self-surrender; there is no rhyme, no echo of the beaten drum, the dancing foot, that would overset my balance." [10]

[8] *Ibid.*, pp. 521–522.   [9] *Ibid.*, p. 524.   [10] *Ibid.*

Yeats wants a "magical" style not in any sentimental sense, but for a specific purpose: on the one hand, to exorcise as far as possible the prose associations increasingly dominant in language since the Renaissance; on the other, to call up, by a subtle use of rhythm, an older collective experience in which all minds become part of a single mind. And it was not enough for Yeats that this shared experience could be imagined in the privacy of a study; he wanted to feel the unity when play, players, and audience are in perfect rapport as a physical and spiritual immediacy. Yet he was so fastidious in distinguishing between proper and improper theatrical emotion that few even of the plays produced at the Abbey fully aroused his gratitude. He demanded a dramatic poetry that tended at one extreme to disappear into wordless ritual gesture—into dance—and at the other to freeze into a mystical lyric symbolism almost, but never quite, algebraic in its intellectual abstraction.

His admiration for Synge, a man important to him in many ways, shows strikingly how Yeats saw the character, philosophy, and language of his friend as parts of an indivisible whole. Something in the depths of Synge's character responded to the still primitive life he found on the Aran Islands and made possible the full expression of his personality. The simplicity of the harsh life, leaving no room for speculation on moral ideals or interest in political argument, released Synge from morbidity and gave him a language perfectly adapted to voice the passionate wisdom born of his personal solitude. He achieved the kind of impersonality Yeats admired, the impersonality of the artist whose ego is absorbed into his traditional subject matter so that his mind becomes part of the Great Mind, just the opposite of the hated impersonality that comes from a mindless surrender of individuality to the mechanical thoughts and feelings dictated by the workaday world.

In Synge's plays the student of drama will be disappointed if he expects "that excitement of the will in the presence of attainable advantages" characteristic of modern drama. Instead he will find a "drifting movement" and an "emotional subtlety" that arise from "the preoccupation of his characters with their dream." [11] Yeats even suggests that the great schools of drama may be distinguished by their particular devices for checking the rapidity of dialogue. Synge's method was to elaborate on the dialects of Kerry and Aran.

The cadence is long and meditative, as befits the thought of men who are much alone, and who when they meet in one another's houses—as their way is at the day's end—listen patiently, each man speaking in turn and for some little time, and taking pleasure in the vaguer meaning of the words and in their sound. Their thought, when not merely practical, is as full of traditional wisdom and extravagant pictures as that of some Aeschylean chorus, and no matter what the topic, it is as though the present were held at arm's length. It is the reverse of rhetoric, for the speaker serves his own delight, though doubtless he would tell you that like Raftery's whiskey-drinking it was but for the company's sake. A medicinal manner of speech, too, for it could not even express, so little abstract it is and so rammed with life, those worn generalisations of National propaganda. "I'll be telling you the finest story you'd hear any place from Dundalk to Ballinacree with great queens in it, making themselves matches from the start to the end, and they with shiny silks on them. . . . I've a grand story of the great queens of Ireland, with white necks

[11] *Ibid.*, p. 304.

on them the like of Sarah Casey, and fine arms would hit you a slap. . . . What good am I this night, God help me? What good are the grand stories I have when it's few would listen to an old woman, few but a girl maybe would be in great fear the time her hour was come, or little child wouldn't be sleeping with the hunger on a cold night?" That has the flavour of Homer, of the Bible, of Villon, while Cervantes would have thought it sweet in the mouth though not his food.[12]

Synge added to the national dignity by the creation of this language which enlarged (or should have enlarged) the Irish vision of their own possible nobility. In his most famous play, *The Playboy of the Western World,* that "solitary, undemonstrative man," in his own peculiar formula combining indolence with a joyous and violent energy, produced what seemed to Yeats "the strangest, the most beautiful expression in drama of that Irish fantasy which overflowing through all Irish literature that has come out of Ireland itself (compare the fantastic Irish account of the Battle of Clontarf with the sober Norse account) is the unbroken character of Irish genius." [13] Yet Synge's fantasy gave the kind of pleasure aroused by great art: "an overpowering vision of certain virtues, and our capacity for sharing in that vision is the measure of our delight. Great art chills us at first by its coldness or its strangeness, by what seems capricious, and yet it is from these qualities it has authority, as though it had fed on locusts and wild honey." The imaginative writer was for Yeats one who showed us the world "as we were Adam and this the first morning." Once the strangeness has worn off, we are compelled to feel as the writer does. Oddly, his very indiffer-

12 *Ibid.,* pp. 334–335.   13 *Ibid.,* p. 337.

ence about others is the mark of his sincerity, for "to speak of one's emotions without fear or moral ambition, to come out from under the shadow of other men's minds, to forget their needs, to be utterly oneself, that is all the Muses care for." [14]

The "self" Synge had revealed to Yeats had the stubborn independence of mind Yeats long struggled to attain for himself. He praises in his friend those qualities produced by the oppositions in human character which always fascinated Yeats. That a brooding, melancholy, silent man should deliver himself of such lusty and brawling offspring was proof of his personal richness. Once Synge had told him that "asceticism, stoicism, ecstasy" ought to be united; "two of these have often come together, but not all three." [15] In Synge they came together.

Knowing that the domination of the actor in the English theater (a situation which Shaw typically both fought against and exploited in the earlier part of his occupation with and in the theater) was the greatest impediment to the domination of the poet in the theater, Yeats early and late insisted on the primacy of what was said over who said it. He wrote in 1902 that he had thought of rehearsing his actors in barrels so that they might forget gesture and concentrate on speech. [16] Then he had seen Sarah Bernhardt in *Phèdre* and thought she realized to perfection the art of stillness. Her rhythmically stylized gestures and those of her partner de Max, with the sculptural nobility of an immobile, white-robed crowd in the background, created "an extraordinary reality and intensity. It was the most beautiful thing I had ever seen upon the stage, and made me un-

[14] *Ibid.*, p. 339.   [15] *Ibid.*, p. 308.
[16] *Plays and Controversies*, p. 20.

derstand, in a new way, that saying of Goethe's [one of Yeats's favorite maxims] which is understood everywhere but in England, 'Art is art because it is not nature.' " [17] As a poet, Yeats was intuitively aware that the concentration of dramatic life came from imagery, both visual and auditory, and that whatever interfered with unity of image would remind the audience of a distracting world it was the business of the theater to make them forget. Obviously against any attempt at naturalistic illusion, Yeats, at least until very late in his life, would have been equally opposed to the alienation effect made famous by Brecht, for this is only another way of arousing the critical "instinct" and returning the audience to the life of opinion and argument Yeats considered the bane of art (and potentially the destroyer of personal happiness as well; remember, for instance, his "A Prayer for My Daughter").

Yeats wanted to believe that in the theater he could make temporary aristocrats out of his Dublin audiences. His rationale was that all men (not ruined by journalism and education) can share the great emotions that only heroes can act upon. Hoping to restore a popular theater on his own terms, he began writing for the Abbey his re-creations of ancient Irish heroes. But Yeats's dramatic aristocrats are hardly members of any recognizable society at all. Childlike, amorous, valiant, their physical strength and their capacity for passionate emotion unquestionable, they pass through the world with a simple-minded disregard of everything not concerned with their chivalric code. In terms of civilization they are at the opposite pole from the neurasthenic Proustian aristocrat. Obviously endowed with the ability to be successful in the world, Yeats's heroes are

[17] *Ibid.*, p. 21.

checked not by psychological alienation or social abnormality, as are so many heroes of modern literature, but by their commitment to extremes of idealism that tend to disintegrate the self-imposed limits of the normal world. They are in search of what might be called a premature immortality. What they learn is the impossibility of reconciling their own values with those of their community. Though most of the plays are laid in the past, the heroes look back to a past still more remote. They are isolated from the world in which they find themselves, but they know too that the standards which govern their lives are sanctioned by a deathless community of which they are members. The elegiac tone is more pronounced in some plays than others; it gives a patina to the verse in all. It was difficult for Abbey audiences to cast their minds back into a past that they were made to feel was exclusively the domain of poets. The relation of the audience to the plays was rather like that of the nonheroic characters to the heroes *in* the plays. Joseph Holloway, the tireless diarist of Dublin theatrical life and an accurate barometer of the general public reaction to the Abbey's work, noted after a 1906 revival of Yeats's *The Shadowy Waters:* "The audience was the smallest of any Saturday night this season. Yeats spells empty benches! Boyle full houses!! Synge cranks at home!!! Lady Gregory popularity!!! I hope Synge's presence means *The Playboy* soon." [18]

Unfortunately Yeats seldom got the kind of criticism that would have been helpful to him. Those who admired him rarely ventured to offer constructive criticism of his

[18] Quoted in David H. Greene and Edward M. Stephens, *J. M. Synge* (New York, 1959), p. 226.

poetry for the theater, whereas those who did not criticized him on irrelevant grounds or from a Philistine point of view, either strident or sheepish about their inability to understand or sympathize with his aims.[19] He was, perforce, his own best critic. His experience in the theater drove him to revise his plays again and again. Frequently he wrote versions in both prose and verse of the same play. From the beginning, as we have seen, language was the crucial problem: how was he to convince an audience that the most dramatic thing in the world was not a battle of wills between people intent on their various worldly misunderstandings, but the effort of an extraordinary person to win the Nietzschean heights from which he could look down on human existence with the cold passion created by his new perspective?

To be sure, it would take a visionary eye indeed to sense anything Nietzschean in the early versions of *The Countess Cathleen, The Land of Heart's Desire,* or *The Shadowy Waters;* not until *The King's Threshold,* first performed in 1903, does the philosopher's influence become unmistakable. There the poet Seanchan defines his vocation in terms of Dionysian excitement:

> And I would have all know that when all falls
> In ruin, poetry calls out in joy,
> Being the scattering hand, the bursting pod,
> The victim's joy among the holy flame,
> God's laughter at the shattering of the world.
> And now that joy laughs out, and weeps and burns
> On these bare steps.[20]

[19] For a symbolic paradigm of the attitude, read between the lines of the brief remarks Robinson makes in his dialogue "Pictures in a Theatre." Lennox Robinson, *Ireland's Abbey Theatre* (London, 1951), pp. 187–188.

[20] *Collected Plays* (London, 1952), p. 114.

The originally happy ending of this play, however, shows how far Yeats was when he first conceived it from the elevated austerity of the Nietzschean vision. *On Baile's Strand*, performed at the opening of the Abbey Theatre on December 27, 1904, was the first play in which Yeats created a mature, thoroughly masculine hero, neither poet nor wise man, whose tragedy is firmly based on an irremediable human situation. It is perhaps Yeats's most sustained effort at "classical" drama: the fatal conflict between father and son, the use of choral figures to place the action in a traditional context and of the Blind Man and the Fool to suggest the enigmatic irony not only of human life in general but more particularly of the isolated hero, and an agon involving not merely death but murder and one of the most harrowing of archetypal recognitions. Yeats returns to the subject of "family murder" at the end of his career in *Purgatory*, but there the father's act is, in effect, part of his prolonged soliloquy and no agon or recognition occurs, though the irony of the son's murder could hardly be greater.

With *On Baile's Strand* Yeats had inaugurated a series of plays, to come at rather widely separated intervals, about the Irish hero who meant most to him. But the kind of play Yeats created was too special a product to provide a model for other playwrights. When Synge, disgusted at the low-minded controversy over his own *In the Shadow of the Glen*, wrote his friend Stephen MacKenna, the translator of Plotinus, complaining that the critics would allow him no alternative but "writing innocently bloodless plays about ancient Irish legendary figures," he had just seen the disappointing failure of Yeats's *Shadowy Waters*, performed on January 14, 1904, at the Molesworth Hall, almost a year before the opening of the Abbey. MacKenna had replied, defending the idea of "a purely fantastic, unmodern, ideal, breezy, springdayish Cuchullainoid *etc.* national theatre." Quite dismayed, Synge had answered, expanding on his ideas for an Irish theater and rejecting the "Cuchulainoid" type of drama in no uncertain terms. He insisted that "no drama can grow out of anything other than the fundamental realities of life which are never fantastic, are neither modern nor unmodern and, as I see them, rarely springdayish, or breezy or Cuchulainoid." [21] Though Synge did not yet know *On Baile's Strand*, which could hardly be described as "springdayish," it would have made little difference in his judgment. To be sure, it is only fair to remark that Synge thought certain individual plays might well be springdayish. "But while life is what it is and men are what they are, I do not think any group of writers will write such work chiefly unless they do so with a wilful insincerity of joy that would make their work useless, and destroy the power of their souls." [22] Wanting Irish writers to "deal manfully, directly and decently with the entire reality of life," Synge could not help regarding Yeats's work as at least a partial evasion of artistic responsibility. Not that he did not respect Yeats for his superb abilities as a fighter for the Irish artist's freedom of conscience and expression and admire him as a poetic genius; he obviously did.

From the very beginning of the Irish dramatic movement there had been disagreement about the kinds of plays that should be written. To name the chief authors who contributed in the early days of excitement to the founding of a new dramatic literature is to list talents so individualistic and so widely varying in temperament and technique that the wonder is how they could have collaborated as closely

[21] Greene and Stephens, pp. 156–157.   [22] *Ibid.*, p. 157.

as they did. Douglas Hyde, Edward Martyn, George Moore, AE, Yeats himself, Lady Gregory, and then Synge —they are a fascinating group. But even before Synge's death in 1909 it was unfortunately evident that Yeats was to have no competitor for his kind of poetic drama. Nor in fact did Synge or the sometimes underestimated Lady Gregory have real followers either. Only in Synge's work, perhaps, were the two streams of mythological fantasy and contemporary reality successfully combined in a way to ensure permanent interest. In Yeats's plays, which already show constant experimentation and change not only from one play to the next but even in different versions of the same play, a singular devotion to *both* poetry and theater produced a splendid variety of drama unified by the belief that the revelations of poetic truth provide the most strikingly dramatic instances of how reality enters life. Yeats deliberately avoided everything the drama he disliked emphasized: the effect of casual conversation arising out of homely situation, interesting little touches of personal eccentricity to "humanize" character, all the critical perplexities any ordinary person might have to face. But he never left out of account the pressure of that usually invisible and inaudible world operating on principles beyond the scope and control of restless, time-bound men but not to be disregarded by them. According to their ability to respond to the challenge, this force might destroy or liberate, or sometimes do both at once. Cuchulain in *On Baile's Strand* is the kind of hero who disrupts established order for the sake of a greater order to which he instinctively belongs. For Yeats, whose curiosity about occult knowledge and ardent desire to master its imagery were life-long pursuits, the writing of such plays was neither insincere nor soul-destroying. For most other writers it might well have been.

[3]

Cuchulain and the Myth
of the Yeatsian Hero

The great mythological battle in which Cuchulain, refusing to heed the omens and warnings strewn in his path, goes
ritualistically to his death is the ultimate result of a tiff between Maeve and Ailell, the queen and king of Connaught,
who many years before had fallen to quarreling one morning in bed over who had the greatest riches. As in the primitive custom of potlatch, except that the goods were not
thrown on the fire, all the riches of each party were
brought out and a census taken. In one item after another
they were found to be equal—eating utensils, jewelry,
clothes, sheep, horses, swine, and finally cattle. But the best
bull in the whole province of Connaught was in Ailell's
herd. Though he had been calved in Maeve's herd, he had
departed, "for he did not think it fitting to be under the rule
of a woman." [1] It was Maeve's anguished search for a rival
bull that led to war between Ulster and Connaught, to
Cuchulain's single-handed defense of Ulster, to the mutual
slaughter of the White Bull of Cruachan and the Brown

---

[1] Lady Gregory, *Cuchulain of Muirthemne* (London, 1934),
p. 178. Her account of "The Cattle Raid of Cooley" is on pp.
175–245.

Bull of Cooley, and finally to the lonely death of our hero, Cuchulain.[2]

The strangeness of this central tale from the Red Branch Saga, one of three great Irish saga cycles, does not come so much from its mingling of the sublime and the ridiculous as from its curious poise between grotesque savagery and elegant elaboration. In the account of Cuchulain's boyhood, given in a "flashback," we learn of the great deeds Cuchulain has accomplished by the time he is a little boy of seven. Leaving home against his mother's wishes (she thinks he is still a little immature), Cuchulain astonishes King Conchubar's elite boys-corps of a hundred and fifty young warriors-to-be by defeating them single-handed, kills the monstrous hound of the smith Culann, and thus wins his name (which means Culann's hound). Taking arms on an auspicious day Cuchulain performs a series of feats sufficient to last a more ordinary hero a lifetime. Inflamed with his triumphs at the end of his first day of knighthood, Cuchulain presents a serious problem: in his fury he will kill all the young men of Emain Macha unless some way is found of cooling him off. The narrator says:

At last they hit upon a method to abate his manly rage (the result of having shed blood), and it was this: Emain Macha's women all (six score and ten in number) bared their bosoms, and without subterfuge of any kind trooped out to meet him (their maneuver being based on Cuchulain's well-known modesty, which like all his other qualities, was excessive). The little fellow leaned his head against the rail of the chariot and shut

---

[2] The death of Cuchulain, however, is not part of "The Cattle Raid of Cooley" in the old Irish texts; Cuchulain's last act there is a moving lament for Ferdiad, the old companion of his youth whom he has slain in the battle of the ford.

them from his sight. Then was the desired moment; all un-
awares he was seized, and soused in a vat of cold water ready
for the purpose. In this first vessel the heat generated by his
immersion was such that the staves and hoops flew asunder
instantly. In a second vat the water escaped (by boiling over);
in yet a third the water still was hotter than one could bear.
By this time, however, the little boy's fury had died down in
him; from crown to soul he blushed a beautiful pink red all
over, and they clad him in his festive clothes. Thus his natural
form and feature were restored to him.

A beautiful boy indeed was that: seven toes to each foot he
had, and to either hand as many fingers; his eyes were bright
with seven pupils apiece, each one of which glittered with
seven gem-like sparkles. On either cheek he had four moles:
a blue, a crimson, a green, and a yellow one. Between one ear
and the other he had fifty clear-yellow long tresses that were
as the yellow wax of bees, or like a brooch of white gold as
it glints in the sun unobscured. He wore a green mantle silver-
clasped upon his breast, a gold-thread shirt. The small boy
took his place between Conchubar's knees, and the king began
to stroke his hair.[3]

This small boy, the king's pet, is obviously something of
a monster. Combining the attributes of a sun-god and an
oriental idol, a becoming youthful modesty and a blinding
heroic violence, this seven-year-old has all too clearly never

[3] Quoted in David H. Greene, *An Anthology of Irish Literature*
(New York, 1954), p. 60. In Lady Gregory's account the description is compressed to the following: "Then they all consulted
together, and it is what they agreed, to send out three fifties of the
women of Emain red-naked to meet him. When the boy saw the
women coming, there was shame on him, and he leaned down his
head into the cushions of the chariot, and hid his face from them.
And the wildness went out of him, and his feasting clothes were
brought, and water for washing; and there was a great welcome
before him" (Lady Gregory, p. 20).

enjoyed a proper childhood. He is a phenomenon thrust upon the world fully created and in a sense incapable of growth. The passage above owes part of its fascination to the original way in which it handles the efforts of the natural world to absorb this ambiguous gift from the supernatural. From something altogether too hot to handle Cuchulain descends by degrees to the little darling fondled between the protective legs of a fatherly king. Fire has been subdued by water to a creature of earth, and the method used has depended on a cunning knowledge of the hero's youthful weakness—a modest terror of the opposite sex. It is the magical third vat of water that restores him to "his *natural* form and feature," with his seven toes, fingers, and pupils, and certainly nothing could be more natural than an excess of physical equipment to match the excess of Cuchulain's other qualities. Small wonder that ten years later he should be able as the champion of Ulster to keep at bay single-handed the entire army of Queen Maeve's Connaught.[4]

The figure that emerges from the old saga stories about Cuchulain (often called the Irish Achilles) is part grotesque primitive and part chivalrous gentleman. In spite of the emphasis on rough games, brutal warfare, and magic spells, we get a picture of a society aware of craftsmanship and beautiful things, valuing the learning and skill of bards and satirists, fond of chess, and much given to courtly etiquette. Cuchulain is a "man" of utter self-confidence depending on no one for help or guidance, full of passion but usually uncommunicative, governed by a code only partly derived

[4] For an excellent summary and interpretation of the Cuchulain myth see Marie-Louise Sjoestedt, *Gods and Heroes of the Celts* (London, 1949), translated by Myles Dillon, pp. 57–81.

from any human authority. His self-imposed loyalties spring from no sense of intimate human relationship. Even in his wooing of Emer, full of ritualistic riddling and fairy-tale obstacles to be overcome before Prince Charming carries off his prize, Cuchulain is a show piece of heroism: the match between him and Emer is marvelous because two perfect creations are being brought, so to speak, into al-chemical union. The hero's fight with his son Connla, ac-cording to the ninth-century text translated by Kuno Meyer, is an unemotionally told account of how Cuchulain, having been warned by Emer that he is probably going to meet his own son if he goes forth to battle the challenger, kills him by a trick after being worsted in fair combat by the boy. So, too, when Cuchulain defeats Ferdiad at the ford it is by the help of the *gae bulga,* a magically irresis-tible weapon, after Ferdiad threatens to get the better of him. Cuchulain's lament for the comrade of his youth, in the great epic tradition, has the proper elevated nobility, but any such lament for the death of his own son is conspic-uously lacking. Like many of the great saga heroes, Cuchu-lain depends on trickery and supernatural powers in his most perilous moments. When he becomes angry he is haloed by his "hero-light" and no mere earthling can with-stand him. In his more benign aspects, however, Cuchulain is so attractive that all the women of Conchubar's court are in love with him. "And all the faults they could find in him were three, that he was too young and smooth-faced, so that young men who did not know him would be laugh-ing at him, that he was too daring, and that he was too beautiful." [5] No wonder the men of Ulster wanted to get him married off in self-defense!

[5] Lady Gregory, p. 21.

Cuchulain lives mainly in an outdoor world of pastoral aristocracy in which heroic bulls, metamorphosed swans, and Amazonian women are part of the familiar setting for the hero's deeds. According to scholars, the period is the century before Christ.[6] Certainly the Christian scribes who wrote out the texts from the eleventh to the fifteenth century and the later redactors and translators have by no means eliminated the pagan flavor of the legends. Nor is it any surprise that such an unchristian hero as Cuchulain, with his doomed inability ever to "knuckle under" to anybody, should have survived as an Irish ideal. Though Cuchulain seems very seldom to be acting in his own interest in any narrow egotistic sense, the altruism of his pugnacity remains vague, and his own and our pleasure in his exploits has little admixture of the moral satisfaction that comes from the triumph of right over wrong. He is an ideal embodiment of unconquerable qualities (until his death, just before which his charmed invulnerabilities fall away from him one by one with the rhythmical inevitability of the steps in some archaic sacrificial dance) opening up a new space in the normally resistant world and leaving it to close again after him. Like Achilles, he knows his time on earth is short but that his fame will be everlasting, and so he must display the maximum of spectacular fireworks in the minimum of time. His deeds are never to be forgotten and never repeated, and for others his example is one to be avoided fully as much as one to be imitated.

A typical hero of romance, Cuchulain is suspended between god and man, capable of human love, suffering, and

---

[6] But Thomas F. O'Rahilly says none of the Ulidian tales has any connection with history; they are wholly mythical. See his *Early Irish History and Mythology* (Dublin, 1957), p. 271.

death but more than human in beauty, strength, and will.[7]
Unlike many heroes of romance, however, Cuchulain has
no great quest to unify his career, at least in the form in
which the stories about him have come down to us. We
hear about his childhood feats, his wooing of Emer, his love
for Fand, his part in the Cattle Raid, his killing of his son,
his final battle and death, but they are all episodes which
for the most part have no necessary connection with each
other, except that Cuchulain is the center of them all. Yet
the hero is always exhibited in riddling splendor, remote
and often terrible in spite of his all-too-human passions.

In his mythological aspect, according to Robert Graves,
Cuchulain is to be associated with Hercules as a type of
sacred pastoral king who assures sexual virility and is the
"male leader of all orgiastic rites." A mighty hunter and
rain-maker, this Hercules is annually married to "a queen
of the woods, a sort of Maid Marian," and each midsummer
is sacrificed by being tied to a sacred oak surrounded by
twelve stones with an altar-stone in front. First he is made
drunk on mead, then secured to the oak "with willow
thongs in the 'five-fold bond' which joins wrists, neck, and
ankles together, beaten by his comrades till he faints, then
flayed, blinded, castrated, impaled with a mistletoe stake,
and finally hacked into joints on the altar-stone. His blood
is caught in a basin and used for sprinkling the whole tribe
to make them vigorous and fruitful." After the roasted
joints have been eaten, the other remains are thrown on a
sacred fire except for the head and genitals. "These are
put into an alder-wood boat and floated down a river to

---

[7] See the now well-known definition of romance in Northrop
Frye, *Anatomy of Criticism* (Princeton, 1957), particularly pp.
186–206.

an islet; though the head is sometimes cured with smoke and preserved for oracular use." [8] Certainly the accounts of Cuchulain's death are well removed from such frank barbarism as this, but the pattern underneath is still discernible, even to the connection Graves professes to see between the Hercules figure and the White Goddess to whom he is subservient.

When the last battle comes, Cuchulain is both aroused and warned by the maiden Leborcham; she and "thrice fifty" queens beseech him not to leave them, and the Morrigu, a fate-goddess associated with battle, even breaks his chariot, for in spite of her conflicts with him she hates to see him leave for the last time. Everything and everyone conspires against Cuchulain who, however, far from having to be made drunk and dragged to his death, proceeds with methodical determination toward his fate. His brooch falls and pierces his foot, his charioteer doesn't want to go, and his marvelous horse, the Gray of Macha, who can talk like the horses of Achilles, "let his big round tears of blood fall on Cuchulain's feet." Cuchulain breaks taboos when he is persuaded by three Crones blind in the left eye to consume food, especially since the flesh is that of his sacred namesake, the dog (hound). He is deprived of his spear by a trick of the satirists three times, and each time it comes back mortally wounding first his charioteer, then the Gray of Macha, and finally Cuchulain himself. The hero gets permission to refresh himself with a drink and goes to a pillar-stone in the midst of a plain and ties himself to it, that "he might die standing up." The loyal Gray of Macha comes to defend him as long as his "hero's light" continues to

[8] Robert Graves, *The White Goddess* (New York, 1948), pp. 100–101.

shine from Cuchulain's forehead. Then the Morrigu and her sister come to sit on his shoulder in the form of crows, and Lugaid, no longer fearful, cuts off Cuchulain's head, though he loses his own right hand when the hero's sword falls on it and in revenge cuts off Cuchulain's corresponding member. The hosts march off bearing the head and right hand of Cuchulain. According to the covenant between Cuchulain and Conal, the latter proceeds to avenge Cuchulain's death, pursuing Lugaid and cutting off *his* head. In the eighth-century version translated by Whitney Stokes, the story ends with a Christian touch. "But the soul of Cu-Chulain appeared there [Emain Macha] to the thrice fifty queens who had loved him, and they saw him floating in his phantom chariot over Emain Macha, and they heard him chant a mystic song of the coming of Christ and the Day of Doom." [9]

Equally in keeping with the mythological pattern is the story of Cuchulain's birth. His mother, the Irish princess Dechtire, conceived him by swallowing the god Lugh in the form of a mayfly. The infant Cuchulain was able to swim like a trout as soon as he was born.[10] Like Hercules, he was precociously strong; his mother should have been glad to get him out of the house. Most famous for his combination of valor and amorousness, Cuchulain could also be regarded as something of a poet. He is most conspicuous in this role in the riddling manner in which he woos Emer, who might be regarded as his Muse. In the *Sickbed of Cuchulain* he has forsaken Emer (The Muse can never be domesticated) and become enthralled to Fand, the queen of the Sidhe, famous for her ideal beauty. But when Emer demands Cuchulain back, Fand relinquishes her claim, ad-

[9] Quoted in Greene, pp. 68–75.   [10] Graves, p. 5, note.

mitting that Cuchulain does not really love her. He is lost as
a poet. As Robert Graves puts it: "An ancient Irish *Triad*
is justified; 'It is death to mock a poet, to love a poet, to be
a poet.' "[11]

As a god of the year, Cuchulain returns to his watery
beginnings by fighting the waves, and in the story of Cuchulain's wager with the Green Knight—according to
which they agree to behead each other at alternate New
Years—the mythological affinities of Cuchulain are again
very clear. Insofar as the story of the War of the Bulls is
regarded as Cuchulain's saga, we see traces of a royal bull-
cult in which his fate is linked with that of the Brown Bull
of Cooley. The two bulls may be interpreted as forms of
royal swineherds, originally priests in the service of the
Death-goddess whose sacred animal was the pig and who
are capable of changing their shapes. Cuchulain was told by
the Morrigu (Fate-goddess) that he would live only while
the calf of Queen Maeve's bull was still a yearling. When
the Brown Bull has succeeded in killing its White-horned
rival and then gone home to die itself, the calf succeeds
it and Cuchulain dies, for in a sense Cuchulain is himself the
Brown Bull.[12] Cuchulain (who mythologically is perhaps
more an Irish Hercules than an Irish Achilles) has many
roles, and not the least of these involves the labor, unfore-
seen by him, of serving as a national symbol for the modern
Irish literary movement.

To pass from the Cuchulain of centuries ago to the literary creations made of him in this century is to face the
problem why Cuchulain was such an evocative symbol of
Irish aspirations not only for Yeats but to a large extent

[11] *Ibid.*, p. 375.   [12] *Ibid.*, pp. 183–184.

for the whole independence movement. Herbert Howarth (who calls Cuchulain the Irish Siegfried!) says that a foreigner cannot help being surprised at the choice of a hero whose career was apparently so gloomy and inauspicious as the model for a hopeful nationalist movement.

On the other hand, he had a total loyalty to his obligations, and an unlimited capacity for sacrifice. His most celebrated feat was to hold the fort against the host of the enemies of Ireland —a Garibaldian feat such as Ireland needed if she was to overthrow an empire. So (although Yeats first used him in poetry for specific personal reasons, haunted by his killing of his son), the literary movement, working from Standish O'Grady's account of him, began to make him a national symbol. The fall of Parnell helped in that determination. Cuchulain's loyalty to land and clan and tabus was counterpointed by his marital infidelity, and that fact chimed with the Parnell associations. Parnell's spirit survived as Cuchulain of the poems and dramas.[13]

This shrewd comment is undoubtedly a helpful insight, but is it so surprising that Cuchulain should be chosen aside from his affinities with Parnell? The heroes of national epics are not a particularly happy lot. Think of Achilles, Aeneas, Roland, King Arthur, or for that matter Siegfried himself. What seems more important is the single-minded heroic energy that drives through to completion its appointed task, no matter what sacrifice is entailed. In fact, the more extraordinary the energy the more extraordinary the personal suffering; such sacrifice puts the seal of authenticity on the hero's life. Then too the special loneliness of Cuchulain, perhaps unique even among epic heroes, gives him a rebellious grandeur very appropriate for the model of a

[13] Herbert Howarth, *The Irish Writers* (New York, 1958), p. 27.

nation wishing to emphasize revolt against authority. (Howarth mentions AE's paralleling of Cuchulain with Prometheus—as well as with Christ.) [14]

The peculiar virtue of Yeats's attitude toward myth lies precisely in his ability to use it as a way of *seeing* his contemporary world. This would not have been possible if he had merely retreated into a more congenial land of dreams. What he did was to conduct a life-long search for a connection between the powerful fantasies that plagued and delighted him in childhood and youth and their source in that greater imagination out of which every man and every civilization has been created. From earliest childhood his outlook was specifically *poetic*, if we think of the poet as being obsessed with the act of creating not only poems but the whole universe that gives them context and meaning. Mythology *was* that universe for Yeats, for in myths peoples and nations had embodied their vision of themselves, and poets had been the custodians of the myths. In trying to construct a system which would provide a place for everything in man's history, Yeats was primarily concerned to account for the way man's desires interact with circumstance to transform his own life, to make and unmake nations, even to bring about the rise and fall of entire historical epochs. The brute weight of the physical world, untouched by imagination, was an objective fact—the kind of fact he mistakenly regarded as belonging to the province of science. When touched by imagination, this inert mass came to life, poetically speaking. For then man understood everything as vitally connected with himself: from moon and stars to his own physical sex, his fate was bound up with the fate of the universe, and his subjective power to

[14] *Ibid.*, p. 27.

comprehend his mysterious relation to everything else was limited only by the energy of his imagination. This ability to focus the world's meanings on himself did not signify, however, that the "subjective" man could make the world according to his liking; it only meant that he might, if will and understanding and desire were strong enough, achieve a completeness of character undreamt of by lesser men, though the very reach of his imagination would make him painfully aware how far he fell short of the perfection his mind conceived.

For such a man, the world was bound to be a theater of conflict. Circumstance was recalcitrant; not only the short-comings of his own character but the inability of other men to see the world with his imaginative intensity stood in the way. At one end of the spectrum was the image of a perfectly realized, self-sufficient beauty; at the other, the mindless existence of mere things, passively waiting to be acted upon by something outside. And all men and times were somewhere in between, more or less blindly moving toward their opposites. Only the heroes could hope, perhaps, to escape from the endlessly turning wheel which brought things around to their beginnings again according to a regular schedule. For oddly enough, despite the imaginative ingenuity of its details, Yeats's system is quite mechanical in its workings. It seems as little dependent on the presence of God as any deist could ask for. Yet the motive that compelled Yeats to create it was far from mechanical, nor does it actually "contain" his mythology. For that we must go to the poems and plays.

But if, influenced by Eastern thought, the neo-Platonic tradition, Renaissance art, modern idealist philosophy, what he took to be the central Irish tradition, and his own varied experience of men and women, Yeats's mythology took on an ever more cosmic significance for him, behind the public and historical concerns remained the image of the beautiful woman, forever beckoning the hero (or poet) to extend himself to his utmost reach. Her fatality for the hero lay in her ambiguous ideality: she aroused his desire to shine in the world with masculine valor at the same time she offered him the chance to forget the world completely in timeless rapture with her. Her love meant transformation; it might bring folly, wisdom, or death, but whether regarded as curse or blessing, it removed the hero who accepted her challenge from his previous condition and gave his energies new focus. As Yeats grew older, his vision of the ideal woman became fiercer, more uncompromising. Love called forth strong images of both aggression and passivity, and the effects on the lover were at the same time more brutally imagined and closer to miracle. The lovers receded further into myth, became more ritualistic, and yet expressed their emotions with greater human intensity.

As Yeats indicated in "Adam's Curse," there is a subtle connection between the labor that it takes to make a beautiful poem and to make a beautiful woman; both involve a kind of soul-toil often unappreciated by the world. Yet it is these "idle trades" that give us the images without which love cannot exist. The more perfect the beauty, it seems, the surer it is to be a source of suffering because the harder it is to attain. The struggle may lead to weary-heartedness and a sense of the futility of the time-bound world—in this mood Yeats may accept the Eastern fatalism of a Mohini Chatterjee—or it may lead to greater activity in the world of affairs. Mythologically, woman may tempt man to his destruction or lead him on to heroic achievement. In her intellectual and moral aspects, woman has represented for man a superior being, a Sophia or Mary (Dante's Beatrice is the most famous literary example); but as a representative of the instinctive and emotional life she is a danger and temptation like Eve or Helen.[15]

In *The Countess Cathleen* and *The Land of Heart's Desire* the heroines, so differently conceived in scale, are alike in their opposition to the inhibiting conditions imposed by worldly circumstance. They are in conflict with Christianity and the moral codes which it imposes, though neither would take, or even understand, an intellectually anti-Christian position. They do not yet have heroes worthy of them, but they represent the pull exerted by the typical Yeatsian heroine: toward some decisive, liberating act that will effectively isolate the heroic individual, leaving him suspended between heavenly and earthly existence. There is little doubt that Yeats's heroines are supposed to set high goals for the hero to aspire to, but it would be very difficult to separate the moral appeal from the emotional, or the intellectual from the instinctive. In fact, Yeats's heroines lead their men into a kind of temptation in which impulse and feeling are much more important than mind, and in which a kind of reckless magnanimity, a complete giving of the self, is more important than the achievement of a predetermined goal. Sometimes, as in *At the Hawk's Well*, the woman-figure represents a challenge to battle that combines a kind of religious commitment with sexual ardor. Cuchulain, in all the vigor of his youthful self-confidence, wants mastery and takes no heed of the price it may cost him.

[15] See, for example, Jung's classifications as cited in J. E. Cirlot, *A Dictionary of Symbols* (New York, 1962), p. 356.

All too seldom is the painfully created beauty that makes
heroes of men described with the serenity of the opening
lines of *The Only Jealousy of Emer*. But here we have
an evocation of the birth of beauty in which storm and
stillness, sea and land, night and day are poised in tremulous
balance; instead of the conscious labor it costs a woman to
be beautiful emphasized in "Adam's Curse," we see vistas
stretching back into the abyss of time in which "the seden-
tary soul" worked "beyond hearing and seeing" to *raise*
loveliness into being. The result was

> A strange, unserviceable thing,
> A fragile, exquisite pale shell,
> That the vast troubled waters bring
> To the loud sands before day has broken.[16]

This beauty is at once human and inhuman, a link con-
necting the generations of men and yet finally a part of
nature, perfect but useless to those who dared wounds and
death to drag this loveliness into being. As one would expect from Yeats, the "bonds no man could unbind" were
the result of imagination, of "the labyrinth of the mind."
Again the creation of womanly beauty is analogous to artistic creation, to the making of a beautiful poem. How much
the image of desire is a product of conscious, willed effort
and how much of the unconscious, ineluctable rhythms of
an impersonal nature is left unsettled, but in the play
Cuchulain, who is an object of feminine desire for Emer,
is "saved" from disappearing forever into the ideal world
where the strength of his dream of beauty has brought him
by the greater strength of those very human emotions
which are the creators of ideal beauty in the first place.

[16] *Collected Plays* (London, 1952), p. 282.

In a sense, beauty is the opposite of the passion that creates it and which it in turn re-creates. Beauty is dangerous because it leads to aggression and conflict or else to a state of mindless ecstasy. Yet without it desire would never be disciplined into civilized achievement.

Cuchulain, even when Yeats has transformed him into a culture hero to serve distinctively modern purposes, retains a certain primitive roughness; and the mythological dramatizations of the feminine ideal sometimes become extreme examples of the counterpointing of primitive and civilized values. So in *A Full Moon in March* the Queen, whose chaste beauty (as in the Renaissance philosophy of love) "can make the loutish wise," is like a savage goddess who must be placated by human sacrifice to ensure the fertility of the crops. Two images, "crown of gold" and "dung of swine," are symbolic of the opposition that paradoxically must be and yet cannot be reconciled. The paradox is expressed by the action when not the swineherd but only his severed head wins the queen's love. For "the pitchers" of love to spill "all time's completed treasure," the play insists, only the sexual "desecration" of holy virginity will do; thus crown of gold and dung of swine are miraculously unified in love-death. This theme suggests the decadence of the nineties and Oscar Wilde's *Salomé*, but there is a crucial difference. Yeats is not interested in the psychology of perverse love; what fascinates him is the mystery of love itself—how pure ideal is wedded to corrupt flesh, how the supernatural and immortal enter into the cycle of nature and mortality, how the sacred and the profane can be one.

For though Yeats was interested in the Fatal Man and the Fatal Woman of Romanticism, he never succumbed to the Romantic obsessions that so preoccupied Baudelaire and Flaubert.[17] Perhaps Yeats was too unchristian; certainly he did not have Baudelaire's sense of Sin. To be sure, the "love" relationship in *A Full Moon* could be described as that between executioner and victim in a literal sense, but there is none of the tortured sensuality characteristic of genuine algolagnia. Yeats would never have thought of sin as the normal state of natural man and virtue as an artificial construct of human reason the way Baudelaire did.[18] It might be said, indeed, that Yeats was insufficiently concerned with the natural man in his work—he was wise not to have become a novelist—and too much concerned with mythical fantasy, but the feminine ideal he projects in his poems and plays never becomes monstrous even when she is cruel, nor does her love inspire her lover to degrade himself. The suffering love causes is romantic in a more old-fashioned way: it is at the heart of tragic experience because mortal capacities can never match immortal longings.

What is longed for? Yeats suggests in "The Gift of Harun Al-Rashid" (1923) that there is a secret wisdom guarded by love, though the loved one is ignorant of it. An old man has found a young girl who loves him. She speaks in trance a wisdom not her own, but the old man is fearful she may discover her "voice" and think he loves her only for that. Then their love would be left in ruins. For him the truth is that the voice and the person who goes with it cannot be separated:

> The voice has drawn
> A quality of wisdom from her love's

[17] For a discussion of these obsessions, see Mario Praz, *The Romantic Agony* (London, 1951), p. 152.
[18] *Ibid.*, p. 146.

Particular quality. The signs and shapes;
All those abstractions that you fancied were
From the great treatise of Parmenides;
All, all those gyres and cubes and midnight things
Are but a new expression of her body
Drunk with the bitter sweetness of her youth.
And now my utmost mystery is out.
A woman's beauty is a storm-tossed banner;
Under it wisdom stands, and I alone—
Of all Arabia's lovers I alone—
Nor dazzled by the embroidery, nor lost
In the confusion of its night-dark folds,
Can hear the armed man speak.[19]

The story has obvious autobiographical relevance to Yeats and his wife, and frequently in his writings the beautiful and desirable woman has a troubling transparency, as though beyond her the hero could see what he was really after—but only if she were there for him to see through. Here Yeats is insisting that the wisdom the sage seeks is "but a new expression of her body"; yet in the next breath the sage is not dazzled by the "storm-tossed banner" of her beauty and hence clearly hears the voice of wisdom, the "armed man" who stands *under* beauty's banner. In the imagery of the verse war, love, wisdom, and beauty are linked. Without beauty there can be no wisdom, but wisdom itself is a masculine thing about which beauty had better not concern itself.

If even the apparently most abstract wisdom is a product of sexual love, if the good of the intellect comes from the inspiration of a longed-for image of flesh and blood, there is also a sadder wisdom that women have to teach. Trouble

[19] *Collected Poems* (New York, 1950), p. 444.

is born of the union of goddess and mortal, as Cuchulain
learned to his sorrow in *On Baile's Strand,* but a still more
cursed inheritance is the lot of man and woman when she
is noble but weak enough to succumb to a suitor who is her
social and moral inferior. In *Purgatory* we see, as it were,
the consequence of mating the Queen and Swineherd of
A Full Moon in March. We descend from the world of
fairy-tale paradox to a no less mysterious but grimmer place
much closer to contemporary Ireland. The mother, who
must relive again and again the sinful moment of her lustful
surrender to the stable boy whom she has married, proves a
baleful gloss on the "desecration and the lover's night" of
the earlier play. Her crime is that she has betrayed the great
house which stands for the Irish aristocratic tradition and
in so doing has set in motion a family curse dreadful as
that of Clytemnestra in the ancient Greek saga. But the
Old Man of *Purgatory* feels sorrow for his mother and
hatred for his father. Caught between remorse not so much
for his own as for his father's guilt and pity for his mother's
purgatorial agonies the only reparation he can offer is the
killing of his own son. At last, and for the only time in
Yeats's work, the mother appears as the loved woman. Although Yeats does not choose to stress the Oedipal implications of the situation in *Purgatory,* making of the play instead a moral parable on the fate of modern Ireland, we can
see a repetition of an old theme with new variations. The
idealized beautiful woman has become all too human: by
not reserving herself for a hero or a poet, or at least for an
aristocratic statesman, she has lost her purity and brought
misery on herself and destruction on her country.

The mischance of the heroic quest for consummation is
farcically treated in *The Herne's Egg,* that late parody of

Yeats's on his own heroic dramas, in which the coupling of two donkeys destines the heroic Congal to be reincarnated as one of their kind, all because man and goddess are not quick enough to perform the act of conception (before the dying Congal's body is cold!) which would have saved the hero for the human world. Even *Purgatory* has its comic moments (as when the Old Man speculates on whether his mother relives the pleasure of the sexual act as well as remorse for it), but now the hero as Old Man can express love only through aggression on his kin and kind. The image of desire, in other contexts the banner of beauty under which armed wisdom stood, has become the incestuously tainted nightmare of a man whose knowledge and love are impotent to rescue him from the torture they inflict. Cuchulain, whose madness returned him to the sea and renewed his desire for perfect, other-worldly beauty, was recalled to the land and resumed his heroic career, but for the Old Man of *Purgatory* his mother's remorse (as he imagines it) is identified with his own; the burden of guilt has become intolerably heavy and the possibility of redemption inconceivable. His love for his mother is so bound up with hatred that heroic detachment is impossible. It is Yeats's bleakest vision of the wisdom woman can bring.

Because evil had seemed to the young Yeats so much a matter of hateful beliefs, he was slow to identify it with the human condition. What Christians called sin all too often coincided with the imaginative energy that Blake (and J. B. Yeats) had taught him to delight in. Ideas of good and evil were essentially aesthetic: the beautiful was good and the ugly was bad, as in fairy tales. Morality, especially official morality, was the enemy of art. So far, at least, Yeats would go with Oscar Wilde and the poets of the *Yellow Book*. The tragic view of life consisted in the realization that ideals are doomed to defeat, mainly because the poet's view does not prevail in a world of shabby rationalists. The moral duty of the poet is to defend tradition—beautiful things, beautiful manners, beautiful ideas—from the egalitarian tendencies of undiscriminating democracy. Yeats never abandoned these beliefs—in fact his defense of tradition is fiercer than ever in his old age—but his sense of responsibility for his hatreds increased. The answers he can never get right in "The Man and the Echo" are responses to moral questions: did certain words of his lead to the injury or destruction of other people? He had long deplored the fanaticism of Maud Gonne at the same time he was attracted by it—now he questions himself. Is it possible that the heroic virtues are morally tainted?

In his earlier plays Yeats was intent on building up illusion, on fortifying the matter of myth against the hostile intrusions of the unbeliever. The Romantic virtues he presented could be regarded ironically only by the enemy, and all the irony *within* the plays is expended on the characters lacking faith in the supremacy of the imagination and unwilling to commit themselves to some image of desirable perfection. In the later plays he is both surer of his ability to create illusion with authority and more indifferent to the need to do so. Consequently he dares to be ironic about myth and finally (in *The Death of Cuchulain*) about himself. *The Green Helmet* (1910) is the last play in which the hero receives unqualified approval. The later plays do not, I think, ever repudiate either myth or romance, but they gain by being read with a sense of humor. They are at once more lyrically intense and more intellectually playful. Yeats trusts his power of incantation more but has less hope that his ideas will be found persuasive.

In the end, Yeats came perilously close to disintegrating the poetic truth of myth in the acid of his irony, but it would be a mistake to think that he ever settled for a serene (or troubled) scepticism. His imagination could not rest in a smaller view of reality than the mythical. What he has done, essentially, is conduct an experiment in stripping away the romantic trappings of myth which so enamored him in his youth to see what is left. What does he find in the foul rag-and-bone shop of the heart (an image, of course, Romantic in itself)?

We might put it this way: man lives by struggling with the question of his relation to the nature within and outside himself. He cannot escape his duality; he is tied to a vulnerable body that ages and has appetites, but his spirit is to an extent independent, or at least determined by some more inclusive and powerful spirit not subject to physical limitation. Nevertheless, this spirit is incomplete too. It requires a body. The bridge joining body and spirit is sex. Pure spirit and pure body are both conceived as masculine, but in between is woman, who draws body upward and spirit downward until they meet. But there is no simple reconciliation. The woman hardly knows what she is doing; she is governed by "unconscious" forces to which she reacts with dreamlike automatism. For man she is paradoxically an end in herself and a means to his own fulfillment. Ideally, sexual intercourse leads to a transcendence of its physical basis, but actually it may be "reflective"—spirit may merely mirror itself or body affirm its instinctive appetite (Attracta in *The Herne's Egg* is ambiguously raped by spirit and body; in a sense it is impossible to distinguish between the two experiences). The ritual fails.

Life, at least for the hero capable of the mythical vision of reality, is a game with strict rules which he must discover—or invent—for himself. He finds out that the solemn rules of society, the conventional morality designed to stabilize the lives of men, to make them comfortable creatures of habit who think alike and act alike, to isolate them from the shock of experience that would make them suffer the paradoxes of their human nature, are at best an irrelevance and at worst a frustration of his own purposes. For him life has become a matter of finding a way to link his destiny with that larger universal rhythm that is before and during and after any particular person, time, or place. That tragi-comic hero Congal has a natural aptitude for the heroic role as long as it involves no reverence for an authority higher than himself; he comes late and reluctantly to an understanding (if it can truly be called that) of the mission incumbent on him to establish contact with godhead. He is duly punished for his recalcitrance. He may get another chance, but it will not be in the next generation certainly.

As we shall see in our analysis of *The Herne's Egg*, the hero's special attitude toward life includes an equally special attitude toward death. He has learned to see himself as a great individual and yet as endlessly renewable, like the seasons. He is somehow sure of his immortality and hence feels no cowardice in the face of death (though Congal is not sure, is mocked in the event, and perhaps emerges as more human because of his uncertainty). Congal is too reasonable; he illustrates what an ironic gift to man reason is. It allows him to be human but makes him aware of insoluble problems. As the action progresses, the ground rhythm of alternating self-assertion and self-surrender on the part of the hero intensifies. In *The Herne's Egg* the actual dying of the hero is drawn out to test the crucial issue: is Congal a mere fool among fools, responding witlessly to the buffets of outrageous fortune, or is he the master of his folly, steadfast in purpose and so unyielding in will that he cannot be denied the title of hero in this life whatever the Great Herne may do with him in the next? Yeats leaves the issue unresolved, for (upon reflection) we see that his irony is remarkably balanced, implying at least as much ridicule of those who would make a donkey of Congal as of Congal himself. Yeats gives us no assurance that the universe is beneficent; that is, organized for the satisfaction of man's ego. He does give us assurance that the pain of life can only be made to yield dignity if we view ourselves with a kind of detached passion, realizing how near akin folly and wisdom are.

[PART II]
THE PLAYS

4

Early Heroines and Heroes

The Countess Cathleen

Yeats wrote to John O'Leary in 1889 that Dowden had urged him to try his hand at a poetic drama for the stage. "I have been intending to write one," Yeats confided, "founded on the tale of 'Countess Kathleen O'Shea' in the folk lore book." [1] In this tale there are two merchants who come to a hotel and do nothing all day but count their gold. The news gets around that they're buying souls. Many come and sell. Countess Kathleen sells all except her mansion and gives money to the poor. But the devils steal her money (she could have prevented them if she could have made the sign of the cross, but her hands were captive). Supplies are coming from the east in eight days, but people can't wait. Countess Kathleen sells her soul. Then she locks herself up in her mansion. Three days later she is found dead in her room. But God nullified the sale because she had saved the eternal souls of her people. Some say that the merchants are chained up in a cave, waiting until they can deliver Kathleen's soul to their master, Satan. The tale is plainly told. No Aleel, no Oona, no Teigue and Shemus and Mary, no climactic scene with angels. And no

[1] *Letters* (London, 1954), p. 108.

touches of nature either.[2] In his notes on *The Countess Cathleen* in *Plays and Controversies,* Yeats refers to a "Christian variant" of the story given in William Larminie's *West Irish Folk-Tales and Romances.* This story, "The Woman Who Went to Hell," tells how a poor woman spent fourteen years in hell to save a boy whose corpse she had revived, when neither the father nor mother could gain admittance, though they were willing to try. When she returns she is recognized only by a magic ring she had taken with her. Her saintliness is proved when she comes up from hell carrying a burden of souls with her which she refuses to surrender either to a tempter who calls herself the Virgin Mary or to another who calls himself God. Only to the King of Sunday does she give them. And he praises her for her resistance to deceit. The theme is pre-Christian, going back as far as Euripides' *Alcestis.* Yeats quotes the French story from Leo Lespes. Here, the heroine is Ketty O'Connor and there are a few extra comments about the Irishness of the story. Otherwise it is identical with the version in *Irish Fairy and Folk Tales.*

What attracted Yeats was, first of all, a structure of meanings as simple and fundamental as the facts of famine itself. The fable is a Christian parable (Yeats called it "the most impressive form of one of the supreme parables in the world"), but it has a pre-Christian flavor as well. The merchants, who (as the sources stress) inexplicably know the Irish language well, are exotic in a way that suggests Arabia and India. Money (in the form of glittering gold) was the devil's lure for the desperate and unwary long before Judas

[2] W. B. Yeats, ed., *Irish Fairy and Folk Tales* (London, n.d.), pp. 232–235 (Item 212 in Allan Wade, *A Bibliography of the Writings of W. B. Yeats* [London, 1951], p. 211).

betrayed Christ for thirty pieces of silver. It is implied, though not stated, that Satan has his headquarters in the Far East. Cathleen, in going beyond the call of a sovereign's duty to save the very souls (and bodies) of her countrymen, at the apparent expense of her own, embodies a great tragic theme that Yeats could not help feeling was a challenge to his poetical powers. And its universality was matched by its local significance. Here was a chance for the proud young poet to give his fellow citizens an object lesson in morality. And those who protested against the play because no Irishman would sell his soul got the point. Irishmen *were* selling their souls, and not only to the English. All compromisers with the ideal were tacitly rebuked, just as all martyrs to the cause of Irish freedom were implicitly praised. Riches were no temptation for Cathleen, and even the beguilements of art (as represented by Aleel) were firmly if regretfully put aside. And Cathleen's lonely isolation (of which a later Yeats would have made so much more) demonstrated that saintliness was a matter of selfless love and active courage more than of humility and asceticism.

Selling one's own soul may be logically self-defeating as well as blasphemous (some of the clergy thought so), but it was the sort of audacity that made the spiritual authentic for Yeats. As he says in his *Autobiography*, if he had been writing the scene where she makes the bargain with the merchants today (1935) he would have had her burst out laughing and horrify all the spectators.[3] But that would not be in keeping with the decorum of the play. Cathleen is so high above everyone else in the play that she views their sufferings with the detachment of a goddess.

[3] *Autobiography* (New York, 1938), p. 252.

Her pity is genuine; she proves that with her life. Nevertheless, her inner passion is far removed from public acts of charity. (The objectors were intellectually misguided but intuitively right to sense that Yeats was offering them no ordinary Sunday-school lesson.) Ultimately, she acts as her vision of what it means to be the Countess Cathleen bids her to, not as her priest, or even her lover, would advise her to do. She has something of the haughtiness of the true aristocrat that Yeats always so admired, though her steeliness is robed in gentle language. It would be wrong to play her as having anything in common with Lady Bountiful.

She belongs to other elements than ordinary humanity as surely as Shakespeare's Cleopatra does. For all her selflessness, she is more in love with herself than she could possibly be with anyone else. She is ancient, mythical, out of time and simultaneously (Yeats thought hopefully) a part of living folklore. It was a combination he found hard to resist. If we try, we can see adumbrated in her, however faintly, the inhuman and statuesque Fand of that much later play, *The Only Jealousy of Emer*. But in this early play her character—and she is only the first in a long line of similar Yeats heroines—remains sufficiently (and properly) vague enough so that it is difficult to distinguish her from the saintly stereotype of the pure and holy spirit, especially without the benefit of hindsight. There is a certain Eastern fatalism in the story as Yeats dramatizes it, as though the human will counted for little in the scheme of things. The action moves towards its preordained end, and the agents of that action, though faced with decisions that mean life or death to them (or perhaps for that very reason), act almost as involuntarily as animals exercising their conditioned reflexes.

How Cathleen saved her country from going to the devil

during the famine is an eminently moral tale, no doubt, but the morality is more subversive than at first appears. Those who profit by the misfortunes of others are evil, in fact they are devils, but they are only acting according to their natures (they have no temptation to be good). The starving peasants should undoubtedly die of hunger rather than sell their souls, but their death would serve no good purpose. In actuality, the famine is good for just one thing: it allows Cathleen to immortalize her soul. The souls of other people count as nothing beside hers; even Aleel and Oona have no individual importance, except to focus attention on the superhumanity of Cathleen. She can do no wrong, not so much because of the holiness of her heart's intentions as because of her sublime self-confidence; it enables her to shake off the dust of this world with a spectacular show of indifference to what all common people cherish dearly. They have no real idea of the value of their souls because their souls do not really have much value. Cathleen knows the supreme value of hers, and, were it not for the drama's sake, would never believe any amount of money could buy it. A soul such as hers cannot be given away; how much less can it be bought. God Himself vouches for that. Cathleen, the first of Yeats's superwomen, is also the most Christian. But it is pretty clear that Yeats is much less interested in her Christianity than in her determination to be every inch a heroine. He did not dedicate the play to Maud Gonne for nothing.

M. J. Sidnell has shown in his study of the early revisions [4] what a great change came over the play after Maud Gonne had refused Yeats's proposal of marriage. Yeats had

[4] M. J. Sidnell, "Yeats's First Work for the Stage," in D. E. S. Maxwell and S. B. Bushrui, eds., *W. B. Yeats: Centenary Essays on the Art of W. B. Yeats* (Ibadan, 1965), pp. 167–187.

been very concerned to make the play stageworthy and Irish. To his source, he added references to supernatural creatures from Irish folklore as well as creating a rural scene with individualized Irish peasants. The Kathleen of the early manuscript versions, a supporter of the peasants' right to steal in times of famine, asserts both her social and religious responsibility to come to the rescue of the poor. No Aleel (or Kevin or Avric) confuses the issue by presenting the claims of private love vs. public responsibility. In composing the play Yeats was very consciously trying to shake off the escapism of which he considered himself guilty in his previous work. Hence the careful attention to natural speech rhythms and realistic detail. Nevertheless, what interests Yeats most in all versions is the pressure of the ideal which forces character to reveal its soul. He never really gave up his interest in escapism, or wanted to. He *did* try to show, however, that "escape" might be a tougher, more masculine process than adroit dexterity in accommodating oneself to the powers that be.

The Land of Heart's Desire

Written for Dorothy Paget, Florence Farr's niece, this faery play is Yeats's least ambitious (excluding *The Pot of Broth*, if that is really his) and most intimate play. It was produced on a double bill with Shaw's *Arms and the Man* in London in 1894. The contrast of two styles could not be greater. Yeats endows the world of amoral, irresponsible play with an inevitable luster; Shaw punctures the "lies" of romance with energetic glee. In *Heart's Desire* the life of drab and Christian duty is threatened by joy. In spite of its poetic delicacy, Yeats's fantasy is firmly in touch with reality; dramatically speaking, it is not in the least ir-

responsible. It uses the changeling theme to make a familiar
Yeatsian point: to deny, or accept, the heart's desire is no
laughing matter. The faery people, tyrannized over by the
repressive institutions of church and state, yet know a way
to get their revenges. They are the guardians of aesthetic
vitality—of the life-giving pleasure that comes from "useless" activity—and they can bring death to any who
respond to the lure of their beauty if the ties of religion and
morality have been sufficiently loosened.

Nature is, literally, just outside the Bruins' door. From
indoors they look out on a night where "the moon or a late
sunset glimmers through the trees." They live in the county
of Sligo at some remote time—a time when things were
much as they have always been in the west of Ireland. A
mother-in-law is complaining of the laziness of her son's
new wife, and the son defends his young bride. The generations are at each other, and Father Hart is there to bring
peace with his Catholic wisdom—and at the same time to
try to lead young Mary to give up foolish dreams and live
exclusively in the authorized world of common sense.
Those who read and write books can be tricked by any idle
boy and never make money. That's what happened to
Maurteen's grandfather. From Father Hart's point of view,
God "gives a little round of deeds and days" and you learn
to be like your neighbors unless you listen to the words of
"some wrecked angel." Mary's father-in-law is sympathetic
to her lonely plight and finds it natural for her to "dream
of the Good People," especially on May Eve. Even Father
Hart, for whom the "Good People" are merely "evil
spirits," approves of keeping "old innocent customs up."
None of these people are far from pagan belief, struggle as
they may to be "sophisticated" Christians.

We would make a mistake to think of the faery people as in any sense "cute" or whimsical. Their life mocks our own, and they are glad to seize any chance to upset the orderliness they despise. Mary is tired of all the tongues that surround her, even her husband's, "a kind tongue too full of drowsy love." Mary is no shrinking bride moping about the house. Even Shawn, who dearly loves her beauty and sensitivity, talks of her "heart that was most proud and cold." But Mary does love her husband's devotion to her and is grateful that he would give her what Father Hart calls "maddening freedom and bewildering light" if only he could. And she is young enough to be very unsure of her own impulses. Maybe she *is* wicked, as her elders would have her believe.

The voice that begins singing of the faeries is reminiscent of the Fiddler of Dooney. Dancing best expresses their utopian abandon and lightheartedness. When Maurteen brings in the Faery Child, even Bridget takes a motherly interest in her, won over by her apparent gentility, her white hands and pretty dress. Underneath, the old and cross have a soft spot for careless beauty, and in a young child it need not be condemned. But it should be, for the child shrieks when it sees the crucifix hanging on the wall. Ironically, it is Father Hart who takes it down, because the young one is so easily frightened. Everyone except Mary is charmed by the faery child; Mary knows all too well that "unholy powers are dancing in the house." And, indeed, because the crucifix is gone the child has power over them. The faery child has come for Mary. No one can save Mary except Mary herself. As Father Hart says, "only the soul's choice can save her now." But his exhortations to duty are of no avail. In the debate for Mary's heart, the call of eternal youth is too strong. Even Shawn's loving arms cannot hold her—and she dies.

To the youthful Yeats, decrepitude and senility were worse than death. He is obviously on the side of the faeries; he abruptly ends the play without giving the others an opportunity to show any human reaction of grief to Mary's death. Yet he shows considerable skill in balancing opposing forces. We understand the position of each character; even cross old Bridget is presented with a certain amount of sympathy. Mary's death is the crowning ambiguity and brings to a focus the shortcomings of the play. Are we to regard her passing as a triumph for "life" or a tragic death? We can do neither, because the attractive Faery Child is too lightweight a representative of aesthetic virtue just as Father Hart is too heavy-handed a defender of moral virtue. *Heart's Desire*, like all the rest of Yeats's plays, is a variety of miracle play, but here the "miracle" is stillborn. In spite of the balance of opposing forces, the melodrama is too violent for its pageantlike context.[5]

It is not hard to see, however, why this play has been, as Yeats tells us, the most popular of all his plays with amateurs.[6] Character and situation are lucidly and charmingly dramatized, the theme is as simple and appealing as a child's game, and the verse is unencumbered by any load of nationalistic significance or abstruse lore. Whether Mary is saved or damned is less important than the reminder that dullness can deal a mortal wound. And even in so slight a play as this, Yeats's characteristic irony is in evidence: the conservative defenders of negative law may be denying life

[5] A. G. Stock, *W. B. Yeats: His Poetry and His Thought* (Cambridge, 1961), p. 36.
[6] *Plays and Controversies* (London, 1923), p. 299.

itself when they try to deny life's impulses toward delight. Their own acceptance of the law they expound is irritable and half-hearted; in fact, their own buried impulses cannot resist temptation, and their yielding is fatal to their cause. Mary is a victim of her own guilty feelings as much as the call to a mindless (and heartless) life of dance and song.

Fand in *The Only Jealousy of Emer* is the Faery Child grown up. But she is unable to win Cuchulain because, unlike the childish Mary, he is old enough to be bowed down by the weight of human memory. And for all its bitterness, he must cherish human love and cling to it. Fand loses when she fails to persuade Cuchulain that a disembodied ideal is better than human perfection. Shawn in *Heart's Desire* is a good-hearted but awkward young man not up to the heroic vocation. He could be made either funny or poignant in performance, and given enough skill, perhaps both. From the standpoint of thematic structure, Aleel's role in *Countess Cathleen* is like the Faery Child's in *Heart's Desire*. But like Fand in the much later play, Aleel loses too. He represents the call of "maddening freedom" from Christian bonds as the faery child does, but of course he is much more human than she is. His love for Cathleen is real, however pitifully inadequate to its task.

Heart's Desire is in the symbolist mode in its insistence on other-worldly values, but it is a symbolist play emerging out of the cocoon of peasant folk-play. The domestic scenes have a homely, if not quite earthy, quality, and a streak of shrewd humor noticeably colors the language. But the play never gathers to a symbolist intensity of mood, though it gropes in that direction. It is too "young" in its conception of the world on the other side of night, too close to the tales of *The Celtic Twilight*, for the intellectual subtlety of a poetics to intervene between experience and the imaginative transformation of that experience. But there are unmistakable signs that the poet who wrote it would never be content to restrict himself to the materials offered by the visible world—everything lesser must be measured against an invisible ideal.

Cathleen ni Houlihan

In *Cathleen ni Houlihan*, as later in *The Dreaming of the Bones*, Yeats has a specific historic occasion in mind—in *Cathleen* it is the landing of the French at Killala in 1798. Undoubtedly history gives the play an added resonance, but it is a myth play as surely as the rest of Yeats's drama. A young man about to be married goes off instead to give his life to Ireland—Cathleen ni Houlihan. The main problem of the play is how to fill up the time until the climax arrives, and we learn that the old woman the Gillanes have given their hospitality to is not a woman at all but an allegorical figure. "Did you see an old woman going down the path?" Peter asks. And his twelve-year-old son Patrick replies, "I did not, but I saw a young girl, and she had the walk of a queen." Yeats had a talent for the strong ending, and this is probably the most famous last line in any of his plays, at least in Ireland. During the *Playboy* riots, Yeats was able to quiet a hostile crowd by reminding them that the author of *Cathleen ni Houlihan* was addressing them.[7] If this is not a propaganda play [8] in any usual sense, it is certainly the most direct appeal Yeats ever made to militant patriotic emotion.

[7] Joseph Hone, *W. B. Yeats* (New York, 1943), p. 231.
[8] Yeats insisted it wasn't. See *Plays and Controversies*, pp. 160–161.

How does he go about it? He uses the by now familiar scene of a peasant dwelling and a family gathering. Instead of being newlyweds, like Shawn and Mary in *Heart's Desire*, the young couple in *Cathleen* are about to be married. Everybody is quite happy at the prospect, though Bridget has some of the typical mother-in-law reluctance to give up her son. Michael is not in the least discontented and apparently very much in love with Delia. Peter, the father, is already planning how the hundred-pound dowry should be spent. Then appears the catalyst of disruption. The old woman seems to the family who offer her charity nothing but a pitiful human derelict, but she "touches" young Michael with her stories of heroes and her singing of their immortality. (Lady Gregory is supposed to have supplied the line, "they shall be remembered for ever," as well as much else.) [9] Under the old woman's spell, Michael forgets about his bride; he is as impervious to argument as Mary was in *Heart's Desire*. He has but a moment's hesitation before choosing Ireland as his bride and abandoning poor Delia.

What is interesting about Yeats's (and Lady Gregory's) contribution to the treasury of Irish patriotism in this piece is its simple austerity. As a recruiting officer, Cathleen ni Houlihan offers nothing better than blood, sweat, and tears. And she is not interested in compromise. "If any would give me help he must give me himself, he must give me all." If you would serve Ireland, you must sacrifice all private welfare and be resigned to failure, hoping that each failure is making eventual restoration of the "four green fields" to their rightful owner inevitable. Compared to an

[9] Donald Torchiana, *W. B. Yeats and Georgian Ireland* (Evanston, Ill., 1966), pp. 78–79.

"affair" with Cathleen, even a loving marriage is no more than a business proposition (Peter's counting out of the bag of money helps suggest this). The absoluteness of the commitment required, of course, is the very thing that makes it romantic. Michael's enlistment in Cathleen's army is no less an escape than Mary's departure for the land of the Sidhe. What the youthful heart desires is immortality and avoidance of the settled comfort or discomfort of crabbed age. Whether fighting or dancing, the adventurer into the ideal has left humdrum reality behind.

It must have been stirring to see and hear Maud Gonne in the title role. She herself speaks as though that first performance of *Cathleen* had been unequaled since, attributing this to Yeats's work at rehearsals.[10] At any rate the effect of the play was so great that the authorities evicted the company from the little hall on Clarendon Street after a week. L. A. G. Strong, who felt that Yeats's plays usually read better than they played, considered *Cathleen* a notable exception. "[It] convinces from the first word to the last, and mounts to a curtain which shook the heart of Ireland and sends a thrill up an audience's spine today." [11]

A Pot of Broth

Nobody would be thrilled by *A Pot of Broth*, which is sometimes thought to be almost entirely the work of Lady Gregory.[12] But Yeats kept it in the collected edition of his plays, perhaps to show the breadth of his dramatic sym-

[10] Maud Gonne, "Yeats and Ireland," in *Scattering Branches*, Stephen Gwynn, ed., reprinted as *William Butler Yeats: Essays in Tribute* (Port Washington, N. Y., 1965), pp. 29–30.

[11] L. A. G. Strong, "William Butler Yeats," *ibid.*, p. 222.

[12] George Brandon Saul, *Prolegomena to the Study of Yeats's Plays* (Philadelphia, 1958), p. 37.

pathies. It is the type of farce where the tricker, or would-be tricker, is tricked. Libby Coneely, a hard-fisted woman who as the play opens is giving her husband John instructions for catching a recalcitrant hen ("Put your hand in the nettles, don't be daunted!"), combines in exact proportions the greed and credulity necessary for the tramp who has dropped by to play the trick of the stone on her. First he borrows a pot and a drop of water and puts his magic stone in the pot. By one means or another he gets the use of cabbage, onions, a ham bone and the hen. Libby is amazed and charmed with the resulting broth. The tramp finally gives her the stone for her kindness, taking only the ham bone, hen, and a bottle of whiskey for his trouble. John walks out to the gate with the tramp, presumably to congratulate him on tricking his termagant wife.

This tramp is a distant relative of Jack the Journeyman (the name occurs in one of the songs he sings) and all those wandering outsiders who live by their wits and are outlaws of society. He is no hero, but the play offers in its narrow scope a surprising opportunity for a good comedian to show his wares. Yeats says, "If it has a lasting interest, it is that it was the first comedy in dialect, of our movement, and gave Mr. William Fay his first opportunity as a comedian. . . . [He] played it not only with great humor but with great delicacy and charm. In some country village an audience of farmers once received it in stoney silence, and at the fall of the curtain a farmer stood up and said nobody there had ever seen a play. Then Mr. William Fay explained what a play was, and the farmer asked that it might be performed again, and at the second performance there was much laughter and cheers." [13] One would have

_____

[13] *Plays in Prose and Verse* (London, 1922), pp. 420-421.

enjoyed hearing Mr. Fay's explanation. Many other plays and playwrights could undoubtedly benefit by the kind of transformation he wrought in his audience.

Diarmuid and Grania

Plays written for the Irish National Theatre Society (established 1902) were usually the product of collaboration, and even before this writers, if not actors, shared in playmaking, for the goal of a truly national Irish drama made even the doughtiest individualists willing to learn from each other. But it is doubtful whether any other collaboration was as lunatic or as far-reaching in its consequences as that of Yeats and George Moore. *Diarmuid and Grania* (completed in December, 1900) is a work neither author seems to have been anxious to claim. It was thought to be lost until William Becker published a typescript that had come into his hands in the April-June number of *The Dublin Magazine* in 1951. Both Yeats and Moore had a good deal to say about the experience of working together. If the play did not add much to the literary history of either writer's reputation, the same cannot be said for the fringe benefits it provided. In the first volume of *Hail and Farewell*, Moore wrote a long and pleasant account of the mismating of impedimented minds.

He regarded Yeats with mingled awe and amusement but could never resist the temptation to make a joke of what Yeats took most seriously. Yeats, who regarded Moore with cautious respect tempered by distaste, hoped he could make a useful ally of him in the struggle to resuscitate Irish literature. According to the compact between them, Moore was to be in charge of construction while Yeats retained the right to have the last word on style. The trouble was that Yeats had plenty of ideas about construction and Moore insisted on arguing about style. Yeats said, for instance, that the first act of a play should be "horizontal" and the second "perpendicular."

And the third, I suppose, circular?

Quite so. In the third act we must return to the theme stated in the first scene; and [Yeats] described with long, thin hands the shapes the acts should take.[14]

In exasperation at Yeats's restrictions on vocabulary, Moore jokingly suggested writing the play in French. To Moore's dismay, Yeats seized on the idea with enthusiasm. Obsessed with his ideas of dialect and the folk, Yeats wanted a "peasant Grania." His subtle mind conceived a fantastic stratagem for "saving" the play from Moore without actually getting rid of him. Moore would write the play in French, Lady Gregory would translate it into English, Taidgh O'Donohue would put the English text into Irish, and then Lady Gregory would translate the Irish back into English again. Finally Yeats would give it the high gloss of style. Moore decided he could not write French in Galway and departed for France. He and Yeats parted amiably. Moore gives a sample of his French—the first scene of the second act. It is an incongruous mélange of businesslike language and romantic subject matter. Moore resolved to give up the whole foolish business, but kept the fragment as a reminder "what a damned fool a clever man like Yeats can be when he is in the mood to be a fool."

The play itself, though it lacks the lyric glow characteristic of Yeats's own heroic plays, is by no means despicable.

[14] George Moore, *Hail and Farewell* (London, 1947), Vol. I (*Ave*), pp. 268ff.

Its construction is workmanlike and its dialogue sounds speakable enough. It does, however, lack the development of situation within each act which one expects in a three-act play. Yeats seems to have lost the battle to make the heroine a "peasant Grania," though she is not much of an aristocrat either.

Like Yeats's later Deirdre, Grania becomes unsure of her hold over her lover after seven years. She would like to see Diarmuid reconciled to Finn, but the dream of herself as the renowned queen of the famous Finn also tempts her. And Diarmuid becomes anxious to meet the fate that hangs over him. Deirdre, by her implacable hatred of Conchubar and her loyalty to Naoise, transcends her lower nature and earns her place in the ranks of deathless heroines; Grania merely dissolves into weeping at the death of Diarmuid. She is little more than a childish bauble who brings bad blood between two brothers-in-arms. The "Helen" theme is one on which Yeats played many variations: the competition between two men for a woman or between two women for a man is the subject of most of his plays; even where it is not central, the sexual triangle is often a necessary part of the background of the story, as in *On Baile's Strand*. But in *Diarmuid and Grania* the heroine is part conniver, part hapless victim, part the adolescent in love with love, but no part true heroine. She hasn't sufficient recklessness and self-abandon to fit the exacting requirements of Yeatsian heroism. She is somewhere in between a Mary Bruin or a Delia Cahel (true peasant girls) and a Deirdre or Emer (genuine queenly heroines). As for Diarmuid, he is the beautiful boy who is also a mettlesome warrior, but really at home neither as lover or fighter. He achieves at best a youthful pathos and dignity but never rises to the grim nobility of a Cuchulain. He might have been an Adonis if he had had a Venus—and they had both been endowed with the tongues of poesy. Either Moore or Yeats might have worked out such a conception in their very different ways, but the "hieratic" Yeats (Moore's epithet) and the Moore who was "more mob than man" (Yeats's phrase) could not do it in partnership.

In *Dramatis Personae* Yeats condescendingly grants that Moore "would have been a master of construction, but that his practice as a novelist made him long for description and reminiscences." [15] Yeats was not sure when the Benson company performed the play at the Gaiety Theatre whether it failed or not: the gallery crowd wanted to displace the horse and pull the cab of Yeats and Maud Gonne through the streets of Dublin, but she, tired of crowds, refused.[16] In a letter to Lady Gregory quoted by William Becker, Yeats tells maliciously how Mrs. Patrick Campbell greeted him after reading the play and hearing that he had done the beginning of the first act, "O Mr. Yeats the opening of Act I is wonderful. Why did you not do the whole play?" Yeats graciously explained "how essential Moore had been" and later confided to Lady Gregory how difficult it was to judge a work "when one has to give up one's own standard as I have had to do in this play." [17] Whatever the virtues of the play, it had the great advantage that each collaborator could blame the other for its shortcomings.

The Shadowy Waters

In spite of the continual help of Lady Gregory, Yeats could never master the country speech. It was a mistake for

[15] *Autobiography*, p. 264.   [16] *Ibid.*, p. 268.
[17] *The Dublin Magazine*, April–June, 1951, p. 3.

him to want a "peasant" Grania (if indeed that is what he really wanted), though his instinct to balance high-flown speech with earthy idiom was surely sound for a dramatist. His natural bent was to gather heroic essence to a greatness until it burst the bounds of the world. *The Shadowy Waters* is the purest example in Yeats's drama of the hermetic sealing off of heroic love from all earthly contamination. It is no accident that the action should take place entirely on the water. Even in realistic works strange things happen at sea. The enforced isolation of a boat magnifies any tension that exists between a captain and his men; loyalty is the greatest virtue at sea. Mad captains have often been the ruination of their men. After a long time at sea, voyagers may find their practical goals have taken on a metaphysical freight of significance. This kind of background is shadowily suggested in Yeats's play.

Forgael is, or was, a pirate in search of treasure. For days he has been following the call of strange human-headed birds (souls of the dead) who have piloted him into little-traveled waters. The sailors are on the point of mutiny. Aibric is still loyal to Forgael for old time's sake, though he no longer understands the weird quest his captain is taking them on. And then everything seems justified. A royal ship appears, carrying a king and queen and laden with a cargo of Oriental splendor. The king is promptly killed and Dectora the queen brought before Forgael. Playing a magic harp, he subdues the reluctant queen to his love. When he plays, the men who would raise arms against him drop their swords. The mystic birds high above seem to disapprove the deceit Forgael has practiced on Dectora, enchanting her to think that they are a pair of mythical lovers who have known each other for a thousand years. He would undeceive her and discovers that his art is more powerful than he is: she will not give up this new lover the harp has created for her. Aibric and the others take over the plundered ship; Forgael bids them to leave him. For a moment Dectora wavers, urging Forgael to go home too. But when he refuses, she unequivocally casts her fate with him. She has become the Ever-living Woman, the ideal symbol of passion fused with beauty, that Forgael has been seeking.[18]

The rhythm of this play has a dreamlike ebb and flow, as if the sleeper were repeating a lesson from the distant past. According to this "oceanic" dialectic, the heart's desire is to go over the horizon into a dream from which there is no awaking, but the dreamer holds back, feeling the tug of life towards the waking world. Finally the alchemy of love distills the quintessence of desire, nothing else matters, and the dreamer cuts his ties with familiar life, enfolding himself in a cascade of golden hair. The golden net of immortality encloses the lovers, and they themselves have become the stuff that dreams are made on. It is a beautiful and subtle conception. Theatrically speaking, the points of view represented by the speakers are always clearly and vividly expressed, and though the shifts in situation are rapid, they are never blurred. The dreamlike quality comes from the uncompromising sensibility of the two lovers, especially Forgael's, and not from any fragmentation of construction or surrealistic confusion of imagery. Yeats's kind of symbolism, even in this most unworldly play, is not of the abstruse and intellectual variety developed by Mallarmé and

[18] This summary is based on the acting version in *Collected Plays*. See Suheil B. Bushrui, *Yeats's Verse Plays: The Revisions, 1900–1910* (Oxford, 1965), pp. 14–38, for a recent account of the revisions.

Valéry. It has, essentially, the appeal of a child's fairy tale. But the precocity of any child who understood Yeats's vocabulary of passion would be somewhat alarming. The interpretation of the play, however, was no simple matter. In the version before 1900, Yeats had so overloaded the play with detail that the story was hard to discover. Richard Ellmann pointed out Yeats's reluctance to explain his symbolic meaning to the editor of the *North American Review*, where the play was first published in 1900. And when Yeats did summarize his understanding of the play to prepare an Abbey audience for it in 1905, he was more concerned to fill the playgoers' minds with the symbolic feast spread before them than to justify his work as stageworthy drama.[19] The trouble was that the play grew between 1885 and 1900 into a kind of dramatic encyclopedia of Yeats's knowledge and theories of symbolism; it was to be the culminating masterpiece of the theater of symbolism. And Yeats himself was uncertain what, exactly, Forgael's victory implied about the supernatural world. Leonard Nathan summarizes the combined interpretations Yeats offered of the play by saying, "Hero and heroine are meant to symbolize any pair of discords that can come to spiritual harmony through love." [20] It is just this kind of summary Yeats took pains to avoid. He really wanted an impossible thing: an audience on whom not a single allusive nuance would be lost and yet who would have this knowledge in their bones so that in a flash of intuition all occult wisdom could be, as it were, concentrated in a single beam of light.

In *The Shadowy Waters* death has lost its sting, and from

[19] Richard Ellmann, *The Identity of Yeats* (New York, 1954), pp. 80–84.

[20] Leonard Nathan, *The Tragic Drama of William Butler Yeats* (New York, 1965), p. 69.

one standpoint this is as it should be—the play is a demonstration of the higher synthesis in which the thesis of death and the antithesis of life have been superseded. But as Nathan says, "The quest for the immortal and the calamitous results of the quest seem to be the fundamental theme at work in *The Shadowy Waters*. . . . Moreover, this theme expressed Yeats's tragic view more characteristically than the surface theme of Forgael's easy victory over the opposition of the natural world and its representatives." [21] Yeats cannot have it both ways. If the supernatural hero is so far superior to natural circumstance that he can take his leave of mortality without a qualm, he becomes a figure of romance. If he is to be a tragic hero, we must feel both the reality and the bitterness inseparable from his choice of sacrifice. For this kind of hero, the crucial decision he makes is tragic because the only thing worse would be not to make it.

Yet if we read the acting version of the play published in *Collected Plays*, I think we can see that Yeats has moved firmly in the direction of romance and away from tragedy, in spite of the fact that he has pruned his play of much romantic decoration.[22] The issues are more clean cut, and Forgael glides toward his predestined conclusion with the assurance of a somnambulist. The only thing that really upsets him is the thought that he has been unscrupulous, that he has "seduced" Dectora under false pretences. This is comic, not tragic, irony. It merely emphasizes Forgael's ignorance; he is not yet aware that Dectora *is* the Eternal Feminine. These two can no more escape each other than

[21] *Ibid.*, p. 75. Throughout, Nathan seems to base his commentary on the version of 1900.
[22] Bushrui, pp. 14–38, shows this very clearly.

Tristan could escape Iseult after that famous couple had shared the love potion. At one stage, when Yeats was undecided about his ending, George Moore helpfully suggested "that the woman should refuse to accompany the metaphysical pirate to the ultimate North, but return somewhat diffidently, ashamed of herself, to the sailors who were drinking yellow ale." Of all Moore's suggestions for reshaping his play, this was "the one that Yeats refused most resolutely." [23] And rightly so, of course. Dectora is no serving girl who, after some brazen insolence to her betters, can be returned red-faced and abashed to her kind.

Yeats is very successful in conveying Forgael's oddly sensual asceticism, and the mastery with which this metaphysical pirate plays on Dectora's moods effectively dramatizes the magical power of a supernaturally sustained love. To be sure, Yeats loses a good deal in sacrificing his poetic evocations of symbolic lore in the acting version of this play that emerges after so many years of toil, but he certainly enhances the unity of mood. It is a mistake, for us as it was for Yeats, to measure this play with the yardstick of tragedy. Unlike Villier's *Axel*, with which it has so often been compared,[24] *The Shadowy Waters* is not an account of a man's struggle to escape the entanglements of "living"; Forgael has already passed that stage when Yeats's fable begins. He is haunted by "that hair that is the colour of burning," and the action of the play is for him to find the owner of that hair in order to cover himself in its glory. Nor is Yeats at fault to leave the supernatural future that

[23] Moore, Vol. I, pp. 217–218.
[24] See, for instance, William York Tindall, "The Symbolism of W. B. Yeats," conveniently reprinted in *The Permanence of Yeats*, James Hall and Martin Steinmann, eds. (New York, 1950), p. 265.

awaits his lovers shrouded in mystery: they have successfully crossed the threshold into a realm set apart from the
life they leave behind; it would be vulgar curiosity to in-
trude on their private bliss.

In fact, the heavy boot of tragedy would be out of place
on the deck of this dream-haunted ship. All that can be
permitted is the remembrance of what tragedy *would be* if
the magic spell should fail. The suspense of the play depends on the *possibility* of tragedy, but its inevitability depends on the exclusion of tragedy. The tragic hero must
suffer the slings and arrows of outrageous fortune in the
natural world into which he was born, however great his
powers of transcendence. In *The Shadowy Waters* the
natural world is overruled, and it is left to the lower orders
to do the hero's suffering for him.

Most critics have remarked the shortcomings of *The
Shadowy Waters* both as dramatic conception and as a
work for the stage.[25] In spite of the changes Yeats made—
increasing the saltiness of the sailors' language, adding motivations to sharpen the clashes in outlook between the
characters, dropping symbolic allusions irrelevant to the
action—the play remained "inhuman." In later days, Yeats
would have made a dance play out of it, equipped it with
opening and closing lyrics, and reduced the cast to three
characters (Forgael, Aibric, and Dectora). Perhaps Dectora
would have been forced to choose between returning to the
land with Aibric and setting further out to sea with Forgael.
She would have chosen Forgael, but at the price of exile and
death, knowing, too, that her choice meant death for her
lover. There would be less humanity in the play, but a

[25] Nathan, pp. 72–74, gives an account of the criticism.

passion colder in its experience and warmer in its full-bloodedness.

The Hour-Glass

The two countries of the mind—the visible world of nature and other people, the invisible order of imagination and spiritual being—are the scene and source of conflict in all Yeats's dramatic fables. In *The Hour-Glass*, based on a tale in Lady Wilde's collection of Irish legends,[26] Yeats is attracted by a variation on the Faust theme of selling one's soul to the devil for some special mastery in *this* life. Lady Wilde's story tells of a priest who has abandoned the church and has twenty-four hours to find a believer in order to be saved. He himself instructs the child who appears from some distant place—an unspoiled believer—to murder him so that his pupils can see for themselves the soul escaping from his mouth. What they see becomes the "first butterfly that was ever seen in Ireland." [27] In Yeats's play, however, the Wise Man, in a sudden shock of illumination, surrenders himself completely to God's will, no longer caring what happens to his own soul. As a result, of course, this precious soul is put into a golden casket as soon as the "white butterfly" flies out of the dead man's mouth and borne straight to the "garden of Paradise."

This little "morality" is much more Yeatsian than medieval. The Wise Man is the inheritor and erstwhile embodiment of that dry and sceptical rationalism Yeats thought of as bringing ruination on modern man. As long as he is possessed by the "devil" (there is no actual devil in the play; he has been completely interiorized in the protag-

[26] *Plays in Prose and Verse*, p. 418.   [27] Saul, p. 60.

onist's mind), the Wise Man dominates everybody by the mocking power of his intellect. But he has been twice troubled by a dream that "the stream of the world had changed its course" and the waters of thought had run back to "some cloudy thunderous spring." [28] If true, this reversal, this "frenzy of the mind," would undo all the work of rational speculation, leaving what he had thought solid reality reduced to the nothingness of wind. The existence of spirit would, ironically, put the existence of reason in doubt, making it as vaporous as he had always taught the beliefs of religion were. In *The Hour-Glass* the ontological conflict is shifted from the watery stage of operatic love-music in *Shadowy Waters* back to the dry land of class-rooms and pedagogy.

It is quite evident that the pupils are no more rational under the Wise Man's tutelage than they were under the old dispensation. They have merely learned to parrot their teacher's arguments and to enjoy the power of beating an opponent in disputation. Their "emancipation" has taught them the delight of sneering at what their cleverness allows them to dismiss as ignorance, but this pleasure is balanced by their abject fear of incurring the ridicule of their master. His desperate efforts to get them to express an honest thought have a satirical charm that has by no means dated. (Yeats has an abiding interest in pedagogy and school children; his ambivalent attitude finds notable expression in plays, poems, letters, as well as in essays and speeches.) One of the major ironies of the play is that argument, so often used to undermine faith, proves so ineffective now in undermining scepticism (though one must admit that the

[28] *Collected Plays* (London, 1952), pp. 302-303.

pupils and Bridget, the Wise Man's wife, are as far as possible from being truly *philosophical* sceptics).

The action of the play is the running out of time and the influx of eternity. The angel gives the Wise Man only an hour (typical Yeatsian foreshortening) to find a believer, and in his "rational" haste the master completely overlooks Teigue the Fool, who could have saved him all the time. When finally the Wise Man does ask Teigue, the Fool refuses to admit his belief—he's not going to be caught in such seriousness—until bidden by the angel. But in that moment revelation has burst upon the Wise Man and he no longer needs Teigue's belief; his own has become perfect. As the sands have run out of the hour-glass, so has the Wise Man's understanding moved from time to eternity. What will happen to the innocently lost souls of his wife and pupils we do not know, but presumably the shock of the Wise Man's death will release them from the error of their ways.

According to Dume, Yeats once referred to this play as "a parable of the conscious and the subconscious life." [29] This seems a better way of regarding it than as a morality play on the model of *Everyman*,[30] though the two views are not mutually exclusive. The intellectual conflict (it hardly seems a moral one, except by implication) takes place exclusively in the protagonist's mind; other people are merely puzzled by his behavior—and this is one of Yeats's best theatrical effects. The only other role of any consequence is that of the Fool. He represents the wise folly that overweening greatness should always be shadowed by; when

[29] Saul, p. 63.
[30] Cf. Una Ellis-Fermor, *The Irish Dramatic Movement* (London, 1954), pp. 108–109.

the emperor has no clothes, the Fool clearly sees so and says so. He has no fear of nonconformity because he lives at the edge (the bottom edge) of society and can never be held responsible for common sense.

Frank Fay played the part to Yeats's great satisfaction, being "beautiful, wise, and subtle." [31] This description suggests a fool who knows more than he tells but who is content to appear the harmless lunatic continually asking for pennies. Certainly the pupils treat him with familiarity and good-natured contempt, as they might a pet monkey. But if he is not the melancholy and pathetic Thin Fool of the Romantic tradition, he does not quite qualify as the Fat Fool of Folklore either, in spite of Yeats's opinion in his note for *On Baile's Strand*.[32] He is hardly "as wide and wild as a hill." He is, if you like, a good representative of the "subconscious" revolt against the tedium of argument and the deference accorded to authority; but he remains gentle and unobtrusive. He is neither a stinging satirist nor an apocalyptic jester.

As usual, Yeats revised and revised. He did not stop bettering *The Hour-Glass* until 1922.[33] He greatly improved the Wise Man, changing him from an over-talkative fellow who is willing to humiliate himself before the Fool to (especially in the poetic version finally arrived at) a man who achieves the dignity of his own vision. Even though his opinion was apparently a minority one at the time, it is hard not to sympathize with Wilfred Scawen Blunt's scathing words in 1903: "The first piece was a ter-

---

[31] *Letters*, p. 409.   [32] *Plays in Prose and Verse*, p. 424.
[33] For the revisions, see Suheil Bushrui, " 'The Hour-Glass': Yeats's Revisions, 1903–1922," in D. E. S. Maxwell and S. B. Bushrui, pp. 189–216.

rible infliction, called 'The Hour-Glass' by Yeats—a stupid
imitation of that dull old morality, 'Everyman,' which
bored me so much last year. What Yeats can mean by putting such thin stuff on the stage I can't imagine." [34] Blunt
might have changed his mind if he could have seen a performance in 1922. Against this reaction of an outsider, we
can put the view of an insider. Willie Fay, Frank's brother,
considered it "the finest of all morality plays, with the possible exception of *Everyman*." [35] How peculiarly Yeatsian
a morality it is, we have tried to show.

[34] Quoted in Bushrui, *ibid.*, p. 190.
[35] W. G. Fay, "The Poet and the Actor," in *Scattering
Branches*, p. 129.

5

The King's Threshold

Yeats had not studied Shakespeare and the other Eliza-bethans for nothing. As he showed in his essay "Emotion of Multitude," [1] he thoroughly understood and valued the resonance produced by the dramatic linking of one fate with many others. His heroes and heroines must be large and exemplary; what happens to them matters, at least potentially, to everybody else. Particularly in *The King's Threshold, On Baile's Strand, Deirdre,* and *The Green Helmet,* Yeats is laboring to give his audience a new sense of society. As he wrote in a note to *King's Threshold,* "It was written when our society was beginning its fight for the recognition of pure art in a community of which one half is buried in the practical affairs of life, and the other half in politics and a propagandist patriotism." [2] Although Yeats was referring to the period of 1903 (the play was produced at the Molesworth Hall in that year), the condition he speaks of did not essentially change for many years to come, if it has changed even now. Yeats was a tireless fighter for the central position of art and the artist in any

[1] In "Ideas of Good and Evil," reprinted in *Essays and Introductions* (London, 1961), pp. 215–216. Dated 1903.
[2] Note of 1911, *Plays in Prose and Verse* (London, 1922), p. 423.

society that pretended to be a great civilization. In this sense, all his plays are propaganda plays.

The hunger strike and other techniques of nonviolence are always the weapons of the political inferior in social power struggles. But they can be used with any chance of success only when the conscience of the powers-that-be is sufficiently tender (and their power sufficiently secure) to permit an alteration of policy on humanitarian and moral grounds. Seanchan in *King's Threshold* is testing the conscience of the king. Yielding to the pressure of his "Bishops, Soldiers, and Makers of the Law," the king has banished the poet from his great council. As is so often the case with those in authority, the king had underestimated the repercussions his act would set in motion. Once having acted, however, he is determined not to lose face by reversing himself. The battle between poet and king becomes a subtle (or perhaps not so subtle) exercise in protocol. A series of persuaders is sent to try to convince Seanchan of his foolishness, of his unfaithfulness to his pupils, of the disservice he will be doing his needy home town, of the stupidity of opposing the king's force, of the disruption he is causing in the orderly functioning of the state, of how good food smells to a hungry man, of how he is betraying the girl he loves. As the temptations to yield become greater, Seanchan strikes back more wildly and aggressively.

The king wants to disguise (even from himself) his role and appeal to Seanchan man to man, all the while relying on his position as his trump card. Seanchan, on the other hand, struggles against the limitations of being regarded simply as a particular man; he not only affirms his role, but is convinced that it is his sacred duty to teach everybody else that poetry matters more than kings or bishops or soldiers or young girls—or even poets. And he succeeds in his attempt. We know this king will never be the same again, even if the kingdom doesn't collapse. And he is unable to go through with his ordeal: instead of executing the pupils, he has them driven out of his sight. In the conflict between the "reason" of society and the "dream" of the poet, the individual will (because sustained by a supra-individual vision) succeeds in overcoming institutional authority—at least for the moment. Seanchan is no wandering minstrel content to sing himself to the land of the Sidhe in order to escape the philistinism of a prosaic world. With only slight distortion, we could say he dies out of bitter exasperation at the shortsightedness of status-mad men of action.

Because Seanchan is a satirist and not just a victim of what he satirizes, his heroism has bite as well as nobility. Though he is a champion of the past *and* the future against the degradation of the present, he insists on exerting power *in* the world, here and now. Unwilling to bypass the enemy, he confronts him head-on, and his opponents are, as a matter of fact, afraid of Seanchan's worldly power. The common sort love him. (What wouldn't Yeats have given for an artist-peasant alliance at this stage of his career! Answer: his poetic integrity.) In Seanchan's final speech, and perhaps even more in the speeches of the pupils, one can feel Yeats's satisfaction in prophesying the worsening of the world and the alienation of the poet, and his still greater pleasure in contemplating the new race of Nietzschean supermen to come and the ultimate justification of the bard's superior wisdom.

The play opens with a speech from the king which has a deceptively conciliatory tone. He presents himself as a lover (and understander) of music and poetry who solicits the help of Seanchan's pupils in dissuading their master from his mad whim of starving himself to death. The king would have them know "how light an issue/ Has put us by the ears," but almost in the same breath reveals that the issue is one of honor—that those who rule the world are more to be honored than those who sing to it. The rest of the play is essentially a debate on this issue.

Like Prometheus tied to his rock, Seanchan never stirs from the king's threshold while a procession of antagonists representing the various claims of worldly compromise try to cajole, bully, or argue him into surrender. But in spite of his immobility Seanchan finds that he is changing, as though "the moon changed everything." As his body grows weaker, his mind gains a new freedom, "moonstruck and fantastical." As the pressures on him increase, his defiance grows bolder, except for a moment of near-surrender to his beloved. His pupils act as a chorus at the beginning and end of the play, explicating the movement from ignorance to wisdom. At first the oldest pupil thinks Seanchan's behavior is as fantastical as the crane's, starving himself at full moon because frightened of his shadow glittering in the water. By a method close to Socratic irony, Seanchan leads the oldest pupil to refute himself. Helplessly, the oldest pupil turns to the others, and the youngest pupil says, "O tell him that the lovers of his music/ Have need of him." Seanchan's answer shows how great a responsibility the poet's vocation involves.

> But I am labouring
> For some that shall be born in the nick o' time,
> And find sweet nurture, that they may have voices,
> Even in anger, like the strings of harps;

> And how could they be born to majesty
> If I had never made the golden cradle? [3]

Seanchan is presenting an old Yeatsian theme: the poet's words allow man to express (and hence come to know) what makes experience humanly valuable. The poet can give wings to a curse and grandeur to a crown. More important, he is the carrier of value from generation to generation. In this sense he is profoundly conservative. Yeats expresses this conservatism not only in the rhythms of his blank verse but in his diction: "labouring," "nick o' time," "sweet nurture," "strings of harps," "golden cradle." Seanchan is a revolutionary against law and order on behalf of "ancient right." His difficult task is to convince others (on stage and in the audience) that poetry is "One of the fragile, mighty things of God,/ That die at an insult." Fragile *and* mighty. In one sense, the task is hopeless: for those who believe poetry is fragile don't believe it can ever be mighty, and vice versa. The play lines up its cast in opposed camps on just this issue. In another sense, however, Seanchan himself is the living image of this paradox. He is fragile enough to die and mighty enough to triumph over the king.

Poetry thrives on sorrow and ruin; it can work the miracle of turning defeat into victory. What Seanchan tells his youngest scholar is, in fact, not only a declaration of the transcendent power of poetry but an excellent definition of Yeats's idea of tragedy:

> And I would have all know that when all falls
> In ruin, poetry calls out in joy,
> Being the scattering hand, the bursting pod,

---

[3] *Collected Plays* (London, 1952), p. 113.

The victim's joy among the holy flame,
God's laughter at the shattering of the world.
And now that joy laughs out, and weeps and burns
On these bare steps.[4]

Catastrophe arouses the hero to the maximum expression of
his capacity to be a joyous victim (tragic gaiety), and
what gives him joy is the sense of a powerful magnanimity
that holds nothing back because he has surrendered all
claims to mortal goods on behalf of a spiritual good beyond
the reach of time. He no longer fears anything or anybody
and so can laugh at the shattering of the world. And yet
this laughter is not an indifference to worldly things in the
deeper sense, for this joy also *weeps* and *burns*. The
laughter is a defense against the swelling pity and rage
which threaten to overwhelm the soul.

Although the poet's main business is not to fight or
make love but to make poems, his language often evokes
intense activity as in this passage where "scattering," "bursting," "shattering," "laughs out," "weeps," and "burns"
carry the forward thrust of the meaning. Seanchan is under-
going the passion that his poetry celebrates. He is in the
peculiar position of being the teacher using himself as an
object lesson ("*And now* that joy laughs out, and weeps
and burns/ On *these* bare steps"). Unless we feel his pain as
a victim, he runs the danger of seeming too godlike or inhuman to satisfy the tragic lust for blood. He must truly
weep and burn.

Yeats turns to comedy at this point partly because he
needs to fill in the "anti-poetic" aspect of experience. And
he certainly can't afford to let Seanchan spend all his eloquence too soon. The mayor, the two cripples, and the

4 *Ibid.*, p. 114.

servant Brian represent selected—perhaps *too* selected—attitudes of the "common people." The mayor's bumbling incompetence emphasizes his provincial self-importance and his complete lack of proper understanding. He is a small-town Polonius, sincerely anxious to restore the *status quo* and win plaudits for his diplomatic skill in bringing town, king, and poet into proper concord. He meets comic obstruction from his own memory (or lack of it), from Brian, and from the cripples. The mayor wants only what is reasonable, and, in the only speech of Seanchan in this episode, receives the crushing retort (with its echo of King Lear):

Reason, O reason in plenty. Yet you have yellowy white hair and not too many teeth. How comes it you have been so long in the world and not found reason out? [5]

The mayor is one of those unfortunates, born neither in a golden cradle nor with a silver spoon in his mouth, who gets his ideas both of authority and of eloquence second-hand and tarnished from his betters. The would-be savior of the kingdom becomes the comic scapegoat. In the "lower" world, he is a symbolic as well as literal representative of the king.

From at least as early as the stage version of *Countess Cathleen* in 1899, Yeats had realized that drama required him to deal with the objective world which he associated with comedy. It is a world that he could describe tellingly, as he proves in his autobiography and elsewhere. During his years of writing for the Abbey, however, he found it difficult to rise above the level of rather wooden caricature in his dramatic representation of characters lacking aristocratic

[5] *Ibid.*, p. 117.

trappings or poetic insight, despite the help of Lady Gregory. Nevertheless, the addition of the scene with mayor, servant, and cripples advances the action and strengthens the drama. It establishes Seanchan's connection with the countryside and helps give balance to the picture of the poet as Yeats liked to conceive him: a man who means as much to the illiterate folk imagination as he does to the educated art lovers at court.

In fact, except for his pupils, no one in the play shows any comprehension of Seanchan strictly as a poet, and even they (as Seanchan would wish) celebrate him as principle more than man. He proves his sincerity as a poet by dying as a man, but the true burden of the play is that the role is more important than any individual. Seanchan is most himself when he is insisting on his separation from the life around him. When the soldier calls him "old hedgehog" Seanchan accepts the figure but transforms it to suit his own meanings:

> You have rightly named me.
> I lie rolled up under the ragged thorns
> That are upon the edge of those great waters
> Where all things vanish away, and I have heard
> Murmurs that are the ending of all sound.
> I am out of life; I am rolled up, and yet,
> Hedgehog although I am, I'll not unroll
> For you, King's dog. Go to the King, your master.
> Crouch down and wag your tail, for it may be
> He has nothing now against you, and I think
> The stripes of your last beating are all healed.[6]

This curious image for a poet is actually one of Yeats's happiest inventions. Here, in a blank verse characteristic in

[6] *Ibid.*, pp. 125–126.

its love of movement, he displays the special talent he had for fusing the lyric and the dramatic. Very much a hedge-hog in the stubborn and bristly exterior he presents to his opponents, Seanchan is indeed "rolled up"; yet within unroll vistas that stretch beyond seeing and hearing—"I am out of life." The lyric moment asserts itself in dramatic opposition to the gross demands that surround it. At the same time Seanchan, a man confronted by other men, is very consciously "in" life and strikes out with sardonic energy at those who would force him to *unroll*. The hedge-hog image is at once grotesque and apt. But a poet can find unexpected uses for the most unlikely comparisons. When it comes to words, the others are no match for him—he demonstrates the fighting capacities of poetry. Never was a kingly antagonist more soundly thrashed by the tragic protagonist than in this play. Seanchan makes of his death a reproach and a challenge to all the lesser men he leaves behind.

When the chamberlain says that he too writes poetry, and therefore wherever he is honored poetry is not entirely disregarded, Seanchan does not question his poetry but his sense of vocation. A true poet must cry out that poetry has given gold and silver their value and man his courage and generosity. It is a poet's duty to defend the "wasteful virtues" his craft has commended,

> And when that story's finished, shake your coat
> Where little jewels gleam on it, and say,
> A herdsman, sitting where the pigs had trampled,
> Made up a song about enchanted kings,
> Who were so finely dressed one fancied them
> All fiery, and women by the churn

> And children by the hearths caught up the song
> And murmured it, until the tailors heard it.[7]

To which the chamberlain replies:

> If you would but eat something, you'd find out
> That you have had these thoughts from lack of food,
> For hunger makes us feverish.[8]

It is the old argument about imagination (incidentally still not settled) as a visionary power capable of re-creating the world vs. imagination as a diseased form of mental activity. If the chamberlain were sincere, he would know that his bejeweled coat was a poor thing compared to a lowly herdsman's song which could make enchanted kings live in the minds of women and children, and endow royal costume with a fiery glamour which, through the repeated words of the song, would finally reach the tailors. Seanchan is claiming no less for poetry than the very creation of reality. Though it may be (*is*, in fact) beyond his comprehension, the chamberlain and his precious coat would not exist if poets had not invested kingly authority and its proper garments with mystery and awe. In the final analysis, tailors only make what poets tell them to. Seanchan invites the chamberlain to join him by lying down on the threshold until the king restores the poet's ancient right, but of course receives no answer. The chamberlain cannot afford to give up the prudent virtues, especially when the wasteful ones lead to such dangerous and subversive activities.

Yeats is surely enjoying himself here. The paradox of the poet's weakness and strength will be explored more subtly in *The Player Queen* and more profoundly in

---

[7] *Ibid.*, p. 127.   [8] *Ibid.*, pp. 127–128.

A Full Moon in March, but never again with such verve and confidence. As with the hedgehog passage earlier, Seanchan has caught up the enemy's weapon and turned it against him. One hopes (without much hope) that the chamberlain will not confuse the poetaster with the poet in the future.

Unlike the chamberlain, who is in love with diplomacy, the Monk has firmly decided against the "wanton imagination" long ago. He is prepared to see Seanchan die without a qualm. But Seanchan is not prepared to let him off so easily. The taunting of the Monk about his "wild God" that is being tamed for the king's comfort is the peak of Seanchan's "sane" aggressiveness; when he horrifies the princess by suggesting her white hand is leprous, a note of delirium has entered his voice (and in a moment he will be staggering on the stage). Behind his scathing mockery of the Monk lies a feeling that the Monk's betrayal of religious integrity is worse than what has come before because religion and poetry should be natural allies.

By a process of "free" association Seanchan is led on from thoughts of God to thoughts of a devilish deity, dispensing his blessings of leprosy from the sky. In a moment of discouragement, this God seems too strong for Seanchan.

> He's holding up his hand above them all—
> King, noblemen, princesses—blessing all,
> Who could imagine he'd have so much patience? [9]

The dead weight of inertia and corruption, inevitable in any settled society where contact with the source of its values has been weakened or lost, is personified in Seanchan's exacerbated state of mind by a supernatural leper. As

[9] *Ibid.*, p. 133.

might be expected, the cripple reduces the meaning of Seanchan's gesture toward the sky:

> He's pointing at the moon
> That's coming out up yonder, and he calls it
> Leprous, because the daylight whitens it.[10]

This gloss is an example of "bad" poetry (the whole play
is a lesson in distinguishing true poetry—and poets—from
their inferior imitations). Seanchan has gone far beyond
the making of fanciful similes out upon "those great
waters/ Where all things vanish away." The crippled imagination has no access to this realm beyond sense.

Fedelm, his beloved, catches Seanchan at his lowest point
of resistance, just when he has most need of her. The pale,
white, whey-faced world of smooth and smiling contamination suddenly gives way to the pastoral world of simple
emotions and unfettered action. And again episodes are
linked by repeated motifs. The first thing Seanchan notices
is his beloved's *hand*.

> Is this your hand, Fedelm?
> I have been looking at another hand
> That is up yonder.[11]

With a Cordelia-like generosity of spirit, Fedelm tries to
shut out the memory of strife and gently lead Seanchan
home to a place of smooth level lawn under an apple-tree.
She would heal his emaciated body and his distressed spirit.
For the first and only time Seanchan almost yields because
Fedelm offers unconsciously (and therefore most power-
fully) the subtlest treachery of all. She would have him
accept an earthly paradise as a substitute for Adam's para-

[10] *Ibid.*   [11] *Ibid.*, p. 134.

dise. In Seanchan's troubled mind the two are briefly confused, but the great rooted blossoms with singing birds in
the tree of which Seanchan sings is not where Fedelm
intends to lead him, and she is too honest to forward the
confusion ("No, there are not four rivers, and those
rhymes/ Praise Adam's paradise"). With an unerring sense
of drama, Yeats has Seanchan remember the poem he wrote
about the "Garden in the East of the World," and not only
remember but bring it alive before our eyes with all the
immediacy appropriate to Seanchan's present desperation
and hunger.

> I can remember now
> It's out of a poem I made long ago
> About the Garden in the East of the World,
> And how spirits in the images of birds
> Crowd in the branches of old Adam's crab-tree.
> They come before me now, and dig in the fruit
> With so much gluttony, and are so drunk
> With that harsh wholesome savour, that their feathers
> Are clinging one to another with the juice.[12]

The two hungers of body and spirit are beautifully brought
together—and the suspense is heightened. Will this country sweetheart be able to take advantage of Seanchan's
weakness to "save" him for his family and friends, but
above all for herself? As the fiery strength of Seanchan's
previous speeches has hinted, she will fail, and he will
choose a life on the other side of death. Yet ironically her
love undoubtedly gives him that spurt of mental energy he
needs to make his triumphant exit from the world.

Yeats's skill in articulating a dramatic action shows itself

[12] *Ibid.*, pp. 136–137.

both in his poetic linkings of opposite sides of experience, in images which (often ironically) reveal the abyss lying between two kinds of vision (literally two ways of looking at the world), and in his acute sense of theatrical contrast. Seanchan's hunger strike precipitates a conflict dormant before but always ready to burst into flame when the unstable balance between "rational" power and "irrational" principle is upset. The lyric vision becomes a dramatic source of unity. As the action rises toward its climax, Seanchan's poetic eloquence increases and, especially in the scene with Fedelm, Yeats demonstrates a new skill in handling rapid shifts of mood.

> Go where you will,
> So it be out of sight and out of mind.
> I cast you from me like an old torn cap,
> A broken shoe, a glove without a finger,
> A crooked penny; whatever is most worthless.[13]

In *The King's Threshold* (as it appears in the final version) Yeats has already achieved mastery of a highly complex dramatic technique. He has easy command of a blank verse that can be as direct and lucid as prose or as highly charged and metaphorical as his lyrics. Moreover, he is able to *use* poetry for the purposes of drama. He gains a resonance difficult for prose but he also gains speed. What would seem too slight unless developed at much greater length in prose possesses a weight and pressure in verse that plunges us immediately into the heart of argument. It is natural for the love scene between Seanchan and Fedelm to take only five pages, and yet it gives us the feeling of summing up a lifetime of experience. Perhaps the chief ad-

---

[13] *Ibid.*, p. 138.

vantage of poetry for Yeats's kind of drama (an advantage he continually learned better how to capitalize on) is that it allows him to "naturalize" those inner workings of the mind that join men together at a deeper level than their normal waking relationships usually offer. Poetry (at least Yeats's variety) is able to do this because it combines distance with intimacy. Yeats gives us almost none of the interesting details of Seanchan's personal life, nor do we expect him to. We accept the elevated plane of his discourse. Yet he shares his most cherished thoughts and feelings with uninhibited abandon. Or if he does not share them, he expounds and exposes them with a delighted exhibitionism. In prose he would certainly run a greater risk of sounding pretentious.

If in spite of its considerable merits we feel a certain dissatisfaction with *The King's Threshold*, the reason may be that it seems to exist in an uneasy no-man's-land between the archaic times it evokes and the present. In a sense, this is surely what Yeats intends. He is speaking to his contemporaries about matters which concern him deeply, and one of his deepest convictions is that man's life is founded on eternal verities. What is valuable in the past can never be obsolete. Unfortunately, it is all too easy to take Seanchan as a spokesman for Yeats, scolding his benighted audience for their incapacity to rise to his poetic occasions. The dice are loaded, and Seanchan is given no opposition worthy of his mettle. There is no devil's advocate to point out that Seanchan's identification of himself with poetry may be tinged with a self-satisfying vanity and not be purely a devoted self-sacrifice on the altar of art.

Yeats's alterations of this play, as usual, improved it, but it was not until 1922 that he gave it its present tragic ending. To us, this ending seems right and inevitable, but Yeats thought otherwise. He said in a Prologue published in *Plays for an Irish Theatre:*

Some think it would be a finer tale if Seanchan had died at the end of it, and the king had the guilt at his door, for that might have served the poet's cause better in the end. But that is not true, for if he that is in the story but the shadow and image of poetry had not risen up from the death that threatened him, the ending would not have been true and joyful enough to be put into the voices of players and proclaimed in the mouths of trumpets, and poetry would have been badly served.[14]

It is interesting that Yeats thought Seanchan "but the shadow and image of poetry" and *therefore* compelled to rise up "from the death that threatened him" in order to make the ending dramatically "true and joyful enough." It is as though poetry would seem to die if Seanchan did— a conclusion strangely at variance with Yeats's confidence in the tragic triumph through death elsewhere. And in fact in 1922 Yeats declared that he had originally conceived a tragic ending but was dissuaded by a friend who argued, "O do write comedy and have a few happy moments in the Theatre." Yeats goes on to explain that his unhappy moments were a result of the fragility of the tragic effect, which can so easily be destroyed by clumsiness in the theater.[15] Nevertheless, when the revised play was presented at the Abbey in November of 1921 it was not a success, according to Thomas McGreevy, who attributed its comparative failure to the predominance of the realistic over the poetic tradition among the actors.[16] The truth is that no changes could make it a popular success in Ireland.

[14] S. B. Bushrui, *Yeats's Verse Plays* (Oxford, 1965), pp. 110–111. See his full account of the published revisions, pp. 78–119.

[15] *Ibid.*, p. 109. [16] *Ibid.*, footnote on p. 117.

6

On Baile's Strand

The revolt against authority in *On Baile's Strand* is fiercer than in *King's Threshold*. Cuchulain's tragedy is both more distant and more intimate than Seanchan's: the famous warrior and lover is shown discovering how unbearably final his isolation from other men is, and just at the point when a new bond of love in Cuchulain's loveless life promises release from the lonely "obsolescence" the hero has resigned himself to, the new hope is "killed" by Cuchulain's own willed and yet unwilling act of violence. In Cuchulain's debate with Conchubar leading up to the taking of the oath, the hero stoutly resists the old king's argument that the time has come for prudence and planning. And yet Cuchulain himself keeps admitting that the great days are gone, that things are not as they were when he and Conchubar were comrades-in-arms.

If Cuchulain is a more primitive, colder, harder (and more lonely) hero than Seanchan—unlike the latter he has no one coaxing him to eat, no faithful Brian, no gentle and loving Fedelm—he is like Seanchan in being absolutely committed to his own integrity and absolutely opposed to the compromises demanded by political expediency. But Cuchulain is confronted with a more difficult and perplexing task—that of discovering the full extent of bitter grief his heroic vocation can exact from him. Seanchan knows from the beginning what he must do, and he does it. Moreover, he gets his reward: as his flesh weakens, his spirit grows, and death is transformed from a defeat into a triumph.[1] Cuchulain has no such luck. He who has always been so sure of himself is suddenly confronted with a situation for which his past career has not prepared him. How does an honorable hero behave when he is convinced his occupation's gone? Cuchulain's very willingness to take the oath—and with no mental reservations—is an earnest of his good intentions. The cruel penalty he has to pay for getting in beyond his intellectual depth in the sophisticated waters of political calculation drives him, in the end, to those deeper waters wherein the unconscious energies that give rise to the love and hate, beauty and heartlessness of the upper world have their permanent abode.

In this play which celebrates not the hatred but the love of father and son, it is the feminine principle which destroys. The song of the three women is a charm, or curse, in which they attempt to exorcise the baleful influence of the black Aphrodite—Muse, White Goddess, Queen of the Sidhe, or simply *la belle dame sans merci*—who, by her singular fascination, is able to beguile the man of her choice away from his loyalties to wife and church and state. Cuchulain is torn between the conservative female of "threshold and hearthstone" and the wild female whom "none can kiss and thrive." The song, significantly, is vivid about the horrors these inhuman women will visit upon the hero-martyr who gives his destiny into their hands, but it has nothing to say about the attractions of the domestic life. The theme is familiar; it plays its part, sometimes dimly but

[1] Cf. Peter Ure, *Yeats the Playwright* (London, 1963), p. 42.

more often glitteringly, from *Countess Cathleen* to *The Death of Cuchulain*.

But in *On Baile's Strand* it has a peculiar ambiguity we have not encountered before. There is no woman in the play to embody the hero's ideal love, though Aoife's ghostly presence may be said to haunt the charged atmosphere and even, by a kind of remote control, to govern the fatal action which will lead Cuchulain to his mad plunge into the waves. It is the young man from Scotland—her son and Cuchulain's—who is the embodiment of love. From what Cuchulain says, we can surmise that he really does recognize his son, and the mother in his son, but that "witchcraft" keeps him from admitting the fact to himself (or, if we want to be cynical, that the exigencies of the plot do). Yet this very "as if" kind of recognition is wonderfully effective in creating for us both the beauty and valor of the young hero. He is judged on his merits (unlike Conchubar's children), not merely held in respect because of the accident of his birth. Father and son are spiritually akin; Cuchulain has been granted his wish for a son worthy of him. But the kind of love the son represents (like his mother before him) is masculine and aggressive. Aoife is not denied her revenge; indeed it is all the more perfect because of the immediate and instinctive love father and son inspire in each other. Cuchulain could never accept family life nor take a housewife as bride. So he must now accept the consequences *his* sort of love entails and which the three women warned of in their choral song (and there is an additional subordinate irony in their later *false* prediction that Cuchulain will be the one to meet his death in the fight).

Cuchulain insists on bodily joy, the warrior's and lover's physical strength and the spiritual courage and vitality that go with it, much more vigorously than does any other Yeatsian hero. In nature men are free of woman's wiles—and curses—and can pit themselves against adventure in trusting and joyful intimacy. In spite of his fear of what Aoife would say, the young man cannot resist the vision of heroic comradeship his father offers. And for his part, Cuchulain would gladly sacrifice his reputation ("O tell her/ I was afraid, or tell her what you will") in order to share his life with his son. It is this amazing and unprecedented offer that convinces Conchubar that "Some witch of the air has troubled Cuchulain's mind." Though Conchubar is in no sense personally effeminate, he is constantly identified with the argument of "threshold and hearthstone," just as Aoife is identified with the opposite. In this play the familiar Yeatsian pattern in which the hero (or in some plays the heroine) is claimed by competing loves is somewhat disguised, but it is unmistakably there. Conchubar and the young man (the single member of the younger generation who offers that hope Cuchulain despairs of finding in the older generation) both want Cuchulain. He is in that middle-aged perplexity in which the conflicting demands of citizenship and individual freedom, fatherhood and bachelor activities, time past and time future are enough to drive him mad. Being a hero, however, he faces his dilemma with a different attitude toward death than we ordinary mortals have. The hero is always ready to fight fearlessly for his life and the lives of others because he knows that death, when it comes, will not mean the "end" of him but the glorious completion of his life's work, something to be remembered long after in song and story. To kill an only son whom he has just learned to love is a much crueler tragedy than his own death would be. *On*

Baile's Strand, Yeats's most militant and masculine tragedy, is also the warmest in human passion.

On Baile's Strand was comparatively well received (Lennox Robinson thought it "perhaps his [Yeats's] most perfect verse-play"),[2] but it is by no means a compromise with poetic integrity for the sake of a *rapprochement* with conventional forms of drama. Cuchulain, about whom Yeats had already planned a cycle of plays, is a hero whose every speech declares him to be a superman well aware of his special pre-eminence. But he has reached a stage in his career where his heroic mettle is to be put to the supreme test. Yeats imagines him as being about forty (though according to legend Cuchulain died as a young man of twenty-seven) and now more of a danger than a help to the kingdom because of his self-centered willfulness and reckless unpredictability.

The design of the play is very simple: Cuchulain is the heroic center of resistance against which all the antiheroic forces of destruction—both inner and outer—are arrayed. The Fool's opening speech describes the very unheroic alliance between him and the "clever" Blind Man, a wonderful instructor in stealing and an excellent cook of other men's chickens. The second sight which allows the Blind Man to foreshadow Cuchulain's fate goes with a complacent indifference to the fall of heroes; clever but not wise, this degraded Tiresias exemplifies the sinister small-minded prudence and greed forever gnawing at heroic pretension. On a higher level, old King Conchubar, once a sharer in the heroic life with Cuchulain, now lives for the generations

[2] Lennox Robinson, *Ireland's Abbey Theatre* (London, 1951), p. 46.

to come and wants to domesticate heroism by the rule of law. The frightened complaints of his children have persuaded Conchubar that he must bind Cuchulain to fealty by a great oath, for "He burns the earth as if he were a fire,/ And time can never touch him." [3]

Unlike *The King's Threshold*, this play begins with the "reflectors" of the main action. Instead of directly opposing the hero—like the mayor, the monk, and the soldier in *King's Threshold*—the Fool and the Blind Man set the scene and prepare us for the action but would not presume to think they could share in shaping great events. What this opening scene does is create the atmosphere of a primitive world close to nature (and to the supernatural), suggest the great distance between ragged outlaws who live by their wits and the big men who determine what the law is while simultaneously intimating that a mysterious destiny links "outsiders" both high and low, and lead us skillfully from storytelling into the suspense of drama.

The "clever" Blind Man—and cleverness is seldom a quality of good omen in tragedy, especially Yeatsian tragedy—knows the little secrets that make the Fool's life easier and more pleasant, but he also knows big secrets. Punished by blindness "for putting a curse upon the wind," he is left the satisfaction of his skill at stealing a living from more law-abiding folk and his knowledge of the shape of things to come. The Fool, who appreciates his good luck in having the Blind Man to look out for him, lacks the intellectual gifts of his companion but is endowed with an intuitive imagination that equally sets him apart from ordinary folk. Boann and Fand may come by on the wind and ask him for a kiss, and he works up his appetite by running

[3] *Collected Plays* (London, 1952), p. 256.

races with the witches "at the edge of the waves." Like the cripples in *King's Threshold*, he is always anxious about filling his stomach. It is all the Blind Man can do to get him to listen to the story he has to tell. Between them these two not only suggest a folklore background but also, and more sharply, display the grim irony which underlies the action to come.

The most striking thing about the first episode between Cuchulain and Conchubar is how even-handed Yeats has made the argument between them. Conchubar is neither a blind man nor a fool; he knows Cuchulain "to the bone"; he takes an unanswerable view of his own solemn duties as High King. To put Conchubar's case more extremely than *he* ever does, Cuchulain, whatever his past services, is behaving like a traitor in time of war. Cuchulain, on the other hand, *has* no rational arguments to answer Conchubar. He is guilty of doing what Conchubar charges him with: "You play with arguments as lawyers do/ And put no heart in them." Cuchulain's case, of course, is equally unanswerable. It is based on his *uniqueness*. But even a man of Cuchulain's arrogance cannot quite argue: look, I am the greatest hero ever, I have no responsibilities to anybody but myself, you ought to be so grateful to have me around that you would be only too happy to let me do whatever I please. But in essence that is what he does say. The strength of Cuchulain's case lies in the fact that he *is* above the law that governs other men, and not through personal willfulness but because it is in his god-given nature to be what he is and not something else. The scene dramatizes the meeting of two immovable objects.

The issue is vigorously and succinctly stated in the following exchange:

Cuchulain.   I'll not be bound.
    I'll dance or hunt, or quarrel or make love,
    Wherever and whenever I've a mind to.
    If time had not put water in your blood,
    You never would have thought it.
Conchubar.   I would leave
    A strong and settled country to my children.[4]

Cuchulain will not be bound because he sees that Conchubar is not the man he once was. He has become that odious thing, an official guardian of the state. He is no longer capable of spontaneous joy or hate, having sacrificed these virtues for grey-haired wisdom. (Incidentally, the sardonic and bitter Cuchulain Yeats gives us here hardly suggests a gay dancer or happy lover; it is as if in his heart Cuchulain knew that the painful indignity of a greater man swearing an oath at the command of a lesser than he was inevitable.) Cuchulain resists Conchubar's "wisdom" with all his might; it is a torment (impossibility, in fact) to be at the beck and call of another, or to "sit at the council-board/ Among the unshapely bodies of old men." The ancient right to sit with lawmakers at the king's council table which Seanchan died to defend would be a kind of death to Cuchulain, whose shins are not "speckled with the heat of the fire."

Yet when Cuchulain asks, "Am I/ So slack and idle that I need a whip/ Before I serve you?" he reveals that serving his country, and even Conchubar himself, is not what he objects to. No, Cuchulain's point is that a man should act according to the law within him and not by compulsion imposed from without. And Conchubar recognizes this. His reply, "No, no whip, Cuchulain," is an effort to make his old comrade-in-arms see that the issue is not personal. But

[4] *Ibid.*, p. 255.

to Cuchulain it *must* be because he finds it impossible to separate his heroic role from his individual self. Conchubar can think of his children, whether pithless or not, as being in some sense equivalent to himself because they will some day occupy his role. No one, it seems to Cuchulain, could ever conceivably do that for him.

Like Ibsen's Brand in his uncompromising hardness, Cuchulain insists on all or nothing. Wearily Conchubar says, "Now as ever/ You mock at every reasonable hope,/ And would have nothing, or impossible things." Conchubar knows that no other woman can ever match Aoife in Cuchulain's mind, and Aoife would gladly destroy all Ireland to get revenge on Cuchulain, the only man who ever defeated her in battle. Cuchulain becomes really angry when Conchubar calls her "that fierce woman of the camp." But his anger gives way to a mood he has not expressed before—a lyric reminiscence of love that both excites and saddens Cuchulain. If only it could have been—

> You call her a "fierce woman of the camp",
> For, having lived among the spinning-wheels,
> You'd have no woman near that would not say,
> 'Ah! how wise!' 'What will you have for supper?'
> 'What shall I wear that I may please you, sir?'
> And keep that humming through the day and night
> For ever. A fierce woman of the camp!
> But I am getting angry about nothing.
> You have never seen her. Ah! Conchubar, had you seen her
> With that high, laughing, turbulent head of hers
> Thrown backward, and the bowstring at her ear,
> Or sitting at the fire with those grave eyes
> Full of good counsel as it were with wine,
> Or when love ran through all the lineaments

Of her wild body—although she had no child,
None other had all beauty, queen or lover,
Or was so fitted to give birth to kings.[5]

This is the moment when, paradoxically, Cuchulain is clos-
est to Conchubar and yet furthest from him. They will
never agree on the definition or function or limits of love;
nevertheless, Cuchulain appeals to Conchubar as though,
if the latter had seen her, he would no more have been able
to resist Aoife's charms than Cuchulain himself was. In
this speech Yeats demonstrates his skill in characterizing
through little pictures. It is vividly clear what kind of
woman Cuchulain does not like—one that would constantly
remind him by her flattery and self-conscious eagerness to
please of her utter dependence on him and, therefore, of
his utter obligation to be faithful, protective, and a good
provider. In contrast, Aoife is remembered in poses typical
of her athletic prowess, her ability to be thoughtful, and,
above all, her passionate beauty as a lover. Yet Cuchulain's
final word emphasizes her fitness to be a mother—of such a
son as he wants. A great deal of self-revelation is pushed
into these supple lines of blank verse which suggest ordinary conversation but, because of their speed and concentration and the urgency of their rhythm, could never be
mistaken for it.

It is almost impossible to read the foregoing scene without feeling how very close it is to Yeats's own concerns:
what should he be willing to sacrifice for family and
country? How can he keep Maud Gonne out of his mind,
or his own desire for a son? Will the country go to the
dogs because of its low-minded attention to family security

[5] *Ibid.*, pp. 258–259.

and its timidity in the face of aristocratic excellence? Certainly he has put a good deal of himself into Conchubar as well as into Cuchulain, and that is one reason for the tough eloquence of the scene. But at this distance, anyway, one need not be distracted by the concealed autobiography nor, on the other hand, is it necessary to know anything of the author. The scene stands firm on its own merits.

The ritualistic scene of three women (like the three fates), chanting their spell against "the women none can kiss and thrive" while one of them tosses fragrant herbs into the bowl of fire carried by the other two, forcibly reminds us how intertwined the heroic realm of Cuchulain and Conchubar is with the most primitive kind of witchcraft and magic. Like the Blind Man and Fool, these three female pillars of society regard destiny as a fearful mystery, mainly in the control of hostile supernatural beings always ready to take advantage of humans who venture too far beyond the threshold and hearthstone. The deeds of a hero like Cuchulain are certainly impressive but they are also reckless. In fact, the admirable energy of Cuchulain seems more dangerous than beneficial. To love such a witch as Aoife is not scandalous or immoral in the same sense it would be in a more sophisticated society—it is nothing less than madness. Aoife is symbolic of all those dark forces which, if allowed to gain the upper hand, will surely tear the community apart.

Against this background, Cuchulain takes the oath. It is a masterly stroke on Yeats's part to introduce this change of pace and style. Otherwise we might tend to forget that the majestic if intense argument between Conchubar and Cuchulain is not primarily a clash of temperaments nor a modern political debate; rather it is a more fundamental struggle between individual right and community right. True, the love theme is too subtle and civilized as Yeats expresses it to belong to a truly primitive community. Nevertheless, it is superimposed on a structural foundation of ritualistic action which does suggest—or should suggest—a community attitude toward the extraordinary individual as far removed from romantic hero-worship on the primeval side as the community attitude Yeats found among most of his contemporaries is on the civilized side. In other words, Cuchulain is no more at home in *his* world than Yeats is in modern Dublin. The parallel is obviously supposed to be there—in the play—but Yeats does go to some trouble to "ground" his drama in a truly ancient and unsophisticated world. That is the reason why it doesn't matter if we don't understand the words of the women after, say, the first four lines. (The stage direction reads: *"They sing in a very low voice after the first few words so that the others all but drown their words."*) [6] The main importance of their singing, at least in the theater, is to suggest the barbaric solemnity of an occasion when the "evil" spirits may be hovering very close to those engaged in exorcising them.

And pat upon the end of the ceremony there is a knocking at the door—and who should appear but Aoife's son. It is a splendid juxtaposition. And the essential failure of the women's magic could hardly be more dramatically emblematized. Cuchulain exhibits a heroic calm reminiscent of Othello. "Put up your swords./ He is but one. Aoife is far away." We are back in the heroic world of weighty words and pride of speech. Assured that the Young Man is a hawk and no sparrow, Cuchulain welcomes the chance to exer-

[6] *Ibid.*, p. 262.

cise his heroic function in the uncomplicated way he knows
best—fighting. It is a relief to forget Conchubar's "wisdom"
for a while.

But the relief is delayed as Cuchulain almost sees the
truth. This boy has the look of a son—and youthful valor
enough to make Cuchulain feel his age. Cuchulain asks,
"Have you no fear of death?"

Young Man. Whether I live or die is in the gods' hands.
Cuchulain. That is all words, all words; a young man's talk.
      I am their plough, their harrow, their very
          strength;
      For he that's in the sun begot this body
      Upon a mortal woman, and I have heard tell
      It seemed as if he had outrun the moon
      That he must follow always through waste
          heaven,
      He loved so happily. He'll be but slow
      To break a tree that was so sweetly planted.
      Let's see that arm. I'll see it if I choose.
      That arm had a good father and a good mother,
      But it is not like this.[7]

Cuchulain feels at ease in a way he definitely has not up
till now. He dominates the situation, at long last he has
discovered a companion worth talking to, and he has a
natural opportunity to display his heroic credentials. For
once he can be the wise man restraining hotheaded youth.
His language is made to go with actions. "That is all words,
all words" goes with a firm but kindly calming gesture. His
exposition of his divine begetting is both an inward remembering and an outward show of proud authority—it is
addressed to the company at large as well as to the Young
Man. Then Cuchulain focuses his attention on the intrepid

[7] *Ibid.*, p. 266.

young challenger, asking to see his arm. The younger man
demurs but Cuchulain insists—"I'll see it if I choose." Then
he compares his own arm for the benefit of all present. He
is enjoying himself, though the Young Man takes it for
mockery.

Nevertheless, as far as it is within his power Cuchulain
allies himself with the son whom he obscurely recognizes.
Though the son is willing, the father will not allow any of
the other kings to fight Aoife's champion.

> Whatever man
> Would fight with you shall fight it out with me.
> They're dumb, they're dumb. How many of you would meet
> This mutterer, this old whistler, this sand-piper,
> This edge that's greyer than the tide, this mouse
> That's gnawing at the timbers of the world,
> This, this—Boy, I would meet them all in arms
> If I'd a son like you. He would avenge me
> When I have withstood for the last time the men
> Whose fathers, brothers, sons, and friends I have killed
> Upholding Conchubar, when the four provinces
> Have gathered with the ravens over them.
> But I'd need no avenger. You and I
> Would scatter them like water from a dish.[8]

Cuchulain's resentment of those who have made him submit
to the oath is typically turned inward to fan the coals of his
imagination until he breaks off the string of mocking met-
phors—quite different from the symbolic hawk with
which he has earlier identified himself—to address his unknown son with a proud boast that yet conceals the pathos
of his appeal for an avenger of the death he foresees for
himself. But in another moment he imagines himself in invincible partnership with the boy. The lines move with a

[8] *Ibid.*, p. 269.

grave majesty which nevertheless permits a considerable flexibility of intonation and sudden turns of thought.

Cuchulain's dream of an embattled but triumphant partnership in which youth and age can scatter time with all its odious consequences of duty to unworthy generations joyless in their servitude to the demands of prudence and security is shattered by a reality even supermen are powerless to resist: the part of themselves that admits the authority of civilized law and order. In the legendary context of the play it is natural, and typical of Yeats, to present this psychological fact as an effect of supernatural witchcraft, though Cuchulain's easy assent to this explanation is both "in character" and dramatically unconvincing.

The unknown challenger from Scotland and Cuchulain give a perfect demonstration of that aristocratic chivalry which the rest are trying to make obsolete. The young man proves before all eyes his right to be his father's son. His brief but fatal initiation into heroism is symbolical of the impossibility of passing on heroism from generation to generation and of the wasteful virtues which ironically condemn heroism to destroy itself. For the loss of his son's life means the loss of Cuchulain's sanity. In a sense, the mark of the hero is that constant grasping after the impossible which to more orderly minds is a sign of madness. Beset by blind men and fools, wives and children, kings and their henchmen, and finally by his own self-division, Cuchulain unconsciously discovers that even Conchubar is not the true enemy. Beyond him lies the very source of all life and passion, the ungovernable sea, and in his mad logic Cuchulain rushes in to do battle with the only opponent worthy of his mettle.

It is no small part of Yeats's tragic effect that the heroic action should be enclosed by the tatterdemalion pair of the Blind Man and the Fool. To the sound of clashing swords we hear the Fool complain that the Blind Man has eaten the chicken and left him nothing but the bones. The Fool threatens to "tell Conchubar and Cuchulain and all the kings" about him. The Fool says the Blind Man is always cheating him, making him "take the windy side of the bush when it blows, and the rainy side when it rains." The Blind Man defends himself:

O, good Fool! listen to me. Think of the care I have taken of you. I have brought you to many a warm hearth, where there was a good welcome for you, but you would not stay there; you were always wandering about.[9]

The alliance between Blind Man and Fool mirrors in a distorting glass the bonds linking Conchubar and Cuchulain. The two worlds intersect and the Fool and Blind Man enter directly into the action.

Cuchulain rushes in with his bloody sword, thinking he has triumphed over witchcraft. Apparently unimpressed, Blind Man and Fool continue their quarrel ("Quarrels here, too!" says Cuchulain) and appeal to the champion to judge their case. From the Blind Man's description of the Fool it is obvious that the latter, like Cuchulain, is a "subjective" man. For "if the moon is at the full or the tide on the turn, [the Fool will] leave the rabbit in the snare till it is full of maggots, or let the trout slip back through his hands into the stream." In spite of the fact that Cuchulain's "father came out of the sun," it is to the "cold, sliding, slippery-footed moon" that Cuchulain has entrusted his destiny. And, like the Fool, he must pay the price in the

---

[9] *Ibid.*, p. 273.

"real" world of his enchantment by the ideal. The subjective man has the advantage that time can never touch
him in the sense that his integrity refuses compromise with
the crooked ways of the worldly—but this also means that
he cannot adapt to change (even when he tries to) and that
time can, and does, touch him with a very heavy hand for
his inability to bow gracefully to shifting circumstance. To
stand still is, at the extreme, to remove oneself from life
entirely. The Fool cryptically refers to these truths (using a
technique reminiscent of his namesake in *King Lear*) when
he sings

> When you were an acorn on the tree-top,
>   Then was I an eagle-cock;
> Now that you are a withered old block,
>   Still am I an eagle-cock.[10]

It is one of the peculiarities of this strange though powerful scene that the symbolic imagery apparently means little
to the characters who give voice to it. They are intent on
their own problems; it is for us to glean significance from
the words and gestures they use, as it were, unconsciously.
So when the Fool, who "likes nothing so well as a feather,"
puts feathers in his hair and Cuchulain indiscriminately
helps himself to the heap beside the Fool and to those on
the Fool's head in order to wipe the blood from his sword,
we realize that fool and hero have a kinship neither would
consciously be aware of. Those feathers (though they are
mere chicken feathers—not the feathers of hawk or eagle-
cock), the worthless prize ironically left to the Fool by the
crafty Blind Man, nevertheless are being used to wipe clean
of the world's bloody stain the bright sword of the hero

[10] *Ibid.*, p. 274.

Feathers vs. blood. A queer opposition to symbolize the subjective man's way of keeping his weapon clean to fight on and on against the inexorable revenges of time. But the Blind Man has his weapon too—a knowledge that half terrifies and half delights him because he knows it is powerful enough to bring the proud hero to his knees. Little by little Cuchulain himself forces the bitter truth out of the Blind Man—who leaves it to the Fool to say aloud the most fatal words. The Blind Man cannot *see* his triumph but he *feels* it. At first he thinks (typically) that the Fool is shaking the bench with his trembling because Cuchulain is going to hurt them. Then the Fool tells him: "It is Cuchulain who is trembling. It is Cuchulain who is shaking the bench." It is a tremendous theatrical climax.

Perhaps never again did Yeats attempt such a rich combination of themes: the idea of historical continuity in the rule of a nation as opposed to ritualistic renewal through resurrection of the heroic spirit, the perspective on the past which reveals fathers as greater than their sons and the younger generation (with the exception of Cuchulain's son) as the pillars of society, the "freedom" of the hero governed by laws more inexorable than any man can devise, and the power of a woman's love to perpetuate heroism and create anarchy. When Yeats returned to the theme of ideological conflict in deciding the fate of a kingdom, as he did from various angles in *The Green Helmet, The Player Queen,* and *The Herne's Egg,* he treated the subject from a comic point of view. Politics always interested him, although his approach is more mythical than historical. Is not Cuchulain a kind of unsophisticated Coriolanus, nearer to Robin Hood in some ways and to Achilles in others than Shakespeare's hero, but potentially comic in his naive response to an ul-

timately incomprehensible world? (We remember that
Bernard Shaw thought *Coriolanus* Shakespeare's greatest
comedy.)

The climax of Yeats's play, however, is neither political
nor comic. It has more of human accident and less of
"divine" surprise about it, at least on the surface, than the
more usual supernatural revelation that, especially in the
later plays, gives the hero a sudden, if terrifying, sense of
enlightenment. Surely Cuchulain represents one of Yeats's
most cherished masks—the man whose poetry is all in the
life of action and whose character is determined by an instinctive courage and courtesy based on a knowledge of his
own strength, of course, but also controlled by loyalty to
the semi-divine standard he has inherited and indeed set for
himself in his younger days. It is a typical peculiarity that
Cuchulain regards himself as already legendary, as the
others also do to a lesser extent, somewhat as though his
youthful self walked the halls of the gods at the very moment when here below he was being asked to enact the
dismal scene of his "growing up" to the mean and unheroic
responsibilities of adulthood. Unlike the protagonists of the
earlier plays, who move in the direction of heroism as the
action progresses, Cuchulain makes the tragic descent from
the mythical world of gallant and reckless play into the
human mire of sad complexity. If this noble savage, acting
out of spontaneous pride, love, and magnanimity, escapes
with his heroism unscathed and even magnified, it is only
because destiny itself has not permitted him to substitute
civilized conscience and social discipline for the joyous
abundance and heroic energy without which life and sanity
are impossible for him.

Cuchulain wins two pyrrhic victories: he escapes the oath

which would have been a testament to the High King's mastery and he remains an undefeated champion. The tragic irony of his predicament is analogous to the artistic dilemma of his creator. Yeats was writing, perhaps without being fully conscious of all he was revealing about himself, a tract for the times, admonishing his fellow countrymen to return to a purer and more imaginative ideal of patriotism; at the same time he was presenting them with a hero almost monstrously indifferent to the responsibilities of good citizenship. The problems Cuchulain faces may be a perfect "imitation" of the perplexities his creator faced at the time he wrote the play, but to most of the Dublin audience it must have seemed suspiciously like a high-minded version for adults of a boy's fairy tale.

Simply as dramatic narrative the play makes an economical and expert structure out of a situation chosen with Yeats's sure instinct for theatrical effect. His style, in both the prose and verse parts of the play, is ample, usually direct, and capable of accommodating itself to the range of expression demanded of it. Yeats never forgets the stage picture he is creating, and though he hated superfluous movement by the actors, he had a good eye for stage business. The ironical interaction of character and event, of what seems like misfortune and a strong sense of destiny, support a complexity of theme which brings together the opposite extremes of the heroic predicament: an isolation from the affairs of other men so complete that only the society of gods and other heroes matters, and an aspiration common to most men but requiring all but the privileged few to sublimate their desires and subordinate their wills, though with secret envy that makes them respond to the hero's fall with a shuddering satisfaction. On the other hand, Yeats's play is thin in all but the most crucial circumstance; in sacrificing epic breadth for intensity of impact he is in danger of turning his hero into a puppet. Even the Blind Man and the Fool are too deliberately symbolic to have a truly choric representativeness.

It is difficult to find the ideal aesthetic distance for plays dealing with mythological subject matter, and Yeats's uneasiness occasionally shows in his language, which must balance between the archaic on one side and the colloquial on the other. Yet, whether "popular" or not, Yeats succeeded in *On Baile's Strand* in doing pretty much what he intended. As he wrote to Lady Gregory shortly before it was put on at the opening of the Abbey, "*On Baile's Strand* is the best play I have written. It goes magnificently, and the end is particularly impressive." [11] Nevertheless, Yeats later made many changes, and the version in *Collected Plays* is very different from what that first night audience at the Abbey saw.[12]

Yeats's revisions clearly show how from an original uncertainty about his purposes he came to an unerring conclusion as to the heart of meaning in his own fable.[13] The problem was how to link the first part of the play—the quarrel between Cuchulain and Conchubar—with the mortal combat between father and son. Originally Yeats

[11] *Letters* (London, 1954), p. 269.

[12] George Brandon Saul, *Prolegomena to the Study of Yeats's Plays* (Philadelphia, 1958), p. 54.

[13] See Nathan, *The Tragic Drama of William Butler Yeats* (New York, 1965), pp. 121–126, for a compact summary of Yeats's dramatic theories from 1903 to 1908; pp. 103–121 for an account of the flaws in the first version of *On Baile's Strand*; and pp. 126–136 for the improvements Yeats made in the second version.

gave too much space to pictures of the idyllic life led by
Cuchulain and his followers, the Young Kings, and Cuchulain himself was uncomfortably close to appearing as a
youthful dreamer rather than a grizzled veteran who could
pose a real threat to Conchubar's authority. And Barach and
Fintain, the Blind Man and the Fool, did not foreshadow
the catastrophe to come—they gave the whole show away.
Yeats said in a much-quoted letter to Frank Fay:

About Cuchullain. . . . Probably his very strength of character made him put off illusions and dreams (that make young
men a woman's servant) and made him become quite early in
life a deliberate lover, a man of pleasure who can never really
surrender himself. He is a little hard, and leaves the people
about him a little repelled—perhaps this young man's affection
is what he had most need of. Without this thought the play
had not had any deep tragedy. . . . He is the fool—wandering
passive, houseless and almost loveless. Concobhar is reason that
is blind because it can only reason because it is cold. Are they
not the cold moon and the hot sun? [14]

This was written before the first version was completed,
and yet we see Yeats already understood quite well what
he was up to. But it was not until the second version, that
of 1906, that he realized in dramatic terms how to make
Cuchulain's hardness both more unequivocal and more
affecting. The solution of the problem was *isolation*. In the
later version Cuchulain really has no followers; even the
Young Kings are on Conchubar's side. The hero faces a
world full of enemies, both natural and supernatural. The
important chorus of women is added, and the Blind Man
and the Fool, who both frame and parody the action of
their betters, are set at an even greater distance from the

[14] *Letters*, pp. 424–425.

hero—and they bring out more effectively the superhuman wonder and terror Cuchulain inspires in lesser mortals. Yeats had said, "The touch of something hard, repellent yet alluring, self assertive yet self immolating, is not all but it must be there." He had gained confidence gradually, and become willing to risk making "the touch" seem the keynote to his hero. And his daring is rewarded: by making Cuchulain's will harder and more imperious, Yeats also makes his hero's involuntary passion for self-sacrifice more convincing and more poignant. And his one moment of heartfelt love doubly moving.[15]

There was great excitement at the opening of the new Abbey Theatre on December 27, 1904. According to Holloway, who seems to have been on hand for every important occasion in Abbey history, it was a wonder that the jittery Yeats did not ruin everything.

On Baile's Strand in rehearsal with W. B. Yeats at the helm. I can say without fear of contradiction that a more irritating play producer never directed a rehearsal. His ever flitting about and interrupting the players in the middle of their speeches, showing them by illustration how he wished it done, droningly reading the passage in a monotonous, dreary singsong; or climbing up a ladder onto the stage and pacing the boards as he would have the players do. (I thought he would come to grief on the rickety ladder several times.) Anon, he would rush on and erase, or add a line or two to the text but ever and always he was on the fidget and made each and all of the players pray backwards.[16]

---

[15] See Bushrui, *Yeats's Verse Plays* (Oxford, 1965), pp. 48–72, for a detailed account of revisions.

[16] Quoted in Peter Kavanagh, *The Story of the Abbey Theatre* (New York, 1950), p. 47.

Holloway's patent dislike of Yeats did not grow less with
the years, but this description provides a good antidote to
the more familiar image of the stately and hieratic poet.
In fact Yeats had every reason to be excited—he was ap-
proaching one of the great moments of his life. Finally he
had succeeded in getting established what was to all intents
and purposes *his* theater, and that against the sneers, doubts,
and stubborn opposition of both high and low in Dublin
town. And he had just written what he regarded as by far
his best play. The response of the first-night audience was
gratifying. Yeats had consulted the stars just before the
curtain went up and "found them quiet and fairly favorable." [17] But of course the attitude of the Dublin press was
suspicious and cynical, with some exceptions. D. P. Moran,
editor of *The Leader*, thought as he entered the theater he
"had strayed by mistake into a prayer meeting of the foreign element in Ireland." All those Anglo-Irish aristocrats!
He was afraid that "Mr. Yeats, shrewd man though he is,
will never touch the Irish heart." [18] And, it must be ad-
mitted, Yeats was much more interested in wounding than
in wooing the Irish heart Moran had in mind.

[17] *Ibid.*, p. 48.   [18] *Ibid.*, p. 49.

[7]

Deirdre

Yeats thought he had made a great play out of *Deirdre*, "most powerful and even sensational." [1] It was simultaneously his most advanced and his most conventional play so far. He had gone further in concentrating his action; he had used his choral figures, the musicians, with greater boldness than ever before to tell the audience that a great fable was in the act of completing itself before their eyes; he had reduced character—and the vanity of characters—for the sake of intensifying the passionate transformation of a young girl into a deathless queen. *Deirdre* is an attempt to lift out of its place in legend a heroic climax, give it a Yeatsian gloss, and return it brighter and more beautiful than it was before. The play is based on one of the oldest of dramatic patterns—the sexual triangle of the old man and the young man who are rivals for the favors of a beautiful young woman. And Conchubar's villainous plotting highlights the melodrama inherent in the tale of the old dragon's revenge on the youthful adventurer who steals the fairy princess. Tyranny foiled of its prey and treachery outwitted are always attractive subjects, and when these can be combined with the tragic death of young lovers, it is a hard heart that cannot be satisfied.

[1] *Letters* (London, 1954), p. 482.

The main interest of this famous Irish story of love and death for Yeats, however, was not the opportunities it afforded for exciting action, or even the chance to write great love scenes, but the challenge it presented him. Could he make a genuine heroine out of Deirdre? Previous heroines, even Countess Cathleen, were pretty much made before the play started; Deirdre was a romantic heroine to start with, but she was far from being a tragic heroine. The problem was quite different from creating a Seanchan or a Cuchulain. Love must be for Deirdre what the poet's right was for Seanchan and what his superhuman integrity was for Cuchulain. And she would have to use a woman's weapons.

Appropriately, three women musicians set the scene. They know the story of Deirdre, already famous for having fled with Naoise to "Somewhere beyond the edges of the world." The first musician's summary of youth's escape from age stresses the mystery of Deirdre's origin. She was

> a child with an old witch to nurse her,
> And nobody to say if she were human,
> Or of the gods, or anything at all
> Of who she was or why she was hidden there
> But that she'd too much beauty for good luck.[2]

This child, who might be a witch, or a goddess, or merely an adopted orphan, is set apart by her luckless beauty. She is the stuff fables are made of, and her escape with Naoise from the King shortly before she was to be married to the old man suggests that Conchubar might be anxious for revenge, but the musicians know nothing about that. They

---

[2] *Collected Plays* (London, 1952), p. 172.

bring with them the beginnings of a tale but no foreknowl-edge of its end. In a rather blunt transition, the second musician says, "The tale were well enough/ Had it a fin-ish." The first musician has more news to tell, but she is interrupted by the arrival of Fergus, who is surprised to find no message from the King. And so the makers of leg-end, who "have no country but the roads of the world," learn that Deirdre and her lover have arrived this very day, and narrative gives way to action.

Fergus, proud of his success in persuading Conchubar to forgive the lovers when all the rest of the court thought this impossible, is so cheerful he would "dance and sing" if it did not ill become his grey head. He is in no mood to be frightened by a musician's reiterated cry of "yet old men are jealous." Nor is he unduly upset by the strange dark-faced men who go to and fro outside, though the first musician says they look like hired murderers. He is sure he knows his man, that Conchubar's oath is his bond, and that the musician's "wild thought" is the mere product of "ex-travagant poetry." And Fergus (here) is the least poetic of men. Fabulous tales and romantic songs are a pleasant ac-companiment to life, but to take their "dazzle" seriously would be to lose one's grip on "common things" and to think "all that's strange/ Is true because 'twere pity if it were not." Fergus is the voice of conciliation and the champion of order and harmony. In this play of violent ex-tremes he will discover that he is a voice crying in the wilderness. His cheerful moderation is counterpointed against immoderate song.

As Fergus goes out to fetch Deirdre and Naoise, the musicians sing of Queen Edain. When she climbs to the top of the tower and looks out on the "waste places of the sky" she cannot keep from crying, sings the first musician. But her goodman answers, sings the second musician,

> 'Love would be a thing of naught
> Had not all his limbs a stir
> Born out of immoderate thought;
> Were he anything by half,
> Were his measure running dry.
> Lovers, if they may not laugh,
> Have to cry, have to cry.' [3]

The musicians join together for the final stanza, which abandons the past and is clearly aimed at Deirdre and Naoise.

> But is Edain worth a song
> Now the hunt begins anew?
> Praise the beautiful and strong;
> Praise the redness of the yew;
> Praise the blossoming apple-stem
> But our silence had been wise.
> What is all our praise to them
> That have one another's eyes? [4]

Music recalls the past, but the very thing music celebrates is now in the making. Praise for yew and apple is appropriate, but for the lovers themselves the present is all-engrossing. Time enough for song when the fatal tale is done.

Naoise and Deirdre are antagonists as well as lovers. He would gladly die for her, yet his honor demands that he live up to a code that, in the final analysis, must be the enemy of love. For love is "Born out of immoderate thought," and the code (dramatically represented by

---

[3] *Ibid.*, p. 177.   [4] *Ibid.*, pp. 177–178.

Fergus) is born out of a social convention that strictly sub-
ordinates individual feeling to a social good. When Fergus
says he has always "believed the best of every man" and
found this enough to make bad men better and even good
men outdo themselves, we can be sure that "good" and
"bad" are to be defined in terms of social obligation. Put
crudely, it is a matter of keeping oaths or breaking them.
But love cannot be bound (as *On Baile's Strand* demonstrated). Deirdre is all woman, and her feminine intuition
is at its keenest because she knows that the thing dearest
to her—her love of Naoise—is beset with danger on every
side. The "problem" of the play is how, or whether, love
can survive in a world of contract, a largely masculine
world where the king's word is law because he is king. The
action is an exploration of possible ways of getting out of
the trap the lovers have walked into at the beginning of the
play, and it is left to Deirdre to take the initiative in trying
to outwit nemesis. Conchubar is only the overt enemy; in
subtler ways she must fight Fergus and even Naoise, un-
witting allies of the High King. In a special and limited
sense, Deirdre and Conchubar are on the same side: both
are willing to practice any deception to gain their private
ends. Naoise, committed to both public and private worlds,
becomes the sacrificial pawn in the game played between
Deirdre and Conchubar. Yeats has devised his most subtle
and complicated play so far.

The musicians serve as a link with the larger realm of
fable out of which the action of the play emerges and to
which it must return, but they also act as a sympathetic but
disinterested companion to Deirdre. The first musician invites Deirdre's confidences in a manner both friendly and
sinister.

> If anything lies heavy on your heart,
> Speak freely of it, knowing it is certain
> That you will never see my face again.[5]

In other words, Deirdre need not fear that she will ever have to confront again someone to whom she has made a too intimate or shameful confession; the fact that they will never see each other again *may* simply mean that the wanderers must be on their way—or it means that circumstances will never *allow* Deirdre to see them again.

> There is nothing in the world
> That has been friendly to us but the kisses
> That were upon our lips, and when we are old
> Their memory will be all the life we have.[6]

The musician (perhaps modestly) does not mention the pleasure they will get and give by their songs of love. Nor does she give Deirdre any straightforward information, forcing Deirdre to interpret her riddling statements, couched in the oracular manner of her kind.

But it is no longer possible to believe in Conchubar's good faith, even for Fergus, once the messenger has made the High King's intentions clear. Fergus would have it out with Conchubar, but Deirdre stops him. Relationships shift as the action tightens, and Deirdre now begins to grow toward her final stature. Addressing Fergus as "old man," she bids him ride quickly and bring his friends. Naoise reacts to the knowledge that they are surrounded by enemies with the calm that both defines and limits his heroism. Deirdre would try to break through to freedom, but Naoise has his mind set on death.

---

[5] *Ibid.*, p. 181.   [6] *Ibid.*

> They would but drag you from me, stained with blood.
> Their barbarous weapons would but mar that beauty,
> And I would have you die as a queen should—
> In a death-chamber. You are in my charge.
> We will wait here, and when they come upon us,
> I'll hold them from the doors, and when that's over,
> Give you a cleanly death with this grey edge.[7]

Deirdre rejects this passive acceptance of death; she fears early and hopes long. Her idea of heroism is an unyielding fight to the finish. But slowly Naoise converts her to his aristocratic view of heroic superiority to death. Reminding her of how Lugaidh Redstripe and his seamew wife met their death, he reaches the climax of his eloquence.

> I never heard a death so out of reach
> Of common hearts, a high and comely end.
> What need have I, that gave up all for love,
> To die like an old king out of a fable,
> Fighting and passionate? What need is there
> For all that ostentation at my setting?
> I have loved truly and betrayed no man.
> I need no lightning at the end, no beating
> In a vain fury at the cage's door.[8]

Then he appeals to the musicians, asking if they could have found an "ancient poem" to praise the living immortality exemplified by that couple, indifferent to life because so concentrated on "the joy comes after." And Deirdre too addresses herself to the musicians as she accepts Naoise's high conception of the way to meet death. Or at least *tries* to accept it. Love should give the strength to make imperfect things seem ugly and unnecessary—including the

[7] *Ibid.*, p. 189.   [8] *Ibid.*, p. 190.

"vain fury" of kicking against the wall of the inevitable. On the other hand, for a woman like Deirdre, love is of the very essence of warm-blooded life. But the thought of the musicians' praise to sound in after times wins her over.

> He's in the right, though I have not been born
> Of the cold, haughty waves, my veins being hot,
> And though I have loved better than that queen,
> I'll have as quiet fingers on the board.
> O, singing women, set it down in a book,
> That love is all we need, even though it is
> But the last drops we gather up like this;
> And though the drops are all we have known of life,
> For we have been most friendless—praise us for it,
> And praise the double sunset, for naught's lacking
> But a good end to the long cloudy day.[9]

Yeats's rhythm of development gives the impression of a kind of intense leisure. The crucial events in the dramatic action happen swiftly, but like the undertow after a wave breaks, the self-contemplation of the actors has a retarding effect. As the essential action moves inward to what is occurring in the minds of the characters, both the tableau before our eyes and the meaning of what we hear contribute to the sense of stasis. A gesture from the world of time is, as it were, being metamorphosed into the attitude (in the Keatsian meaning of that word) of eternity. From the time Conchubar's messenger appears until Naoise and Deirdre are left alone with the musicians, a great deal happens: it looks as though all were well and Fergus begins to celebrate his vindication with joyful relief, Deirdre insists the message is not finished, the truth comes out, Naoise immediately accepts it but Fergus still clutches at straws until

[9] *Ibid.*, pp. 190–191.

Deirdre punctures his fantasy and sends him for help. Naoise reenters having been foiled in his attempt to get at Conchubar by the mocking messenger, and Fergus declares his intention of protecting, or at least revenging, the lovers imperiled by his drastic error in judgment. Then the bustle ceases and Naoise (*"who is calm, like a man who has passed beyond life"*) sets the tone for what is to come until the lovers sit down for their last game of chess: "The crib has fallen and the birds are in it."

Here is a different kind of action. Without Naoise's eloquent vision of heroic transcendence expressed in this scene we would be inclined to think him a trifle obtuse, no matter how high-minded. Yeats rights the balance and makes him a paramour worthy of Deirdre while still allowing him a suggestion of boyish naïveté. He says proudly to Deirdre, "You are in my charge," and successfully enforces his domination. He is resolved not "To die like an old king out of a fable,/ Fighting and passionate" because he has seen beyond such "ostentation" to a stillness that far more grandly completes the action of their lives. The escape from present suffering is aesthetic detachment, and if Deirdre's "heat" seems more lifelike than Naoise's "cold," *that* imbalance will be ironically righted too when Naoise is brought in like a fluttering bird in the fowler's net. Yeats has gone to some trouble to prevent his lovers from seeming *too* distant. They are fabulous and on their way to becoming more fabulous. Nevertheless, Yeats shows them to be humanly erratic as they grope their way toward their final consummation.

It is growing dark, though *"there is a clear evening light in the sky."* Sitting with Naoise at chess, Deirdre tells the musicians not to make a sad music, but "a music that can mix itself/ Into imagination" without interrupting the concentration "the hard game needs." It could be Naoise speaking, so thoroughly has she adopted his stance. The musicians do indeed sing an appropriate song, but not one that helps Deirdre to keep her mind on chess. They sing of love as a longing for something life can never satisfy because "love-longing is but drouth/ For the things come after death." It is a song that might well comfort lovers absolute for death. For it commits true (i.e., immoderate) love irrevocably to fulfillment on the other side of time. And it serves to pull the action toward that consummation Deirdre both desires and dreads.

> Love is an immoderate thing
>   And can never be content
> Till it dip an ageing wing
>   Where some laughing element
> Leaps and Time's old lanthorn dims.
>   What's the merit in love-play,
> In the tumult of the limbs
>   That dies out before 'tis day,
> Heart on heart, or mouth on mouth,
>   All that mingling of our breath,
> When love-longing is but drouth
>   For the things come after death.[10]

It is a song easy to mock if looked at in the harsh light of day—love is an old bird flying off into the sunset, for the weary sun is dimming; no wonder, because the joy of physical contact can't even last out the night and is, in any case, a fraud practiced on the soul thirsting for insensible

[10] *Ibid.*, p. 191.

pleasures. In dramatic context, however, it seems a perfect response to the great amount of life the lovers have been living through in such a short span of time. The peculiar combination of ecstasy and melancholy Yeats achieves hauntingly suggests the trembling balance of the lovers, poised at the outer edge of day for their plunge into the dark. Though "the merit in love-play" is questioned, the sensations of physical passion are tellingly evoked before they are by implication rejected. Deirdre's response to the song is a tribute to its power to disturb. She would deny the import of its question, and so she has risen from the board and is kneeling at Naoise's feet as the singers conclude.

For all her resolution, Deirdre is not yet capable of denying the warm blood in her veins. Naoise would prevent her, but she cannot hold in a last passionate outcry. Begging him to recall their first night in the woods together, she does it for him (and us). In the early grey dawn when the birds came awake he bent over her, thinking her still asleep. But the eyes he bent to kiss were open. It was a moment when "love-longing" *did* reach content in time. For Deirdre, "that old vehement, bewildering kiss" still lives to be renewed.

> Do you remember that first night in the woods
> We lay all night on leaves, and looking up,
> When the first grey of the dawn awoke the birds,
> Saw leaves above us? You thought that I still slept,
> And bending down to kiss me on the eyes,
> Found they were open. Bend and kiss me now,
> For it may be the last before our death.
> And when that's over, we'll be different;
> Imperishable things, a cloud or a fire.

And I know nothing but this body, nothing
But that old vehement, bewildering kiss.[11]

Without this simple and moving testimony on behalf of
body, the soul's victory would be too easy. Deirdre is pro-
testing not, perhaps, the burden of the musicians' song but
its "fabulous" distance from the actualities of love as she
has known it. She would rather be human than heroic.
During the action of the play there has been no opportunity
for a demonstration of love; it seems that at last the lovers
will seal their undying passion with a kiss. But we never
know whether Naoise would have yielded to Deirdre's
importuning because Conchubar appears and the mood (as
so often in this play) is abruptly broken. What a shrewd
theatrical stroke this is on Yeats's part! For if Naoise had
yielded and the lovers had kissed, the austere beauty of
Naoise's cold passion would have been marred. Yet if he
had refused to kiss Deirdre we might doubt the reality of
his love for her. The way Yeats handles it, both heroism
and humanity are preserved—and the baleful effect of
Conchubar is underlined.

Conchubar thinks he completely controls the situation
and is willing to bargain in order to get Deirdre to walk
into his house voluntarily. At first she cries out against
being separated from Naoise, but it is obvious Conchubar
is not going to give up the reward of seven years of planning and deceit. Deirdre fights for her lover's life (though
the way she puts her offer of self-sacrifice seems almost
calculated to arouse Naoise's strongest objections). Naoise,
true to his belief in eternal love, reminds her of the impossibility of bargaining with "Love's law."

[11] *Ibid.*, p. 192.

O eagle! If you were to do this thing,
And buy my life of Conchubar with your body,
Love's law being broken, I would stand alone
Upon the eternal summits, and call out,
And you could never come there, being banished.[12]

Naoise has recovered his heroic implacability. There is
nothing left for Deirdre to do but kneel and beg Conchubar
for mercy; and there is nothing for *him* to do but have
Naoise killed. That he is executed behind the curtain while
Deirdre is praising his worth to Conchubar is only the last
and most horrendous of the cruel ironies Deirdre has had to
suffer on her way to becoming a fit subject for the harper's
song.

Appalled at Deirdre's icy calm when she realizes Naoise
is dead, Conchubar can only stand agape at his own handi-
work. Deirdre has succeeded in turning the tables on him—
now he is the victim of her irony. She pretends to be an
ordinary specimen of her sex, ready to love whatever male
proves himself cock of the walk for her sake. "There's
something brutal in me," she says, "and we are won/ By
those who can shed blood." Thrown off balance, Conchubar is torn between taking immediate possession of his prize
and allowing her to make her private farewells. Deirdre
has now achieved the "inhuman" heroism just beyond her
reach while Naoise still lived, and Conchubar is no match
for this wily female whose wits are sharpened by her steely
will. She argues that her memory of her lover as a corpse,
"All blood-bedabbled and his beauty gone," will make her
love for Conchubar more sure. Conchubar does not believe her; she must goad him further. She mocks him for
refusing her first request. "There is no sap in him;/ Nothing

[12] *Ibid.*, p. 197.

but empty veins." She says he will go down as a laughing-stock who dared murder and yet "trembled at the thought of a dead face!" Hard pressed, half knowing the truth that Deirdre has a knife concealed on her, Conchubar is shamed into letting her go to Naoise unsearched. This small gesture of kingliness is, ironically, his fatal mistake. Having based his seven-year pursuit of Deirdre on fraud and deceit, at the critical moment he weakens into magnanimity: "Go to your farewells, Queen." What else could he do? Deirdre could be humiliated, but not his *queen*. The musicians know that the lovers have won—"Eagles have gone into their cloudy bed"—but Conchubar is able to confront Fergus, who has returned with a mob armed with scythes and sickles, with what the High King still believes to be a triumphant *fait accompli*. He had "to climb the topmost bough, and pull/ This apple among the winds." Now no one can rob him of her. When the curtain is drawn back revealing her body, he cannot believe she has "escaped a second time." Fergus will not allow him to touch her, though nothing is left "but empty cage and tangled wire,/ Now the bird's gone." It is Conchubar who stands isolated at the end. Denied the privilege every common man has of keeping his wife, surrounded by "traitors," Conchubar retreats into the royal dignity he has so long abandoned.

> Howl, if you will; but I, being king, did right
> In choosing her most fitting to be Queen,
> And letting no boy lover take the sway.[13]

If *On Baile's Strand* is Yeats's most masculine tragedy, *Deirdre* is the most feminine. No wonder Mrs. Patrick Campbell was anxious to play this part,[14] though Yeats was

[13] *Ibid.*, p. 203.   [14] *Letters*, p. 475.

not at all sure she was right for it. Deirdre is the most psychologically complex of Yeats's heroines (with the possible exception of the player queen, a part Yeats wrote with Mrs. Campbell in mind) exactly because her struggle to *be* a heroine is the essential action of the play. The climax when Deirdre "passes over into immortality" is unlike the masculine analogues in other plays: her virtue is no less wily than her opponent's villainy. She is neither ecstatic nor maddened, but a woman who has found a way of fully possessing her own nature. I think we should feel about her that both Conchubar and Naoise have good reason to be taken in by her ruses, for she is a wild creature of violent moods and subtle transformations, only *one* of which is her joy in being worthy to be sung by the musicians. While Naoise was alive it was impossible—or at any rate very painful—for Deirdre to imagine herself dead. She resisted being absorbed into legend with all her might. She wanted the reassurance of Naoise's kisses to keep her love warm; she agreed to the game-of-chess attitude toward death only to please him. Once he is dead, her fear of Conchubar (part of which might have been that she really *would* feel attracted to him) is changed to a clear and unambiguous hate. Now the full meaning of her love for Naoise is defined. She must seek her friends in the next world, for in this world she has none. Extreme love and extreme bitterness combine to give her her greatest strength. And her last stratagem does not fail. She is a heroine who needs—and has—her wits about her to the very end.

This blend of dove and eagle, of innocent coquette and amorous warrior, of cunning deceiver and queenly lover Yeats had neither tried nor achieved before. He succeeds in retaining the moment of passionate revelation, but the revelation is more of character and less of a new super-natural dimension than is usual with him, though individual greatness is once again shown to be at odds with a society too small to contain it. Deirdre is as assuredly feminine as Cuchulain is masculine, but her true stature at the beginning of the play is as unknown to herself as it is to others. The fate of the lovers is sealed as soon as they agree to return from Scotland, but Deirdre's character remains in suspense until the moment before she goes to her death. Yeats had a perfect right to regard his new play as "most powerful and even sensational."

Part of its power comes from the skill with which Yeats has focussed his story. With the musicians, we happen upon a legend in the making, and once the action begins Yeats never lets us forget that what happens is momentous be-cause it belongs to the universal repository of myth. The musicians are there to get the story right and even to help the action along, though they do their best not to interfere with the destiny it is their business to record. Each episode is a little action which rises to its own climax and leads on to the next. The suspense is cumulative. But even more im-portant is the thematic use of imagery to suggest the vio-lence out of which love comes and the serene heights to which it aspires.

As the play progresses the imagery of transcendence grows steadily more insistent. Naoise apologizes to Fergus for Deirdre saying she "has the heart of the wild birds that fear/ The net of the fowler or the wicker cage." But when Naoise himself is in the net, he addresses her as "my eagle" and asks, "Why do you beat vain wings upon the rock/ When hollow night's above?" And finally the first musi-cian speaks of the lovers as eagles who "have gone into their cloudy bed." Balanced against this upward-looking imagery is the imagery of blood, beasts, and dark-faced men, which also gathers power as the tragic climax approaches. The seamew with her "cold sea's blood" gives way to Deirdre, whose "veins being hot" must stir up giddy passions, and Naoise himself becomes, as he supposes, the hunter ready to carve up the beast. Deirdre speaks (ironically) of admiring those "who can shed blood" and pictures (for Conchubar) her lover's "blood-bedabbled" body. And those murderous dark-faced men who bothered Fergus are the "dark slaves" who would have searched Deirdre had Conchubar ordered them to. Dark is ambiguously the lovers' night and the murderous aspect of humanity. Chess, a game in which queens are lost, is a perfect image of aggressivenes contained within a courtly etiquette of high formality. In this play where the savagery of love and its power of stillness are equally given their due, one could almost say that the action becomes image and the imagery action.

In Synge's later *Deirdre of the Sorrows,* where reality is firmly rooted in nature and the pity of love is that the young must grow old, it is important that we get the sense of the passing of time. Deirdre is a child of nature, capable of queenliness but quite unfitted to be happy amidst the cold formalities of the royal court. The idyllic seven years she spends in Scotland with Naoise come to an end essentially because she fears the inevitable day when Naoise's love for her will no longer be unforced and sincere. In the last act Deirdre accepts death because she cannot imagine life without Naoise. (I have kept Yeats's spellings of names in discussing Synge's play.) But death will be a cold and ugly contrast to the life the lovers have had together.

Yeats begins at the point Synge arrives at in his third act, but even where they overlap their treatment is very different. In Synge's play there is no hint of personal immortality, and the only pleasure left the aged is caring for or regarding the young. When the lovers appear, it is Naoise who takes the gloomy view of the shabby place Conchubar has prepared for their reception. But they have little time for brooding; Deirdre discovers a newly dug grave behind a curtain and urges Naoise to take her away at once. He refuses to abandon his two brothers, Ainnle and Ardan (who do not appear in Yeats's play at all). With self-pity he taunts Deirdre, advising her after he is dead to remarry if she gets the chance, and not to go on lamenting him forever. But she is determined to die when he does. In all this the lovers show no desire for, or even consciousness of, being figures in legend. They are entirely concerned with the devastating prospect of an end to the happiness they have known together.

Synge's characters are human, all too human. Conchubar is no ogre dealing in magic but an old man obsessed with the idea of having Deirdre to solace the desolation of his last years. He is cruel through self-pity. Naoise is a bold and beautiful youth, loving as he must and fighting when he must, but not at all desirous of dying with heroic propriety. And Deirdre, sorrowing over lost youth and love, casts life aside not with the hope of joining her lover in some cloudy nest but only with the clear knowledge that any conceivable future can only mar her perfect memory of what has been. The greatness of Synge's play lies in its supreme evocation of the joy and misery of humans mired in time.

In Synge's conception of tragedy nature and fate are as important as artifice and will are in Yeats's conception. Not only does Synge evoke the woods, the moon, the sky; he makes character seem almost a part of the landscape. The grave itself has a chilling physicality. Deirdre says, "Draw a little back from the white bodies I am putting under a mound of clay and grasses that are withered." She balances the terror of cold earth against the grey horror of spending her declining years in hopeless lamentation. In a sense Synge uses the story of the lovers as a pretext to write the plotless tragedy of *all* human existence. Yeats's tragic pattern has its stoical element too, but in the total design the limitations that bind humanity to the cycle of nature are less important than the laws man imposes on himself. The extraordinary individual finds himself obliged to defy the laws governing ordinary mortals in the name of a higher law that allows him to be true to himself. His tragic fortitude is a response to the efforts to drag him down from the heights into ordinary humanity. Synge, on the other hand, could not help regarding heroic pretensions with a sceptical eye. Though he offers no real homage to pagan gods—or any gods—his feeling for nature is suffused with something very close to pagan mysticism. The man who can attune his life to the seasonal rhythms of nature will not escape sorrow and solitude, but he will be worthier of admiration in Synge's eyes than lords and ladies who have insulated themselves from the hardships and glories of living close to earth and sea and sky.

It was natural that critics should come to opposite conclusions in their judgment of *Deirdre*,[15] because it "invades"

---

[15] See Ure, *Yeats the Playwright* (London, 1963), p. 43, for a convenient summary of criticism, and for a fuller account see Bushrui, *Yeats's Verse Plays* (Oxford, 1965), pp. 152–153.

the territory of the realistic playwright to a greater extent than Yeats had done before and at the same time insists on the virtues and techniques of poetic drama. Instead of leaving the imitations of an immediate and humorous self-interest in the ordinary vexations of life to a cast of "low-life" characters, Yeats has simply eliminated them from this play—but not the interests they represent. The four main characters have their "high" purposes, but the exigencies of the situation force them to attend to what Samuel Beckett calls "the little things of life" as well. One might say, in fact, that the forward motion of the play toward the resolution of uncertainties contends with a backward pull to fix attitudes in timeless gesture. From this point of view, Naoise is the play's center of gravity. He is the voice and soul of honor—even to the point of a certain lovable stupidity; he is so above deceit that he falls into every trap with punctual ease—who reminds the others that the etiquette of living and dying is the proof of greatness. Against his immobility of character, and depending upon it, the others conduct their maneuvers.

Yeats believed that the portrayal of character belonged to comedy, not tragedy. Peter Ure goes so far as to say that *Deirdre*, indubitably a tragedy, would, judged by Yeats's own criteria, have to be considered a comedy.[16] Because Deirdre's character is so obviously the center of interest in the play, staging it has sometimes presented problems. Lennox Robinson says that even an adequate performance is enough to guarantee success,[17] but this seems unlikely. Yeats thought it necessary to engage an experienced actress from

[16] See Ure, pp. 58–59, for the contrast of Yeats's theories of tragedy with his practice in *Deirdre*.
[17] Gwynn, *Scattering Branches*, p. 92.

England, Miss Darragh, to play the title role and thereby caused a considerable flurry among the regular Abbey players, who understandably enough resented a "star" being brought in who had to be paid a good salary and who got the lion's share of the advertising. Nevertheless, the play was well received by both audiences and the Press, which "hailed it as the best of Mr. Yeats's verse plays." [18] Yeats would have had mixed feelings about the reason given by Willie Fay for its popularity: "The fact that it was not in any way mystical, but a straightforward treatment of a favourite story from the epic of the Red Branch, helped to make it popular, for the publication of *Gods and Fighting Men* and *Cuchulain of Muirthemne* by Lady Gregory had lately aroused in the Irish people a fresh interest in the early history of their country. This was the first verse play that gave us the feeling that the audience was with us and really liked it, and there were signs that with time and trouble Frank's scheme for a verse-speaking company was a possibility in the near future. We were hopeful in those days." [19] That was in 1906. Two plays later the Fays had left the Abbey. Perhaps *Deirdre* was the high water mark of the Abbey's popular success with a verse play.[20] But a very different kind of critic, the poet Sturge Moore, also praised the play, seeing in it something quite apart from what Willie Fay saw. "How I should like to see it adequately rendered! I think it would produce the effect of a religious mystery by the perfections of its seclusion from the world and the rare distinction of its self-decreed limitations." [21]

[18] W. G. Fay and Catherine Carswell, *The Fays of the Abbey Theatre* (New York, 1953), p. 209.
[19] *Ibid.*, pp. 209–210.
[20] Joseph Hone, *W. B. Yeats* (New York, 1943), p. 227.
[21] Quoted in Hone, p. 225.

The contrary tendencies in the play—toward psychological realism and toward ritualistic stylization—gave Yeats a good deal of trouble in working out his strategy of attack. Though he was pleased with the original performance of the play, the news that Mrs. Campbell would like to do it with the Abbey company the following year sent him scurrying back to his desk, inspired to make substantial revisions in the first half of the play.[22] He did not stop making revisions until 1934, when the *Collected Plays* appeared. The final version, as usual, was far superior to that used in the original production. Motivations were sharpened, unnecessary decoration cleared away, and new words added where they could strengthen dramatic impact. In general, the contrast between Naoise and Deirdre was given firmer definition. Against the greater naturalness of the speech, the songs of the musicians and the crucial moments of dramatic conflict stand out in bolder relief. But the play, in whatever version, depends on Deirdre more than any previous play had depended on its protagonist. Essentially, the men are not very interesting, and Fergus in particular has a thankless role. Yet a good enough Deirdre could make an audience forget other inadequacies. Stephen Gwynn, who saw Mrs. Patrick Campbell do the part in London, felt that she came between play and audience,[23] but Yeats toward the end of his life looked back on her performance as one of those moments when he had seen tragic ecstasy greatly played—"Mrs. Patrick Campbell in my 'Deirdre,' passionate and solitary." [24]

---

[22] See Bushrui, pp. 126–152, for a detailed account of revisions.
[23] *Ibid.*, p. 151.   [24] *On the Boiler* (Dublin, [1939]), p. 14.

8

A Bridge to
The Player Queen

The Unicorn from the Stars

The idea that Yeats had hoped to embody in *The Unicorn from the Stars*, and which he knew he had failed in doing, was "bringing together the rough life of the road and the frenzy that the poets have found in their ancient cellar, —a prophecy, as it were, of the time when it will be once again possible for a Dickens and a Shelley to be born in the one body." [1] In its first form, *Where There Is Nothing*, it was written hastily to forestall George Moore, who had threatened to "steal" the plot.[2] Lady Gregory took care of the Dickensian part of the play and Yeats provided the infusion of Shelley. Since Yeats himself felt that *The Unicorn from the Stars* had far more of his spirit in it than the earlier version did,[3] and since he put it in his *Collected Plays*, I will address my remarks to *Unicorn*.[4]

[1] Quoted in Nathan, *The Tragic Drama of William Butler Yeats* (New York, 1965), p. 146.

[2] *Letters* (London, 1954), p. 503.   [3] *Ibid.*

[4] For an extended summary of *Where There Is Nothing*, see Nathan, pp. 93–99, and for a favorable criticism see Una Ellis-Fermor, *The Irish Dramatic Movement* (London, 1954), pp. 104–107.

What is most recognizably Yeatsian about the play is the familiar opposition between civil order and divine disorder. In Martin Hearne's dream, heaven is emphatically not a place of restful reward for a life misspent in dutiful toil. As he says in his "candle" sermon just before his death by accidental shooting—

Father John, Heaven is not what we believed it to be. It is not quiet, it is not singing and making music, and all strife at an end. I have seen it, I have been there. The lover still loves, but with a greater passion, and the rider still rides, but the horse goes like the wind and leaps the ridges, and the battle goes on always. That is the joy of Heaven, continual battle.[5]

This has (shade of Yeats forgive me!) an almost Shavian ring to it.[6] But Martin is neither a Don Juan nor a Joan of Arc. And he needs to be something of the sort if the play is going to rise to the height of its vision.

Realizing that the boy had an unusual restlessness of spirit, his guardian Thomas, with the advice of Father John, had sent him to a monastery in France (of which we have only report in this version of the story). Martin has returned and been working hard on a carriage—Thomas has taught him his trade, and the boy is a good worker. He had been gilding a lion and a unicorn to put on the top of his coach when he went into a trance. Father John says when he picks up the ornament, "It was a ray of sunlight on a pewter vessel that was the beginning of all." [7] When Martin comes out of his trance he can remember unicorns trampling grapes, but he can't remember what he was com-

[5] *Collected Plays* (London, 1952), p. 381.
[6] In fact, Shaw admired *Where There Is Nothing*. See Ure, *Yeats the Playwright* (London, 1963), pp. 132–133.
[7] *Collected Plays*, p. 329.

manded to do. It is through the mouth of a beggar that the mystic command is recovered. When he is caught trying to make away with a bag of money (Martin's money), Johnny Bocach lets it fall to the floor and woefully exclaims, "Destruction on us all!" [8] Then Martin remembers his mission to break down the wall "that comes between us and God." [9] Consequently Martin becomes the leader of a band of beggars, every working man in town is made drunk, and all hell breaks loose. Two great houses are burned. Since this is not a movie, we get to see none of this excitement.

In the third act Martin is thought to be dead and laid out for burial. He has been the unlikely hero of the daring deeds performed during the night, and the tinkers (or beggars) are determined not to let him (or his corpse, as they first think) fall into the hands of the hated British constabulary. Father John arrives and says that Martin is not dead, he is in a trance, but he refuses to awaken him this time as he did before, feeling guilty about interfering between Martin and his mystic communion with divinity. Maybe all the destruction Martin has wrought was the Devil's work, and not God's; and maybe it was all Father John's fault for waking him. But at the climax of argument about what to do, Martin awakes of his own (or God's) accord. He had indeed heard the music of Paradise, "made of the continual clashing of swords." [10] Unfortunately for his hopeful followers, though, the kind of warfare Martin is to undertake has nothing to do with the happy violence of burning houses and driving out the hated English tyrant. To their dismay, Martin tells them, "What have I to do with the foreign army? What I have to pierce is the wild heart of time.

[8] *Ibid.*, p. 345.   [9] *Ibid.*, p. 346.   [10] *Ibid.*, p. 377.

My business is not reformation but revelation." [11] None of them know what to make of Martin—is he touched or a sacred fool or a nervous wreck? When he is shot, Martin and all the others are released from an impossible dilemma. The main thing wrong with the play is that the Nietzschean idea of joyous destruction has no real intellectual content, and yet the whole action hinges on Martin's vision. Lady Gregory undoubtedly saw the comic possibilities of the play but was inhibited from exploiting them except in a tentative and half-hearted way, probably for fear of offending Yeats. Elizabeth Coxhead feels that Lady Gregory put some of her best work into the play and that in the beggars she attained "an almost Syngean note," but it is hard to agree.[12] At this distance, anyway, the characters seem at best occasionally amusing stereotypes. Andrew, the brother of Thomas, who sympathizes with Martin when Thomas is merely disgusted with him, provides a humorous link between two uncompromising opposites, for Andrew is against dull work and in favor of drunken excitement when the opportunity offers, but of course he has no more real understanding of Martin than anybody else does. (O'Casey could have done wonders with Andrew.) Father John, who once had a vision somewhat akin to Martin's, was squelched by his bishop and has remained subdued ever since. His uncertainty, however, is only mildly humorous. The makings of a grand farce of misunderstandings are in this play, and later Yeats was to use some of the same materials to write just such a piece—*The Player Queen.*

The idea of catastrophe and renewal combining joy and

[11] *Ibid.*, p. 378.
[12] Elizabeth Coxhead, *Lady Gregory: A Literary Portrait* (London, 1961), pp. 109–110.

terror—the coming of a new dispensation—had preoccupied Yeats since the early stories of *The Secret Rose*.[13] It
continued to preoccupy him for the rest of his life. Giorgio
Melchiori has shown how the symbolic meaning of the
unicorn developed from Yeats's studies in magic and the
occult.[14] It stood for the complex of ideas Yeats associated
with the shock of transition from one era to the next. It
combined "raging violence and newborn joy, tragedy and
laughter in instantaneous synthesis, . . . the very essence
of all his greatest poetry, . . . actually the things that make
that poetry great." [15] It was violent because the times required violent destruction, and joyful because it heralded a
new age of exalted creative energy. Combining the virtues
of power, passion, and purity, it was a perfect instrument
of catharsis. And in *The Unicorn from the Stars*, where the
symbols of lion and unicorn occur together, the unicorn
takes on the added meaning of being the emblematic champion of Irish independence against the lion of British im-
perialism.

As the unicorn crushes the grapes into the wine of
Dionysian inspiration, it also elevates the clash of opposing
forces from the physical realm to the metaphysical—and
here is the capital opening for misunderstanding. There is
all the difference in the world between the high and solitary
intelligence of the unicorn (who spirals the plenty of all
being into one horn) and the mindless enthusiasm of a mob
bent on releasing their frustrations in wanton acts of
destruction; it is the difference between divine intoxication

[13] Cf. Ure, pp. 128–130.
[14] Giorgio Melchiori, *The Whole Mystery of Art* (London,
1960), pp. 35–73.
[15] *Ibid.*, pp. 56–57.

and ordinary drunkenness. The one illuminates intuition, the other merely dulls the intellect. It is out of this confusion that Yeats made the splendid farce of *The Player Queen*, but in *Unicorn*, where the sober Martin is in no way superior to his surroundings except, maybe, when he is in a trance, the play really becomes an unintentional parody of Yeats's idea of the hero. It is an adventure story in which most of the adventure takes place off stage; the lengthy exposition prepares us for an abortive melodrama. In the end there is neither tragic gaiety nor comic enlightenment, only an undignified muddle. Nevertheless, the play has the negative virtue of defining for us as it did for Yeats a dead end of his talent. He had not found the way to bring Don Quixote and Sancho Panza together.[16]

The Green Helmet

In *The Green Helmet*, a verse play based on the prose *The Golden Helmet*, Yeats does achieve a new and successful form. He writes a dramatic ballad based on an anecdote from folklore and gives it theatrical unity of place. In a log house by the edge of the sea, Laegaire and Conall are secretly waiting for the return of the Red Man, a god-figure from the sea, who has a claim on Laegaire's head. Like the green knight in the medieval romance of *Gawain and the Green Knight*, the Red Man has challenged a hero to play the game of whipping off of heads. Beheaded, he has walked off with his head, promising to come back in a year to collect his due. Twelve months ago he returned and was refused. Now Conall and Laegaire are terrified lest

---

[16] Cf. Yeats's note on the play in *The Collected Works* . . . (Stratford-on-Avon, 1908), III, pp. 220–221. Quoted in Nathan, p. 147.

he tell everybody they are afraid and so ruin their reputations. It is a moonlit night, and the Red Man may come any moment. Instead a young man appears, astounds them by being able to force his way inside, and then reveals himself to be their friend Cuchulain, who has been away in Scotland. When he is told of their plight, he agrees to stand with them and confront the Red Man. The Red Man comes, a mighty figure carrying a mighty sword. He explains that he was only joking, admits that maybe he jokes too grimly when he is in his cups, and leaves a green helmet as a gift for the bravest. Immediately argument begins, but Cuchulain fills the helmet with ale and says they must drink to sharing the prize.

At this moment there is a terrible hubbub outside. The heroes' chariot drivers and their wives are arguing about which of the three heroes is the greatest. Stable boys and scullions are carrying horns and ladles and other instruments with which they try to drown out the arguments of the opposition. Then the three wives dispute who shall enter the house first. Always trying to keep peace, Cuchulain orders that holes be cut in the walls so that the three rival wives can come in simultaneously! Once this is settled, a quarrel breaks out about the meaning of the order in which the heroes drink from the helmet. Cuchulain flings it back into the sea; then he is accused of depriving the others of their lawful right. Just when it seems there is no hope of avoiding bloodshed, black fingers reach in the windows and the lights go out—and even the moon is dimmed. When light reappears, the Red Man is in their midst, and two of his shape-changers carry the sword and the green helmet respectively. Who will offer his head? Cuchulain agrees to the sacrifice, despite the keening and suicide threats of his

young wife, Emer. When Cuchulain kneels down to receive the fatal blow, the Red Man places the green helmet
on his head, explaining

> I have not come for your hurt. I'm the Rector
>   of this land
> And with my spitting cat-heads, my frenzied
>   moonbred band,
> Age after age I sift it, and choose for its
>   championship
> The man who hits my fancy.
> [*He places the Helmet on Cuchulain's head.*]
>   And I choose the laughing lip
> That shall not turn from laughing, whatever rise
>   or fall;
> The heart that grows no bitterer although betrayed
>   by all;
> The hand that loves to scatter; the life like a
>   gambler's throw;
> And these things I make prosper, till a day come
>   that I know,
> When heart and mind shall darken that the weak
>   may end the strong,
> And the long-remembering harpers have matter for
>   their song.[17]

Unlike *Unicorn*, where the dazed Martin becomes a kind
of hero by the accident of circumstance, *The Green
Helmet* shows us a hero, the young Cuchulain, completely
self-possessed in the midst of a dazed world. He makes no
false moves and never hesitates. He possesses all the military
virtues and yet is statesmanlike by instinct. Alone, he is
able to rise above personal considerations of prestige and

[17] *Collected Plays*, p. 243.

identify himself with the common weal. The threat of the Red Man is subtler than that of an ordinary shape-changer; Conall and Laegaire are sufficient where no more is required than strength and daring, but here the control and detachment of a man who is in a sense "beyond life" are needed. Cuchulain is a match for the Red Man not because he could defeat him in an epic battle—he obviously could not—but because his confidence in his own destiny is so great that he can afford to be careless of his life. If Cuchulain were not there, the dark day when "the weak may end the strong" would be much closer. In Yeats's other plays about Cuchulain, the hero is in one way or another at odds with sovereign authority; he is, or seems, eccentric—an outlaw in conflict with the conventional wisdom of society. In *The Green Helmet* he *is* the central authority, for a triumphant moment anyway. The uncrowned king is actually crowned; the hero in a public ceremony receives divine sanction. And yet Cuchulain is allowed a lightheartedness that appears nowhere else. He is not on an heroic quest—he just happens along, so to speak, at the right moment and takes over Conall's unfinished business. Cuchulain undergoes the ritual ordeal of kingship without realizing what is happening. He is solely concerned with bringing unity to his divided people.

Yeats calls the play "an heroic farce." This is a very exact generic description. In the center of the play stands the hero, a moral pillar of strength surrounded by the squabbling of fools. The absurdity of their human weakness stems from their complete involvement in the present moment. In their barbaric rivalry for an individual distinction they are comically obsessed with the name of honor; the heroes and their wives cannot see how very inglorious their pursuit of glory is making them. And they steadily force Cuchulain to retreat from one stratagem to another in his effort to keep the peace until darkness supernaturally descends. The Red Man thoroughly proves his case: unless they could find a superman ready to sacrifice himself, a man bold enough and generous enough to play the game with the Red Man, they would be in a sorry plight indeed. As so often in farce, tragedy is held at bay but lurks in the background. The Red Man is a benevolently inclined guardian spirit—as things turn out. But he is grim and awe-inspiring too, and he predicts a day of inevitable catastrophe. Cuchulain is caught in all the splendor of his flourishing prime. He is able to laugh away bitterness and tragedy (though he doesn't do much actual laughing in the play). Never again will he be so carefree.

Though it comes much later in Yeats's career and is certainly not modern in its ballad rhythms, the lively experimentalism of *The Green Helmet* suggests analogies with Eliot's chronologically later *Sweeney Agonistes*. Both are attempts at comic stylization of primitive material and both employ a strategy of combining sophistication and naïveté. And both are joyously satirical at the expense of modern vulgarity. But of course there is no hero in *Sweeney Agonistes*, only the distant allusion to Greek drama to suggest a contrast to the sordid scene of modern post-war London. Yeats is presumably writing about the legendary past, and in fact he gives the feeling of staying closer to his folklore sources here than in any other of his plays; nevertheless, the application of his tale to the contemporary world would not be lost on a perceptive modern Irishman. Though Cuchulain is not forced to sell his soul to save those of his countrymen the way Countess Cathleen was, he *can* keep his integrity and uphold that of his country only at the cost of offering self-sacrifice. It is a hard job to be a hero under any circumstances—unless it is made supernaturally easy. The ironical energy so evident in both *Helmet* and *Sweeney* finds expression in highly accented verse, and the underlying pattern of ancient ritual, though used in very different ways by Yeats and Eliot, suggests a common dissatisfaction with "cultivated" poetic drama and the need to get at something more theatrically fundamental. Unconsciously, Yeats was preparing the way for such later plays as the *Player Queen* and *The Herne's Egg*. Eliot, however, was to turn toward comedy of manners, though his fables never completely lost touch with their mystical origins.

According to Bushrui, the earlier play, *The Golden Helmet*, "came immediately after *The Playboy* riots and was meant to satirize the mob mentality and conduct of Synge's enemies." [18] Certainly Yeats, never democratic by temperament, had a scorn for the mob equal to Shakespeare's and Ben Jonson's, and though he hoped for larger audiences at the Abbey, he wanted them on no terms but his own. He had used grim humor before, notably in the Blind Man and the Fool of *On Baile's Strand*, to satirize the "low" type of common mind, but the *Helmet* plays were the first in which the hero was able to rise above circumstance by virtue of what we might christen as "comic gaiety." Encouraged by his recent victory over Dublin Castle in the matter of staging Shaw's *Blanco Posnet*, Yeats could perhaps imagine a good deal of himself in the Cuchulain he had portrayed, and perhaps something of his friend Synge.

The inspiration for the irregular Alexandrine meter came

---

[18] Bushrui, *Yeats's Verse Plays* (Oxford, 1965), p. 178.

from Wilfred Scawen Blunt's *Fand*, which had been written at Yeats's request and presented at the Abbey in 1907. Blunt says in his diary that Yeats "told me he had been converted to my use of the Alexandrine meter for plays in verse, but that he had such a difficulty in finding rhymes that a rhymed play would take him two years to write." [19] The effort was worth it. *The Green Helmet* (a specifically *Irish* helmet) has the edge over its predecessor both in narrative gusto and in satirical bite, though sometimes the meaning is clearer in the prose version. As an example, here is the ending of the play in the prose version (which can be compared with the poetic version quoted above):

I will not harm you, Cuchulain. I am the guardian of this land, and age after age I come up out of the sea to try the men of Ireland. I give you the championship because you are without fear, and you shall win many battles with laughing lips and endure wounding and betrayal without bitterness of heart; and when men gaze upon you, their hearts shall grow greater and their minds clear; until the day come when I darken your mind, that there may be an end to the story, and a song on the harp-string.[20]

Despite the great differences between Yeats and Shaw, there is an interesting parallel in the relationship of the protagonist to the other characters in the works of both playwrights. I think it was Ronald Peacock who first pointed out that whereas Molière isolated the unreasonable character, Shaw isolated the reasonable one. "Molière gives us a series of characters who offend our idea of rational behaviour: Harpagon, Alceste, Arnolphe, Argan, Tartuffe are

---

[19] Quoted in Bushrui, p. 184. See pp. 183–208 for a comparison of *The Golden Helmet* with *The Green Helmet*.
[20] *Ibid.*, p. 187.

examples. Shaw, on the other hand, gives us a series that illustrates his own idea of rational behavior: Dudgeon, Caesar, Tanner, Dubedat, Undershaft, Shotover, Magnus, Joan, and so on—all characters with a head, with their eye on the point, piercing illusions and grasping reality." [21] The last phrase unexpectedly applies to the Cuchulain of *The Green Helmet*, much as Yeats might have objected to considering his hero a rationalist. Cuchulain shows up the folly that surrounds him just as much as Shaw's Caesar does. And this is usually true of Yeats's heroes and heroines, as much as it is of Shaw's. To be sure, the conception of *reality* is different. The Yeatsian hero rises above the natural (i.e., social) world to confront a supernatural reality. The Shavian hero finds it necessary to clear away romantic illusion in order to challenge the ugly realities of the everyday world and so change them. The two Irishmen would seem to be at the antipodes from each other—and certainly they often thought of each other that way. But there is a curious kinship. The detachment of Cuchulain—his sense of belonging to a purpose greater than his own self-advancement —gives his idealism that same touch of coldness Shaw's heroes are often accused of having. Both authors exalt a certain magnanimity of spirit that liberates the hero from the meanness and triviality of those poorer souls wholly preoccupied with securing their rights and prerogatives. And, in their undoubtedly different ways, the heroes of both men are concerned for the honor of the human race. It is merely one of the ironies of history, one of which both Yeats and Shaw were well aware, that the human race is ungrateful. Of this irony Shaw made comedy throughout

[21] Ronald Peacock, *The Poet in the Theatre* (New York, 1946), p. 89.

most of his career. At first Yeats was inclined toward a romantic and tragic view, but as he grew older tragedy more and more often approached farce on the one hand and apocalyptic vision on the other.

9

The Janus Face:
The Player Queen

From the beginning *Player Queen* suggests the unreliability of our knowledge about the world. Two old men, waiting for the dawn of a new day, question each other about sights and sounds. One sees better, the other hears better. But their failing senses report more than their minds can assimilate. The old men exchange derogatory opinions about their juniors. The young and the middle-aged are up to some mischief; they don't know the value of sleep and "are always in a passion about something or other." Lacking the strength and health the old men had, the younger generation wear themselves out—they will never live to be ninety. Footsteps approach. The old men agree to pull their heads in their respective windows, for "the world has grown very wicked and there is no knowing what they might do to us or say to us." Down below in the street one of the middle-aged appears, the poet Septimus. He is drunk—and remains more or less drunk throughout the play. Disenchanted with his wife, his occupation, and indeed the whole world, he cannot find even the modicum of Christian charity he seeks—a place to sleep out the rest of the night. Instead an old man tells him to go away and an old woman pours water on him. Drenched, wretched, shivering, drunk, and disregarded, Septimus presents a comic image of the *poéte maudit*.

One aspect of the comedy is that Septimus, far from being the proud and self-reliant hero of Byronic melodrama, is a worried husband anxious for the esteem of "his betters" and consumed with self-pity for his neglect by others. His attitude wobbles as his body does. At one moment he sees himself as a passive victim of malevolent circumstance; at the next he is the aggressive peacock, chastising his inferiors for their bad taste and lack of vision. Whether he is passionately defending the Unicorn or complaining of mistreatment, he is never quite himself—whatever that self may be. He is capable of comparing himself, however ironically, to Jesus—"Bring me to a stable—my Saviour was content with a stable"—though at the next moment, after dissociating himself from "bad, popular poets," he professes to care for no one "except Venus and Adam and the other planets of heaven." Like Hesse's Steppenwolf, he despises the philistine world for its complacent mindlessness and seeks salvation in the transcendent realm of art, yet he cannot do without the natural comforts bourgeois existence, and especially marriage, provides.

From one standpoint Septimus is that traditional fixture of sexual comedy, the deceived husband; unable to adapt to a rejuvenated world, he must be cast out at the end of the play. But from another standpoint his conservatism represents integrity, a refusal to submit to the dictates of his bad, flighty wife. Originally, Yeats conceived the poet-figure who developed into Septimus as a goodlooking but shallow and stupid man, and Septimus retains a certain stupidity that even drunkenness can do no more than turn into pseudo-profundity. Septimus favors revolution, so long as it is safely spiritual and poetic, but in the world of action and politics he is a hopeless bungler. He appeals to women, or at least to Nona and Decima, but he is no more prepared to make Decima his Beatrice than he is to be a proper breadwinner for Nona. He is a truly alienated man, but he is just as truly useless to himself or anybody else. And yet for the play to succeed we must feel that he still possesses a spark of nobility the world can ill afford to lose.

The main vehicle for creating this effect is, of course, Decima, the Player Queen. Septimus, without intending the consequences, has made not only a woman of her, he has made a queen. He has endowed her with a "divine discontent" that enables her to become a master of illusion and more truly a queen than the *real* queen is. The poet is overwhelmed by the reality of the gross world, but Decima rises to the top because she has learned to *play* with reality. She is a born opportunist, but it was poetry that gave her the imaginative self-confidence to dominate reality. And yet if Septimus had agreed to expel Nona from his bed and his heart, Decima would willingly have obeyed him in all else. But Decima refuses to compromise with reality —she will have her way or she will commit suicide. The crowning of Decima brings to climactic focus all the ironies of the play.

It indicates first of all that the state, like the individual, cannot do without an ideal image of its destiny. Where a vacuum exists, sinister fantasies flood in to fill the gap in nature. A queen who denies her presence to her people becomes an obscene witch born out of popular superstition. By cutting out the rather elaborate development of specific grievances about taxes that existed in earlier versions, Yeats puts the emphasis where he wants it—on the *unicorn* of imagination. To the popular mind, this fabulous beast is all too real, but it is monstrous, a symbol of those unholy pagan powers which lead straight to the devil and damnation. Ironically, the queen herself is most afraid of those dark, sexually tinged passions that the populace imagines her to be indulging in behind the castle wall. Her saintly ideal—a complete abnegation of the powers and dominations of the world—unfits her for true martyrdom as much as it disables her as queen. Her fear of the world is as great as *its* fear of her. And in both cases sexual obsession dominates the shaping of fantasy. A little cool rationality could do the state a great deal of good here. Instead, one form of overheated imagination is poised against another.

Septimus's extravagant defense of the Unicorn is in fact a justification of his own ideal of artistic integrity. And at the center of that ideal is chastity. Like the queen, he is unfitted for the world because only the transcendent is pure enough for him. His drunkenness is a sign of his estrangement from earthly concerns; he tries to persuade others—and himself—that it is a divine intoxication which both provides a vision of reality and guarantees its authenticity. Yet he knows and we know that his bad, flighty wife is at the bottom of it. Nothing is more deflating to the "image" of the Romantic poet than having even the best of wives as a partner of destiny. Septimus may indeed have a wisdom denied to more ordinary men, but unfortunately his wife seems more real than his Unicorn. And to be an unsuccessful family man is not the same as being a successful Bohemian. His struggle to assert his dignity merely emphasizes his comic absurdity; the more Septimus insists on his role as inspired bard the drunker he seems.

The strength of his position depends on an absolute refusal to compromise with the ways of the world—but he has already fatally compromised himself when the play opens.

Comedy, on the surface, celebrates the triumph of a younger, more vital order over the deathlike rigidities of the old. But underneath it may be saying that the more things change the more they stay the same. On the surface, Decima triumphs at the expense of Septimus, but unlike a figure of romantic comedy she does not marry a young prince but an elderly, undistinguished, and thoroughly "realistic" prime minister. It is a marriage of convenience. She provides the poetic image that the mob craves and demands, and the prime minister will, presumably, provide the necessary bureaucratic know-how to keep the kingdom running. Decima has arrived at the top by a combination of luck and pluck. But she would never have been capable of making her imagination dominate the world around her without the schooling given her by Septimus. He has taught her to see herself as a member of that charmed company of whom legends are made—kings and queens able to command the devotion of poets and thereby assure themselves of a kind of immortality. (It is too bad that Yeats did not give us a scene in which we could watch the eloquence of Septimus working on the girlish imagination of Decima, transforming her from a mischievous hoyden into an "artist" * in her own right.) We do not know whether the bad, flighty wife, having found her proper role, will become a good, steady queen or not, but we do know that she is realistically aware of the implications of her break with Septimus—who will always

---

* With strong emphasis on the secondary meaning of this word as cunning trickster, practical magician.

be king of that interior country of Decima's mind to which we can be sure the prime minister will never gain access. By refusing to swear allegiance to Decima, Septimus asserts his integrity—and rises to his saving moment of heroism. Decima has lost him by trying to force his loyalty; her mask has failed her. So her success with the crowd is a settling for the second-best, and her power to avenge humiliation by banishing the cause of it mocks her as well as her victim. The beggar has found his straw, the donkey has brayed, and the new dispensation has arrived. Ironically, it has no religious significance whatever. The crowd has what it wants—an image of authority to adore and reverence. This is what the crowd always wants. The revolution has ended with the usual accommodation between the ideal and the real, between poetry and politics.

In her farewell words to the players, the new queen makes a statement of policy that deliciously combines cynicism, idealism, authority, and scepticism. The banished players will be well paid, but of one thing they will permanently be deprived.

A woman player has left you. Do not mourn her. She was a bad, headstrong, cruel woman, and seeks destruction somewhere with some man she knows nothing of; such a woman they tell me that this mask [of the sister of Noah] would well become, this foolish, smiling face! Come, dance. [*They dance, and . . . she throws them money.*] [1]

Is Decima trying to comfort her fellow players? Bribe her own conscience? Secretly confess her guilt to Septimus? Reassure her new followers of what a good sober queen she will make? Or mock the hollowness of her new role?

[1] *Collected Plays* (London, 1952), p. 430.

Her first official act as sovereign, far from announcing a bright new lucidity, only weaves a more tangled web of illusion around this gaudy butterfly. For the populace, what looked like a really nasty crisis has been pleasantly averted. Septimus and Decima, at least, have learned a more unpleasant fact: the old high truths of romance are not for them. Perhaps we can read Septimus's drunkenness as a symbol and symptom that he has really known this before the action of the play began. At any rate the concluding dance is a ritual not of union but of separation. The innocent illusion of the players is exiled lest it cast doubt on the sophisticated illusion of the player become queen. The powerful, chaste, and dangerous imagination of the Unicorn, glimpsed by a poet impotent to make his vision prevail, has faded from men's minds and the world is once again, for the time being, made safe for mediocrity.

The Player Queen is a curious play because it is so crowded with odds and ends from the Yeats workshop. Its fable emerges out of mythology, bearing the earmarks of the magical transformation of life by supernatural agencies so central to Yeats's conception of drama, but the plot is not descended from any well-known legend. In fact, it works in a kind of dialectical opposition to myth, though immersed in the very element it would destroy. Yeats is very fond of stories where a kingdom is at stake, where love comes into mortal conflict with commitment to a higher conception of the self, where royalty asserts its prerogatives at the expense of its own greatness, where king and poet battle for their rights, where marriage is rejected for something closer to the heart's desire. All these familiar themes reappear in *Player Queen*, but they are deliberately

vulgarized and made consciously theatrical. In spite of
Yeats's theory that *character* belongs primarily to comedy,
even Decima and Septimus are not substantial in the way
the earlier Countess Cathleen or Seanchan or Deirdre or
Cuchulain are. Nothing in the play is substantial for that
matter. Though we are present at the dawn of a new day,
a kind of midsummer day's dream unfolds before us. Something of the play's strangeness comes from the almost
mundane clarity of its parts—nothing that we see or hear
is shadowy or obscure on the surface—and the baffling
movement of ideas underneath. The motives of each character seem quite clear; we understand the games they play
with each other and the reasons for their feelings. Even
more esoteric matters, such as the doctrine of the mask,
the meaning of the Unicorn, and the idea of historical
phases are sufficiently explained by the play itself. The
difficulty lies elsewhere.

One might describe the action of the play as "to find the
queen." The irate revolutionists, fearing their celibate
queen will leave no heir, need only the scandal of her sexual misbehavior with a unicorn to release their violence.
They pay no attention to Septimus's high-flown defense
of the Unicorn, but they are terrified of the beggar whose
itching back is prophetic of a revolution. Why, if they
want revolution, should they dread the portent of its coming? For the same reason, perhaps, that they wanted revolution in the first place: their fear of *all* irrational behavior.
What they see in the beggar is the embodiment of their
own lunatic itch to force a comforting stasis on an intolerable instability. But in this dark mirror where their own
violence is reflected in an uncanny calm, they are compelled to recognize their dilemma: to destroy one uncer-

tainty is but to create another. The beggar is, in fact, the very *principle* of irrational mystery. Through him speaks the voice of "God," or whatever we want to call that tendency in the universe to impose a meaning on the shape of things, a meaning that teases the mind by constantly receding into incomprehensibility. The beggar is that familiar figure in Yeats's work, the medium—a creature that must be evacuated of humanity in order to make room for divinity. The First Citizen puts it this way:

His eyes become glassy, and that is the trance growing upon him, and when he is in the trance his soul slips away and a ghost takes its place and speaks out of him—a strange ghost.[2]

As for the beggar, he himself achieves neither knowledge nor power. He is, so to speak, an inanimate bridge over which inhuman mystery crosses to manifest itself in human affairs. He is both sinister and comic, for Yeats has taken pains to contrast the terror he inspires in those who fear him because he is nothing more nor less than a symbolic projection of their own panic before the unknown with the harmless amiability he shows to any who dare engage him in conversation. Having more important things to worry about, neither Septimus nor Decima is afraid of death. The Old Beggar offers them no show of violence. And he confides to Decima that he is the reincarnation of the donkey who carried Christ into Jerusalem. He dissuades her from driving the scissors (a significant variation of the more romantic dagger) into her heart because, he says, she might be reincarnated as a seer who could foretell the death of kings, and he "could not endure a rival."

[2] *Ibid.*, p. 399.

When she asks about the fate of love and lovers in the after-life, he cannily (?) admits "another secret."

People talk, but I have never known anything to come from there but an old jackass. Maybe there is nothing else. Who knows but he has the whole place to himself? But there, my back is beginning to itch, and I have not yet found any straw.[3]

It is in the nature of things that this reincarnated jackass should know no more of heaven than himself. And yet his remarks have an ambiguous effect very characteristic of Yeats's tone in the play as a whole. The irony of having "God's fool" speak the most devastatingly sceptical lines in the play, not about the existence of supernatural reality but about its content, demonstrates how far Yeats is now prepared to go in playing with his most precious toys. *Player Queen* does not so much show a dialectical work-ing out of fundamental oppositions—though that pattern is there—as the kaleidoscopic shifts in the "color" of an idea as it twists this way and that.

For the people, finding a queen is essentially a matter of interposing a warmly human symbol of authority between themselves and the fearful unknown. Though some of them, especially the Third Countryman, want to combine being "with the people" and seeing justice done to the queen, they find that reason and due process of law stand no chance against the pull of unreason. And the most fa-natic of all, the Big Countryman, has an irresistible penchant for strangling witches; naturally he does not want his spe-cial talent to rust unused. The significance of the anecdote, told by the Third Countryman, about the young man of

3 *Ibid.*, p. 425.

twenty-five who one day refused to get out of bed and
never left it again until he was carried to his grave forty-
four years later, is that a non-violent protest against the
tears in things might be a more blameless way of rebelling
against the injustice of life than the violent way of revolution. If the queen has withdrawn herself since the death
of her father (which is all they can be sure of), "small
blame to her maybe." But this sort of anti-social behavior is just the kind of thing you would expect from
witches, retorts the Big Countryman. The Third Countryman insists that the man he knew "was no witch, he was
no way active." Parson, priest, and doctor tried him, but
he would not budge from his position that "life is a vale
of tears." The First Citizen interposes with "We'd have
no man go beyond evidence and reason"—and then offers
the Tapster's wild and sex-obsessed fantasy as *evidence*
that "we cannot leave her alive this day—no, not one day
longer." The pressure of irrational purpose is like a wave
that inexorably gathers strength to break upon the shore.
The pretence of reason is but a spume that plays on the
surface.

While the crowd seeks an end to nightmare in a revolution inspired neither by common sense nor by idealism,
Septimus seeks an end to the intolerable disunity of his
own being. He would see beauty wed to chastity, the wild
imagination domesticated, poetry honored by the ignorant.
He wants an impossible utopia. He sees clearly enough the
stupidity of the crowd, yet he actually craves their charity.
To his mind they have been led astray by "bad, popular
poets" and he would gladly set them straight, but it is
painfully obvious that their Unicorn and his can never
coincide. His drunkenness allows him to see with extraor-

dinary (and childlike) lucidity the difference between good and bad, but unfortunately his distinctions are so subjective, so closely bound up with his own needs and inadequacies, that they seem just as irrelevant to the historical crisis he has happened upon as the objective, "journalistic" lunacy of the dim-witted crowd. He, too, seeks the comfort of a queen who will shield him from the rigors of a too-naked confrontation with the mysteries of his own vocation. He is as much a player poet as Decima is a player queen. Unlike Seanchan in *King's Threshold*, he no longer has the support of the populace; and with good reason, for he is a "rootless" man, a vagabond player who has traveled the world and perhaps played before Kubla Khan but who is certainly not the poetic guardian of a community heritage. For the crowd the "revolution" in *Player Queen* provides a happy ending *instead* of a revelation; they have been spared the shock the Old Beggar had seemed to promise them. No longer Christian *or* pagan, neither rational *nor* religious, they eagerly accept a facsimile queen and a king of her (apparent) choice who has no legitimate claim upon the throne. What do these people lack? An image of greatness. And that is what their poets should provide them.

Septimus puts "the great secret" this way:

Man is nothing till he is united to an image. Now the Unicorn is both an image and beast; that is why he alone can be the new Adam. When we have put all in safety [he tells Nona] we will go to the high tablelands of Africa and find where the Unicorn is stabled and sing a marriage song. I will stand before the terrible blue eye.[4]

4 *Ibid.,* p. 420.

Here Septimus is projecting in fantasy the true marriage of flesh and spirit, idea and reality, which is mocked by the counterfeit marriages of the play. And who is his stage audience? Nona, the complete embodiment of the domestic virtues, whose highest aim is to serve genius, not to inspire it and certainly not to understand it. But Decima, in rage and despair, is listening too. She knows that Septimus has betrayed himself as well as her in accepting Nona's "goodness" and rejecting her "badness." It may be all right to worship the Muse and write poems in praise of her; to be *married* to her is something else again. She has driven Septimus to drink and must take the consequences.

The scene which follows *could* be the funniest Yeats ever wrote, though it would take a Septimus of extraordinary range and control to pull it off. For Septimus must be detached, almost dignified, and yet obviously in need of drink to sustain that courage which should be natural to followers of the Unicorn. He must be both judicious and wily, above the battle and yet keenly interested in the outcome. He must display not only the qualities which make him appealing to both women—a combination of mastery and helplessness—but also reveal those traits which attract him to both of them. In this scene the fates of all three are being decided—the key to the gates which Decima holds is the key which will unlock their futures. But while the gates remain locked and death is apparently racing toward them, Decima, determined to arrive at a moment of truth, holds the flux at bay. Her ultimatum to Septimus is in the best melodramatic tradition: truth and falsehood, good and bad, will be forced to drop their disguises and show forth their native whiteness or blackness.

Septimus must commit his loyalty wholly to her, or they will all die together for his treachery. But the real question is: Can Decima put an end to play and compel "seriousness"? Can she uncover behind the bewildering variety of masks a single sincerity, and petrify the free play of imagination into a fixed and necessary truth? Of course she cannot. The action which she initiated by her playful refusal to take the part of Noah's wife will be completed by her playful acceptance of the role of queen. It is possible to exchange one mask for another; it is not possible to go without one. She has acquired her power over Septimus by turning her passion into a cold mystery—a "mask of burning gold with emerald eyes"; to remove the mask is to lose her power over him. Play can be just as inexorable as law.

Septimus points out the error of her logic when he answers her charge of infidelity. Having fortified his wisdom with another drink from his bottle, he makes his oracular declaration:

I am only unfaithful when I am sober. Never trust a sober man. All the world over they are unfaithful. Never trust a man who has not bathed by the light of the Great Bear. I warn you against all sober men from the bottom of my heart. I am extraordinarily wise.[5]

When Septimus is sober, the discrepancy between the dignity of his calling and the indignities he must put up with becomes too much to bear. He is glad to surrender his privileged position as slave of a devilish Muse and embrace the comfort of a too-human breast. But this sober frailty disappears when he has drink taken; then his vision of the

5 *Ibid.,* p. 422.

Unicorn is bold and free. He is at one with his vocation
and everything he says can be trusted. Sober men, absorbed in their petty schemes and fearful of any profound
vision which might upset their conventional way of seeing
things, can never be trusted—they will practice any deception or self-deception to save themselves from the
shock of revelation. Septimus is asking Decima to trust the
poet who has taught her the value of the mask, not the
man who has made her jealous of Nona. By trying to
decree by legal means a loyalty that can only be assured
by unsatisfied desire, Decima has made the fatal mistake
of dropping her mask. Septimus refuses to become the
sober man Nona urges him to be—one who would practice
any deception to escape trouble. "What I promise I perform, therefore, my little darling, I will not promise anything at all." Poor Septimus, shoved aside, knocked around,
ordered about, has at last asserted his heroism.

In the battle between them, Decima has lost because her
"badness" was no match for his "goodness." By an adroit
tour de force Yeats has made conventional morality the
butt of the joke. When Decima is most "sincere" she is
most wrongheaded, or rather when she mistakes matri-
monial possessiveness for "divine right." She has lowered
herself into the world of sober men. But when by her
bitchiness she drove Septimus to drink, she *was* fulfilling
her proper function—to jar him out of complacency and
drive him to inspiration. And this scene proves she has
done her work well; she has enabled Septimus to reject the
tyranny of his "little darling" while reaffirming his loyalty
to the Muse. Yet the balance maintained in the scene is
delicate. Septimus's promise of performance is undercut
by his drunken bravado. Indeed his drunkenness through-

out the play suggests loss of control equal to loss of in-
hibition, and an escape from responsibility as much as the
influx of divine afflatus. Perhaps in the modern world the
poet *must* appear as a drunken buffoon. Because of "the
machinations of Delphi" the Unicorn is unable to become
the new Adam, and an example of those "machinations"—
the fatal split between spirit and body, reason and appetite,
high and low inaugurated by the Greeks—is being dramatically exhibited in the conflict before us. It is appropriate that Nona should succeed in snatching the key from
Decima just after the would-be player queen had descended—as she thinks triumphantly—to the level of personal vengeance. By invoking law in the cause of personal
ambition, Decima has unwittingly allied herself with the
politicians, those who manipulate images in order to hide
the truth and advance their own ends—and thereby perpetuate the fatal division between man and Unicorn.

Against the false unity of the politician, Septimus urges
the true unity of the poet. He was at first unwilling to use
force against Decima, despite Nona's efforts to egg him
on, because his wife's fierceness made her beautiful and
reawakened his love. Her mask had not yet really dropped
for him. His decision a moment later to take the key from
her after all is (perhaps) an admiring response to her
love and an effort to save her from the consequences of
her jealousy more than acquiescence to the promptings of
Nona. But by the time Nona has seized the key by stealth,
Septimus is quite willing to use strength against his flighty
wife because she has clearly gone over to the enemy. He
has the strength of "a violent virginal creature" because
he has kept faith with his Unicorn and remained "unfor-
sworn." Decima and Nona have become merely two jeal-

ous women quarreling over a man. Even Decima's final desperate offer to make a compact of faith with him is useless. For she has already broken the higher faith— fidelity to her mask—which really matters. Still she retains her attractiveness, and Septimus leaves her regretfully. "A beautiful, bad, flighty woman I will follow, but follow slowly," he says, as he prepares to do the opposite; and he takes the "noble, high-crowned hat of Noah" but leaves the "drowned, wicked mouth" of the mask of Noah's sister behind as he moves slowly out the gate after Nona, abandoning the forlorn Decima to her own devices. The self-conscious dignity of his exit suggests a drunken imperviousness to the painful reality of Decima's situation that seriously (and comically) qualifies any credit for heroism we might be inclined to give him. Ironically, Nona is the only one of the three who is really victorious —her (comparatively) common sense view knocks the egoistic stilts out from under her more romantic betters.

But fate, of course, is only playing with Decima in order to prepare her to play with it. If this were tragedy, Decima would coalesce with the Unicorn and become for Septimus the inhuman, amoral ideal of spiritual beauty that Fand is for Cuchulain, in *The Only Jealousy of Emer*. Instead, both Septimus and Decima are struggling to shed their incongruities, like impure essences distilling themselves. Each is a false image for the other; the yoke of marriage must be severed. In this comedy of anti-romance two lovers learn the trick of falling out of love as a prerequisite for realization of their separate subjectivities. Both are incapable of the kinds of chastity each demands of the other. And the implication of their disunity is that the powers of politics and poetry will not mix.

It is an old Yeatsian theme. And so Decima finds room at the top, though not without a moment of true existential despair to urge her onward. Reversing the usual scale of values to point his ironic ambiguity, Yeats puts his two idealists, seven and eight, below his two pragmatists, nine and ten. Decima finds greatest difficulty giving up Septimus; Octema (the saint on whom the queen models her unworldly ambitions) actually helps Decima by disabling the queen from fulfilling her duties of office; Nona is exiled with the other players; Decima reaches the top rung of the ladder. There she is in a position to make her wishes into commands, except for one—she cannot have Septimus beside her on the throne but must make do with the Prime Minister. Septimus has indeed "wronged" her, and at this inopportune moment he keeps stubbornly insisting that the new queen is his wife, and a bad, flighty one at that. Decima has resumed her mask, but now she will be public Muse to the "poets" of the multitude. She fully accepts the banishment of her *own* private freedom when she says, "My good name is dearer than my life, but I will see the players before they go." Donning the mask of the sister of Noah (which Septimus had refused to take with him when he took Noah's hat), Decima foreswears her former flighty ways; she pronounces execution on her former self. In her apology to the players she is in effect saying that she has put away childish things and made the compromises necessary to enter on the responsibilities of adult existence. With this twist, Yeats makes his final comment on morality: Decima's new "goodness" has been won at bitter cost indeed; for the sake of law and order she has sacrificed love and art. And her motive was the opposite of Countess Cathleen's. Underneath the gay transformations of character and sudden changes of fortune lies a sorry fable indeed.

Player Queen allows the sardonic and playful side of Yeats's dramatic genius, held in check in the earlier plays by his conscious effort to create a model of heroism for his Irish audience, to emerge in full force. To get the full impact of this negative inversion of the heroic design Yeats had so laboriously constructed, it is necessary to know the earlier plays. Decima, for instance, has something of Countess Cathleen's sublime egoism but none of her moral scruples; she has, too, something of the Faery Child's anti-Christian gaiety in *Heart's Desire* but completely lacks the Child's ingenuous ignorance of what it is up to; above all she has Deirdre's sense of rising to a great occasion, but for Decima greatness is not a matter of embracing immortality for love of another but of mastering others here and now for her own sake. Decima is at the awkward age where the charm of the spoiled child alternates uneasily with the imperious will of the merciless lady. Likewise Septimus has Seanchan's conviction of the high status of poetry but conspicuously lacks Seanchan's ability to fight for his beliefs; he has Cuchulain's aversion to knuckling under to authority and to swearing oaths of loyalty but none of Cuchulain's power to match deeds with words; he shares with Teigue in *Hour Glass* the seer's vision of irrational truth but is too infected with the woes of worldliness to possess the natural integrity of the Fool. Septimus is a poet who can regain the strength of innocence only by resorting to the weakness of intoxication. Essentially what Yeats has done in *Player Queen* is to lower hero and heroine into the mire of life. No longer able to confront the vulgar enemy with the purity of heart born of a natural confidence in their own superiority, both Septimus and Decima, in their different ways, are the victims rather than the masters of circumstance. They are not allowed the tragic destinies their romantic souls yearn for. They *want* to belong to the world of myth but find themselves firmly anchored in the natural world, with all its imperfections and corruptions. Nonetheless, however incongruous the disjunction between their godlike aspirations and their human follies, they remain distinct from, and superior to, those who totally reject or accept the world as it is. The queen, paralyzed by fear of sexual contamination, is hardly too good for this world; she is simply unequal to coping with it at all, as a martyr or otherwise. And Nona, a kindly conformist when her domestic passions are not aroused, is a creature of comfortable habit who neither asks nor cares what the greater world is up to.

If fantasies of greatness are indistinguishable from private illusions and reality is no more than collective delusion, all values float aimlessly on the stream of relativity. Has Yeats rejected the struggle for unity of being as a basis for his dramatic structure in *Player Queen?* Has he used the Renaissance metaphor of world as stage to imply the futility of the struggle for roles? The play *does* suggest a certain cynicism about the tricks of human imagination, but the remarkable detachment Yeats has achieved here does not entirely conceal the indignation beneath the surface. For if *Player Queen* is in some sense a parable of the fragmentation, deception, unreliability, even disintegration of modern life, Yeats clearly does not approve of what is going on. If the world has reduced Septimus and Decima to actors who can only play at heroism, their virtues rejected by the sceptical and their vices encouraged by the gullible, so much the worse for the world. We may be amused at the spectacle, and Yeats intends us to be, but we should realize the implications of his comedy. In such a world tragedy is no longer possible.

When Yeats, beginning with *At the Hawk's Well*, again takes up the tragic form, he no longer places his hero in a social situation. In some isolated spot where we can be sure no crowds will ever assemble, man confronts his lonely destiny and discovers the peculiarities of the vocation that will forever separate him from his more ordinary fellows. Action has become less a matter of performing, or refusing to perform, certain deeds and more a matter of opening the heart and mind to the critical alternatives represented by opposing life attitudes. The young are initiated into the mysteries of a supernatural reality that makes them cruelly aware of the painful costs of any extreme and uncompromising commitment to an ideal (*Hawk's Well, Dreaming of the Bones*); the more experienced, having already suffered from such a commitment, submit their further fates to the charity and judgment of some person or persons who have been vitally affected by the hero's past behavior (*Only Jealousy of Emer, Calvary*). The opinion of the "general public" is given sometimes poignant expression in the words of choral characters, but there is no suggestion that hero or heroine can, or would, pay any attention to the shock or sorrow or even the sympathy his or her actions have evoked. An impassible psychic barrier lies between those who have boldly stepped over the threshold of the transcendent regions and those who have stayed safely at home among familiar faces, though the hero is never allowed to forget his humanity. To truly attain the moral indifference either of a Faery Child or the queen of the Sidhe would be as complete a disqualification for heroism as failure to succumb to the lure of an impossible and timeless perfection. Longing to attain the artifice of eternity, the hero yet cannot bear too much of that reality. In the mythical world of these chamber plays, chance and choice, fatality and freedom, manifest themselves with a lucidity and force unknown to the inhabitants of our lower world, where clear-cut distinctions are lost in the random hurly-burly of our mixed existence. As art in general is to the life it reflects and orders, so is myth to a looser and more gregarious art. Myth simplifies, heightens, and focusses the central ambiguities at the heart of life. All Yeats's drama is in the service of myth, but *Player Queen* has the special interest of *dramatizing* the problem of the artist's attitude toward myth itself.

It is as though Yeats had asked himself how anyone could be expected to suspend his disbelief in the unlikely and old-fashioned symbolism of heroic revelation sufficiently to care what happened to his heroes and heroines and had then come up with an answer: such carelessness deserved the playful punishment of being shown the consequences of its scepticism in a distorting mirror. He would demonstrate the lower workings of passion and imagination when they are deprived of proper sustenance, even though he must parody his own deeper thought to do so. His premise is that man's mind is so constituted that he cannot get rid of myth. So he shows that if man can no longer raise his understanding to the level of heroic myth, then myth will lower itself to the level of popular understanding. Whatever pleasure this demonstration gave Yeats, it was at the same time an admission of artistic perplexity. Must he give up tragedy in order to accommodate himself to minds who would rather have a play about Noah and his shrewish wife than make the effort to respond to transcendental resonances? For a hero like Yeats the answer was clear: he would abandon *this* audience so that he could free a Septimus or a Decima for their proper roles once more. But in the future his tragedy would be both more uncompromising and more sardonic—and his comedy more grotesque and shocking.

Indeed *Player Queen* points forward toward *Herne's Egg* as much as it looks back toward the earlier tragedy. The later farce like the earlier throws scepticism and superstition, private fantasy and public credulity, into grotesque juxtaposition. But the occasional vulgarity of *Player Queen* is replaced by licentious barbarity in *Herne's Egg.* And the uncomfortable ambiguity which mars *Player Queen* because Septimus and Decima are at once so flamboyant and so lightweight, so full of themselves and yet granted so little real dignity, is no longer a problem in *Herne's Egg,* where the decorum allows a freer, more fiery language, and absurdity does not destroy but oddly enhances the dignity of man's rebellion against irrational power. By a kind of comic catharsis, Yeats in *Player Queen* is purging himself of the noble rhetoric fashioned to win over a people still imaginatively attuned to the rhythms and imagery of Romantic self-assertion. Confessing himself unable to find in the theater that simple soul uncorrupted by the filthy modern tide who would glory in the tragic self-realization of an archaic queen, Yeats revenges himself by showing the easy triumph of a player queen over a mob who must think in unison because they lack the courage and intelligence and imagination to think otherwise.

In the plays to come Yeats will show us heroes drawn to their destinies by a power ambiguously outside and inside themselves but quite independent of their roles in society. Or to put it another way, the later hero seeks his metaphysical identity, usually through the medium of a feminine inductress to supernatural reality, and cares nothing for authority and honor bestowed by a position of social consequence. From the Christ of *Calvary* to the Swineherd of *A Full Moon in March* (and these two certainly represent opposite extremes) the hero either is, or is quite willing to be, an outcast from society. And there is never the slightest question that domestic tranquillity and the pursuit of personal happiness are incompatible with the heroic vocation. More and more, Yeats insists on the absurdity, even the horror, of being "chosen" a hero as judged by the standards of common sense and conventional morality. It was difficult and dangerous enough for Countess Cathleen and Cuchulain and Seanchan and Deirdre to take the heroic leap, but their motives were unimpeachable and their actions carried the sanction of a comprehensible tradition. In the later plays, however, an abyss has opened between the hero and all nonheroes. Until we get to the self-possessed Cuchulain of Yeats's last play, we have a series of spiritual adventurers who would qualify for the lunatic asylum if they were not insulated by myth —and of course the Swift of *Words Upon the Window-Pane* does qualify. Within their contexts, however, Yeats succeeds in giving his protagonists an irrational logic, sometimes very like a kind of animal instinct (as in *Full Moon*), which wins our assent because we are able to identify the protagonist with a necessary principle of order however savage and unruly he himself may be. In *Player Queen* Yeats is going in the direction of that sophisticated formula of symbolic primitivism at which he later arrived, but Septimus and Decima are firmly caught in the toils of a society whose values they cannot alter; although Decima "succeeds" and Septimus "fails," they both must bow to the power of "democracy." Nowhere else in Yeats's drama are his featured players subjected to this humiliation.

My interpretation of *Player Queen* is not the conventional one (if there *is* such a thing). For instance, Wilson takes as gospel the story that the old Queen has been co-habiting with the Unicorn and assumes that he will transfer his affections to Decima when she is the new Queen.[6] He identifies Decima with the harlot figure who represents for Yeats "all that is cast out in this era, all that will be justified in the era to come." [7] The two Queens are exact opposites, and the old Queen (though young) represents the almost extinguished Christian era which will presently give way to a new era, "from whom divinity will beget a race of new men, pagan but heroic, incontinent, virile and proud." [8] This may be, but it suggests that the real drama lies entirely outside the play Yeats has given us. In fact we need the contrast between the mythic resolution that *might* have occurred and the comic resolution that *does* occur to get the peculiar dissonance Yeats has created for us. In Vendler's opinion Decima is waiting "until the time

[6] F. A. C. Wilson, *W. B. Yeats and Tradition* (New York, 1958), p. 180.

[7] *Ibid.*   [8] *Ibid.*, p. 183.

is ripe for her new master, the elusive Unicorn, to possess her." [9] She is angry at Septimus and accepts the Prime Minister with nonchalance. The fact of the matter is, though, that it is really Septimus who rejects her and the Prime Minister who determines the marriage. Whether they are about the Unicorn's business without knowing what they are up to must be left to speculation, but as a character in the play Decima is hardly experienced enough to be a harlot nor inhuman enough to be a full-fledged Muse. She is certainly working in the right direction, but we catch her at the awkward stage where she must *play* at those roles as she does at being queen. Part of her comic charm lies—or could be made to lie in a good performance —in her alternating dependence on others for food and occupation and love and her struggle to assert her independence. And when she actually attains the crown at the end of the play we must not discount entirely Septimus's stubborn insistence that she is still his "bad, flighty wife." She is queen because it fits the convenience of everyone but Septimus that she should be queen. It may also be true that the caterpillar has metamorphosed into a butterfly and that, ironically, the new dispensation of the Unicorn has arrived after all. Again, however, we should remember how elusive the Unicorn appears from *inside* the play this time and should exercise, perhaps, a certain caution in assuming that Yeats's statements elsewhere about the Unicorn and related matters provide the key to his meaning here. One point he is making by the inflated rhetoric and dubious auspices under which the Unicorn makes itself known is that the Unknown is truly unknown.

[9] Helen Hennessey Vendler, *Yeats's "Vision" and Later Plays* (Cambridge, Mass., 1963), p. 135.

One of the most persistent difficulties is the *tone* of the play. The gaiety rings false and encourages commentators to ferret out the philosophical meanings which Yeats had been at such pains to dissolve into symbol. His "cruelty" to his main characters stirs readers to construct a defense for them which will give them tragic dignity. If people are to be made uneasy by a drama which cuts man down to size, they at least expect the playwright to indicate his point of view clearly. But in *Player Queen* it is hard to be sure which is more absurd, man or his masks. Worse yet, the play has something of the romantic idiom of an old-fashioned costume piece where hero and heroine ought surely to be joined rather than separated. Here is a symbolic play in which the melancholy if obscure elevation other symbolist plays have led audiences to expect of the genre is present, but present only to be rudely jostled by abrupt transitions which at one moment suggest the stupidity of the vulgar populace and at the next the vapidity and equal vulnerability to self-deception of their so-called betters. There is no center of feeling with which the spectator can safely afford to identify himself.

In spite of all this, the play has undeniable life. Even those baffled by its air of mystification respond to the tensions of its mystery. When Lennox Robinson produced it at the Abbey in 1919 it was, says Peter Kavanagh, "the most notable offering of the season." It attracted an encouragingly large audience, though "after the performance everyone was asking one another in the foyer what it was all about. No one knew, and everyone assumed it to be high art." [10] Such are the dubious rewards of fame.

[10] Kavanagh, *The Story of the Abbey Theatre* (New York, 1950), p. 120.

In Ireland Yeats could count on reverence, perhaps in proportion to his incomprehensibility, for his dramatic efforts. What he surely could not count on was a production as boldly experimental as his play was. For of all his plays *Player Queen* has the widest range of effects and makes the fullest use of theatrical devices. More than his other plays it requires production to reveal its meanings because there are so many possible emphases to be tried out. The temptation is to try to "level out" its disconcerting variety, to impose a factitious unity on it. The very skill with which Yeats has hybridized his two-headed fable challenges a director to integrate production by forcing waywardness to obey the rule of a single dominating style. But to make the play a burlesque extravaganza, for instance, would be to betray its richness no less than to inflate its tragic implications by making Septimus into Hamlet and Decima into Cleopatra. Alienation is built into the play— the people from their sovereign, their sovereign from life itself, the poet from his audience, the actress from her role, husband from wife, and (probably) the Unicorn from a world he never made—and the problem is to prevent the malaise and general readiness for irritation that hangs over the play from damping the eager animal vitality shared by all the characters except the queen.

If the theme of the play is man caught midstream by the necessities of revolution—a revolution cosmic, political, poetic, religious, sexual, and personal—the reaction of the characters is by and large aggressive. In the comic push-and-pull between the opposing forces of a comfortable familiarity and an eerie unknown, between the old order and the new, the characters vibrate with nervous expectancy. But unlike the people in some absurdist drama, most notably that of Beckett, they are quite confident that *some* energetic activity is called for. And they have no difficulty in finding someone to fight, curse out, or rail at. To each a scapegoat. Uncertain of themselves, defensive about their motives, they run the gamut between the outright sadism of the witch-strangling countryman and the almost voluptuous masochism of the guilt-ridden queen. No one sighs after the good old days or feels the pull of a lost love. Such backward-looking, tragic emotions are swallowed up by the more restless emotions of war-like anticipation of victory over an external enemy and internal frustrations. Even the perhaps elegiacally inclined Septimus looks forward to the miraculous moment when the Unicorn will give its terrible love and lose its chastity. Nevertheless, against the brisk and overwhelming forward movement of the play we need to feel the retardation of those moments when Septimus harangues a surly or recalcitrant listener or listeners about the strange and wonderful attributes of the Unicorn. The poet's drunkenness symbolizes not only his own ambivalence but the ambivalence of the whole play. At once sinister and expansive, ridiculous and majestic, fantastic and inspired, this intoxication reflects and focusses the paradoxes of this coldly charming play.

10

Plays for Dancers

In the kind of drama Yeats turned to with his dance plays, he devised a form that continued earlier principles and practices. What is new about these plays is the greater concentration of effect: action is more remote from everyday experience, character is brought down to the expression of a single passion, language becomes quieter but more tightly packed with meaning. We are more aware of artifice, both poetic and theatrical, and yet these plays have an impressive unity. In spite of their subtlety and allusiveness, everything works toward a single end. Some fundamental, even universal, polarity in human experience reveals itself in terms of a decisive judgment made by the protagonist which suggests a destiny shaping the history not only of two or three individuals but of whole races and nations. We are made sharply aware of the almost equal power of the opposing principles by the immensity of sacrifice the hero's crucial decision entails. As in the earlier plays, he must give all for his single dream. Immortal glory will not abide with mortal comforts.

Dominated by a few powerful images, using masks to suggest the impersonality of "fixed" passions, creating a lonely scene through the lyrics of the musicians that gives the effect of being on the edge of the world, inducing through the ritual of a dance a trancelike state in which the veil separating time now from time always is dropped, these plays (at their best) bring the subtle intensity of poetry and the stark power of drama into indivisible accord. They combine a bitter astringency with delicate beauty, a sense of urgency with the stillness of contemplation. The bustle of the world, which Yeats (with the help of Lady Gregory) had tried so hard to work into some of the earlier plays, is gladly discarded, and the emotion of multitude is replaced by the emotion of solitude. No longer concerned to promote either the Abbey Theatre or a high-minded patriotism, Yeats uses his Irish material with even greater freedom than before to satisfy his own imaginative desires.

He wanted both intimacy and strangeness. In the closeness of a studio or drawing-room he was able to see the Japanese dancer whom he later used in *At the Hawk's Well* as a "tragic image."

There, where no studied lighting, no stage-picture made an artificial world, he was able, as he rose from the floor, where he had been sitting cross-legged, or as he threw out an arm, to recede from us into some more powerful life. Because that separation was achieved by human means alone, he receded but to inhabit as it were the deeps of the mind. One realized anew at every separating strangeness, that the measure of all arts' greatness can be but in their intimacy.[1]

Certain conventions of the Japanese Noh theater appealed to Yeats because they gave re-enforcement to old ambitions. When he wrote such plays as *On Baile's Strand* or *The King's Threshold* he had no time to re-create the mysterious suggestiveness of the scene, "to bring again to

[1] *Essays and Introductions* (London, 1961), p. 224.

certain places their old sanctity or their romance."[2] The Noh, with its insistence on a connoisseur's knowledge of artistic tradition, seemed akin in its ideals and values to the recent European movements in art with which Yeats had most sympathy. "The men who created this tradition," thought Yeats, "were more like ourselves than were the Greeks and Romans, more like us even than are Shakespeare and Corneille. Their emotion was self-conscious and reminiscent, always associating itself with pictures and poems."[3] And he was impressed by the playing upon a single image to create "lovely intricacies." The Noh offered an example of a highly civilized poetic refinement that yet retained the attraction of simple fairy-tale or folklore. Here was a way to bring together the culture of "the people" (which Yeats never ceased to champion) and the aesthetic distinction of the knowledgeable artist without sacrificing the virtues of either.

Pound, with his zeal to establish a new polyglot tradition, interested Yeats in the possibilities of the Noh. Yeats's goal of creating a ⁺heater of opposite tendencies from that of Ibsen and Shaw was of long standing, and the ideal of beauty aimed at by the Noh seemed admirably fitted to his purposes. Realism, the delight of the common people, would be more honest if more complete, and Yeats hoped it could rid itself of insincere idealism; a "true theatre of beauty," however, replaces the mimicry of naturalism by a rhythm that intensifies by stylization the connection between gesture and thought. Speaking of the Noh tradition, he says:

The interest is not in the human form but in the rhythm to which it moves, and the triumph of their art is to express the rhythm in its intensity. There are few swaying movements of

[2] *Ibid.*, p. 233.   [3] *Ibid.*

arms or body such as make the beauty of our dancing. They move from the hip, keeping constantly the upper part of their body still, and seem to associate with every gesture or pose some definite thought. They cross the stage with a sliding movement, and one gets the impression not of undulation but of continuous straight lines.[4]

This art, a projection outward of inner meaning, depends on mastery of an imaginative discipline. An anecdote traditional among Japanese players illustrates their teaching. A young man, ambitious to play old women in the Noh plays, followed a stately old woman through the streets, observing her movements carefully. "Why do you follow me?" she asked. When he explained, she told him he would never learn what he needed from observing life. "He must know how to suggest an old woman and yet find it all in the heart." [5]

Whether or not Yeats understood the Noh as a scholar might, the evidence of what he took from the Noh is plentiful in the later plays. Hiro Ishibashi gives a convenient and succinct summary in his pamphlet for the Dolman Press.[6] Here are a few representative examples: the use of natural objects as images symbolic of spiritual action or states of mind, like the well in *At the Hawk's Well* or the house and tree in *Purgatory;* sudden transformations of personality, like those that determine Cuchulain's fate in *The Only Jealousy of Emer* and the "possession" that takes over a medium as in *At the Hawk's Well* and *Words Upon the Window-Pane;* the intersec-

[4] *Ibid.*, p. 231.   [5] *Ibid.*, pp. 231–232.

[6] Hiro Ishibashi, "Yeats and the Noh: Types of Japanese Beauty and Their Reflection in Yeats's Plays," Anthony Kerrigan, ed., The Dolmen Press Yeats Centenary Papers, No. VI (Dublin, 1966).

tion of past and present, as in *The Dreaming of the Bones* and most strikingly in *Purgatory* and *The Death of Cuchulain;* the use of music and dance to embody a climax "beyond words," as in *The Only Jealousy of Emer, A Full Moon in March,* and *The Death of Cuchulain;* and the evocation of a "ghost" as in *The Only Jealousy of Emer, The Dreaming of the Bones, Words Upon the Window-Pane,* and *The Death of Cuchulain.*

The most obvious difference between what Yeats is up to and the Noh is that he was trying to "manufacture" a tradition instead of following one. The Noh is very impersonal, and its ideal of beauty as developed by Zeami allowed freedom only within very strict limits. Yeats admired this impersonality but nevertheless, as in his previous drama, used his plays as vehicles for his personal preoccupations. He indeed wanted a "pure" art, free of moralizing and immune to popular opinion, but the aesthetic distance of the Noh was *too* great for his purposes; on the other hand, the intimacy it could achieve with its well-initiated audiences was also impossible for Yeats. The Noh is, at least in its highly developed form, an allusive and aristocratic art especially designed to appeal to the philosophic and religious convictions of the nobility and the warrior class, but Yeats's audience, even when aristocratic, had no such common ground—they came to see the latest effort of a famous personality and poet. The "tradition" was really novelty (more so than it had been in his plays for the Abbey), and the connoisseurs who appreciated what Yeats was doing appreciated Yeats, not an anonymous communal tradition.

Most important, Yeats was a poet (with no Japanese) who insisted on the primacy of words in spite of his use

of music, gesture, mask, and dance. Though he wanted
a passion of solitude and, from the dance plays on, moved
in the direction of a stylization further away from the
imitation of "reality" than ever, he always based his dramatic conflict on the pull between the natural and the
supernatural. The Noh celebrates emotion over intellect,
and with this Yeats was in entire sympathy, but its aesthetic ideal is "precious"—a passion that obtrudes the
uglier and more violent side of humanity must be distilled
until an evanescent and nostalgic sorrow is all that remains.
Poignancy but not catharsis is the goal. Ishibashi suggests
"calm, graceful, grave, detached, mysterious, elegant" as
descriptive of this beauty.[7] In the Noh the Main Player
dominates the action completely, but in Yeats, as Ishibashi
notes, a minimum of two strongly opposed characters is
required to develop the action. Though Yeats's new form,
compared to Shakespeare and in fact to the whole Western
tradition of tragedy, is rarefied and pure, it cannot do
without the savagery and "ugliness" evident in such plays
as *A Full Moon in March*, *Words Upon the Window-
Pane*, *The Herne's Egg*, and *Purgatory*. Yeats's dream
plays retain more of a nightmare element than the Noh
would tolerate.

The Noh is a significant aspect of Yeats's interest in the
East, evident in his early poetry and lasting throughout
his life. And certainly the later drama is distinguished from
the earlier partly by the devices Yeats took over from the
Noh. But continuities are at least as evident as disconti-
nuities. The language of the major tragedies—*King's Threshold*, *On Baile's Strand*, *Deirdre*—is nearer to Shakespearean blank verse than is the language of the later plays, but

[7] *Ibid.*, p. 132.

the Yeatsian vocabulary of praise and scorn, the imagery of birds to suggest qualities of soul, and the emphasis on heroic isolation, for instance, remain constant. And so do the Irish themes, though with a difference. From *Countess Cathleen* to *The Green Helmet*, being willing to die for Ireland, the heroic Ireland with which heroine or hero can identify, is unquestionably admirable. This heroic Ireland does not disappear in the later plays, but (except for Cuchulain) the problems of being an Irish hero are too great to be surmounted, and the protagonists of *Words Upon the Window-Pane* (Swift), *The Herne's Egg* (Congal), and *Purgatory* (the Old Man) are left in miserable and ridiculous predicaments, fates worse than death. If it were not for *The Death of Cuchulain*, we might think that Yeats had decided the chasm between legendary Ireland and contemporary Ireland had become too wide to be bridged.

By turning to a form of drama where exposition is reduced to a minimum and yet the action itself requires to be read as a symbolic commentary on (among other things) the futility of all action in a world that nevertheless demands action, Yeats put his powers as dramatist to a new test. Depending much less on Irish legend to carry his meaning and much more on his "private" philosophy, he yet contrived to keep his dramatic parables simple in one sense however profound in another. For whatever they may mean intellectually (and they radiate meaning in many directions), they always tell a story of fundamental passions shocked into awareness of the bitter paradoxes of human existence. This is the narrative pattern behind all Yeats's drama; only in the later plays time is discontinuous or almost irrelevant, whereas a considerable part of the suspense in the earlier plays depends on our sense of time running out for the protagonist. One might say for purposes of contrast that the earlier plays aim at persuasion and the later plays call for contemplation. All these are matters of emphasis and degree, not absolutes.

At any rate, in his plays for the Abbey, Yeats worked continually to make his language more dramatically functional, which often meant raising the lyric temperature as well as improving the logic of theatrical exposition. He tried to develop an "even richness" (as he says in discussing revisions of *Deirdre*) which could serve all his purposes simultaneously. But he was seldom satisfied with the way his "prose" purposes meshed with his poetry, and often he felt obliged to print two versions of a play, one in prose and one in verse. In his later plays, where he makes more use of lyrics disengaged from the rest of the verse (his choruses stand aside to comment on the action or speak for the characters, but they don't *enter* the action), the poetry is never sacrificed to prose necessity. The discontinuity he learned from the Noh is deliberate, and the highly condensed exposition does not need to be logically motivated; it is simply (and often beautifully) placed before us. Once the "facts" are given, Yeats is able to concentrate on working out the conflict largely in terms of image and symbol. Because he is not worrying about a (hopefully) large public audience any more, but writing to please himself, he is more peremptory in exposition and subtler poetically.

As we have seen in the Abbey plays, Yeats was successful in forging a blank verse supple enough to accommodate passionate argument and ecstatic revery. And his ability to write dialogue that drives the action forward becomes very impressive. But compared with what he achieved later, his language is the speech of public persuasion, and its violence is often (and often appropriately) declamatory and oratorical. The verse of the later plays typically "acts" as though the characters were concerned entirely with themselves or each other, and there were no necessity whatever to proselytize. In general, Yeats's rhetoric grows simpler and often harsher, his rhythms more sharply defined, his repetitions more insistent, and his allusions more complex. In dialogue his effect is brisker and more colloquial; in the lyrics he achieves the effect of trance and otherworldliness. The dance plays are dream plays of a sort, but the austerity of style and structure is very far from the seemingly random looseness of free association.

At the Hawk's Well

At the Hawk's Well poses the "Achillean" question—is it better to take a chance on a short but glorious life or settle for a slow but hopefully comfortable growing old among familiar faces? The musicians first "call to the eye of the mind" a bare place and a man to match it: "A man climbing up to a place/ The salt sea wind has swept bare." The lyrics give us an emblem of the hero in his scene and then ask questions like the one in "Among School Children": what would a mother think if she could see what life had done to the old man she once rocked as a hopeful infant at her breast? And just as the well of immortality is located at a lonely spot where land and sea meet, so are day and night meeting at the intersection of sunset as the play opens. The outer scene mirrors the inner reality of the contradictions of the heart, which "would be always awake," and yet longs to "turn to its rest." Time and place are auspicious to force the moment to its crisis.

What is a life for? Waking or sleeping? Presiding over the scene is the death-like figure of the Guardian of the Well, "covered by a black cloak." The Second Musician voices everyman's reaction: "I am afraid of this place." The musicians expand on the heart's opposed longings while an old man enters and starts a fire going beside the dry well. This ends the introduction.

Upset by the guardian's stony dumbness, the Old Man half guesses what is about to happen because it has happened before—the immortal waters will appear and disappear and he will never get a drop. He will fall asleep. But an unexpected companion has entered; the Young Man (Cuchulain), inspired by the story of the well, has hastened hither, full of confidence in his "luck." He has never had to wait long for anything he wanted. The Old Man warns him to go away. Cuchulain is sure *he* will not fall asleep—he has a restless heart. He would gladly pierce his foot to keep awake, a painful act the Old Man would never have thought of, for the Old Man's heroism is merely one of passive endurance. The Young Man wins this miniature agon, and his decision to stay is punctuated by the Hawk's cry of the Guardian of the Well.

To the Old Man, this desolate spot seems a strange place for an amorous young warrior to look for adventure, but Cuchulain has been led here by the hawk-woman herself. His account of the hawk's attempt to drive him away and of his desire to hood it is a symbolic paradigm of Cuchulain's kind of heroism, an aggressive blend of warlike domination and sexual conquest. Again the Old Man warns Cuchulain of the perilous course he has embarked

on. The Woman of the Sidhe puts a curse "On all those
who have gazed in her unmoistened eyes." And the Old
Man accurately predicts the kind of curse that will darken
Cuchulain's future. When the hawk-cry sounds again, the
Old Man, fearing to be deprived of his last chance to get
the water, begs Cuchulain to go, though Cuchulain responds by offering to share whatever comes, even if it be
only a few drops. But Cuchulain has looked in the Guardian's eyes, which the Old Man cannot face, for "they are
not of this world." The Old Man falls asleep once more,
and Cuchulain has completed the second stage of his initiation.

Now he is ready for the dance which will irrevocably
seal his fate. Cuchulain boasts that he will not leave this
sacred place until he has put on immortality—and in an
ironic sense he keeps his word, for despite the fact that
the "madness" descends upon him and that his determination to perch the grey bird on his wrist leads him to turn
aside from the plashing water he hears and go out "as if
in a dream," his acceptance of the heroic challenge *does*
assure his immortality. Only there is no short cut. Immortality must be earned by mortality, and a grievous mortality at that.

As the musicians point out, Cuchulain has forfeited this
life for the life to come.

> He has lost what may not be found
> Till men heap his burial mound
> And all the history ends.
> He might have lived at his ease,
> An old dog's head on his knees,
> Among his children and friends.[8]

8 *Collected Plays* (London, 1952), p. 217.

But it was obvious from Cuchulain's first entrance that he was not the type to live the life of ease. And neither was the Old Man, whose fate is worse than Cuchulain's. The Old Man has been called but not chosen, which means that he has wasted his life for nothing. He has been cursed with a living death, and yet no name will live after him in history. Both mortality and immortality have been deceptive illusions because his desire destroyed his will instead of strengthening it. He has escaped both the hate and the love of the Sidhe and been more bitterly cursed by their indifference. When Cuchulain returns, he wastes no time bemoaning the loss of the precious drops of water, but responds with martial ardor to the fierce cries coming from the mountain side. The Old Man's plea to Cuchulain to stay with him *now* has no deception; it rings with the bitter sincerity of an intolerably lonely man. But Cuchulain is in full possession of his *arete*. He goes out to face these supernatural women of the hills with joyous abandon, "*no longer as if in a dream*," but fully conscious of his capacity to live up to the heroic part his successful initiation has proved that destiny has assigned him.

The closing lyrics re-enforce our sense of the distance between the hero who has crossed the divide that separates man and god, and the rest of us who can take comfort in the familiar human surroundings that offer us a common security. The heroic life is seen entirely in terms of its sacrifice, not at all in terms of its glory. It almost seems that the sleepy heart has nothing in common with the wakeful heart. Nevertheless, the praise of the happy pastoral life is ironic; it is given by "the empty well" and "the leafless tree." The heroes of the earlier plays were exhibited in all their tragic glamour. In this play Yeats has

done an extremely difficult thing: he has shown the young
Cuchulain at the start of his career, impulsive and valiant,
convincingly innocent of any self-doubt; he has given us
a devastating picture of the horrors of the heroic vocation;
he has been ironic at the expense of both heroism and non-
heroism; and at the same time he has managed to convey
a weird sense of tranquil beauty.

Cuchulain's whole tragic career is adumbrated in this
play that shows his setting forth. He is surrounded by the
doubts, fears, and misgivings of those who do not and
cannot share his vision. One thing that proves he is a hero
is the *sangfroid* with which he encounters what others turn
away from in horror. And at this stage he is the least introspective of young men. The momentum of his forward
thrust comes from a complete and intuitive faith in his
"luck." Unlike the heroes in many more leisurely stories
of heroic initiation, Cuchulain has no fear at all. We must
get the necessary sense of dread entirely from the responses of the musicians and the Old Man. And we must
not allow our knowledge of the suffering in store for
Cuchulain to obscure the young man Yeats gives us in
this play. Surely part of Yeats's irony depends on the contrast between this eager young neophyte (very like
Cuchulain's son in *On Baile's Strand*) and the bitter old
veteran he is to become.

But a still greater irony lies in the fact that *experience*
is utterly incompetent to pass judgment on *innocence*. The
bitterness in the play is not directed at Cuchulain but at
those who, incapable of heroism themselves, would drag
all heroes down to their level. They are praisers of all the
"wrong" things. Yeats's play, however, is much subtler

than a spiritual melodrama that neatly divides "good" from "bad." He is showing us opposed longings as inseparable as the systole and diastole of the beating human heart. Cuchulain will feel the terrible wrenching of opposed desires with a fullness unknown to nonheroes. But not in this play. Yet with the knowledge of his whole life before him, Cuchulain could not be different than he is. And Yeats is showing us this too. To have Cuchulain's certainty of purpose and heroic energy is to *be* Cuchulain. And no matter what the consequences, Cuchulain (at least as Yeats sees him) never wishes to be other than he is. In spite of what he learns from experience, the hero of *The Death of Cuchulain* is recognizably the same haughty but magnanimous person he is in *At the Hawk's Well.* The "tragedy" of this first dance play is not Cuchulain's but the Old Man's. Those who merely *wait* to have immortality thrust upon them neither win fair lady nor conquer themselves. And Yeats deftly but unequivocally portrays the Old Man as selfish, greedy, fearful, and irresolute—a child of (say) ninety whom his mother would indeed be shocked and grieved to see.

The tone of desolation evoked by the opening lyrics and borne out by the action is qualified by elevation. The well "long choked up and dry" and the boughs "long stripped by the wind" are first called "to the eye of the mind," but they are matched by a face with "lofty dissolute air" and the man to whom the face belongs, "climbing up" to a high place exposed to the "salt sea wind." One gets the impression of weather-beaten man and nature, worn down to the bone, impotent and infertile. The heavy, emphatic rhythm and the repetition of words (eye, mind, long, call, wind) suggest the weariness of age and the per-

petual round of eroding nature. But it is not "natural" for
a man to *climb up*, even if a kind of somnambulism is
hinted at. The man in this landscape is making an effort,
however futile, to counter the nature that surrounds him.
The musicians ask whether he would be better off dead,
and imagine the dismay of his mother if she could see her
ninety-year-old son. Presumably she would be moved not
just by the physical appearance of decrepitude but by his
lack of a family and friends. This man has stopped the
cycle of generation that is to a mother the chief justification of her labor pains. He should rest, but he has chosen
the wakeful heart—and as we learn later, been punished
by sleep when he least wants it. Yeats has created a feeling
of expectancy by putting a man before our mind's eye
who seems to be doing something nonsensical and for that
very reason must be suspected of having the strongest
motives for enduring an almost intolerable situation.

The dominating images of the play operate in a similar
manner. The hawk, an aggressive bird of prey, is associated with a quiescent well, the unmoistened eye of the
Guardian of the Well is contrasted with familiar faces, the
bareness of a lofty and lonely place stands in opposition
to indolent meadows, and the very contradictions of the
heart, which "would wander always like the wind" and
yet feels it is "time to sleep"—all these present a world
of conflicting duality. And the Old Man and the Young
Man, who identify themselves by their opposing positions
in argument, become emblems of disillusionment and
idealism (though we should note that the Old Man is still
there after fifty years and shows no intention of leaving).
Empty well and leafless tree are in the mind's eye at the
beginning and the end of the play, but each image and

thought in the play seems to call out to its opposite in a kind of dialectical rhythm.

The dry well *does* become damp (thus attesting its authenticity) and Cuchulain passes through this barren place like a refreshing wind, bringing not rain but assurance that the desiccated heroic tradition can be rejuvenated. He is the hero the Guardian of the Well has been waiting for, and if he is a victim who has fallen into the trap of the gods he is also the agent who restores the broken contact between the natural and the supernatural. The "stillness" of Yeats's play contains a dynamism all the more impressive for being strictly controlled by the grave and mysterious lyrics of the musicians, who in spite of their detachment yet subtly change from neutral commentators and "voices" for the contradictions of the heart to awestruck spectators, fearful of unmoistened eyes and only too thankful to "choose a pleasant life." Not the least of Yeats's ironies is the way he has re-enforced the human rejection of the hero by imagery, tone, and the very rhythm of his songs.

In his fascinating and valuable book, F. A. C. Wilson interprets *At the Hawk's Well* as a peculiarly Yeatsian reworking of the grail legend, with an admixture of Buddhism and Kabbalistic doctrine. He arrives at the conclusion that Yeats's spiritual life was at low ebb when he wrote the play and that it expresses his complete disillusion with the possibilities of the way of the sage. It is a play "where action is seen as evil and resignation as the sole good," and it requires of the audience less pity or compassion for *either* Cuchulain or the Old Man than an "emotion of winter." [9] This certainly makes sense, but it seems one-sided. It is hard to see any resignation of a *spiritual* kind in the play, and still harder to see, even as a "dramatic fiction," Yeats flattering the audience (no matter how select) that they have mastered a "self-discipline" which the characters in the play have not. I think Yeats's artistic integrity and his imaginative investment in Cuchulain as a mythical embodiment of an Irish ideal would never permit him to suggest that his audience was in a position to look *down* on Cuchulain instead of *up* to him. Certainly the play says nothing to suggest that Yeats *equates* the Young Man and the Old Man. It is very dangerous to take the choral representative in Yeats, Shakespeare, or even the Greek tragedians, as a mouthpiece for the author. And while it is undeniable that Cuchulain is no Galahad, Yeats nowhere suggests that he should have been. Wilson's difficulty comes from trying to squeeze a total heroic pattern of action into what is after all only an episode in a hero's life.

From a certain point of view, *all* human action is a snare and a delusion, and perhaps every tragic hero is entitled to think at one time or another that it would be better never to have been born. Cuchulain (unlike some Greek heroes) never seems to feel this way, however. His reaction is to fight or make love or, if necessary, to die. To make him over into a failed saint is self-defeating ingenuity. Cuchulain does not drink the water that plashes for him in the well because, to put it playfully, he has better things to do. This does indeed mean that he is preparing

[9] F. A. C. Wilson, *Yeats's Iconography* (London, 1960), pp. 30–31.

a tragic life for himself, and the reaction of the musicians (and the Old Man) provides a preview of what Cuchulain is in for. He has chosen (or been chosen for) the rugged path up the hill where he will fight and love in the company of immortal women; he has "rejected" (the choice was never really offered) the path down into the valley where the only "struggle" is to get the cows milked and call the children in to supper.

The Only Jealousy of Emer

The hawk-woman who assured both Cuchulain's *eventual* immortality and his *immediate* mortality, who guaranteed his heroic devotion to an ideal impossible of attainment and proved his "cursed luck" meant an unending battle with divinity, has assumed the form of Fand in *The Only Jealousy of Emer*. A sadder and wiser Cuchulain is now tempted by the claims of the "restful heart" which he would have scornfully rejected when young and impatient. And Fand is prepared to offer him an end to all "intricacies of remorse." Though Fand represents that ideal beauty impossible of human embodiment which Yeats identified with his fifteenth phase of the moon, her direct appeal to Cuchulain does not seem to be based on beauty at all. Rather she promises the oblivion of human memory, a release from the pain of feeling. Cuchulain is "that amorous, violent man" reduced to a strange passivity by the workings of the curse which he has experienced; at low ebb, he would be glad to give up that heroic career he had embraced with such vigor in *Hawk's Well*. It is Emer who, because of her love for him, recommits an unwilling Cuchulain to his heroic, and accursed, vocation.

The opening lyrics, as in *Hawk's Well*, set the theme

of conflict. Woman's beauty, a frail and unserviceable thing, is born of man's passionate aspirations and, once created, promises deceptive peace. But any man capable of the vision of matchless beauty is by the same token *not* capable of stilling his restless heart. Whatever additions in subtle erudition Yeats has achieved during the interim, his theme is fundamentally the same as the one that haunted *Countess Cathleen* and *Land of Heart's Desire*. Man would like to seize the moment of most perfect beauty, pleasure, peace and forget his heartache, but he is bound to the wheel of life and cannot stop its turning. That still point at the center lures him, and his very efforts to reach it keep the rim steadily whirling. For beauty comes from "soul toil" but cares nothing about the suffering and effort that made it possible. To consummate a union with beauty is, in human terms, not only to give up love but life itself. Strictly speaking, beauty should feel no love for anything, much less for human imperfection, but perhaps we can see Fand's love of Cuchulain as necessary for her to prove the strength of beauty's frail perfection. For Yeats, at any rate, beauty is abstract only insofar as it is beyond flesh and blood; he *images* it as a beautiful woman. Cuchulain cannot be faithful to a mortal woman exactly because he *is* faithful to an immortal ideal. But that in itself is a paradox, because morality has, and can have, no application in the realm where human memory is obliterated.

A prostrate Cuchulain, in a state of suspended animation between two worlds, seemingly has no power whatever to determine his own fate. It is as though the three women who love him were three fates in charge of deciding his destiny. Emer is the love that persists through time by virtue of memory and hope, Eithne Inguba is the momentarily fortunate shadow of the ideal which lies beyond embodiment, and Fand is the dream of ultimate aesthetic perfection. Until he awakes, Cuchulain is in a trance like that in *Hawk's Well* which, though comparatively brief, was decisive for his career. Now, however, Cuchulain is in the keeping of the Country-under-Wave and can only be released by Bricriu, the fomenter of discord between gods and men. He is the principle that assures, and here presides over, the conflict of opposites. In the deeps of his mind, Cuchulain responds to Emer's longing for him. Fand hastens to the scene to exert her counter attraction. But Cuchulain is not as "dead" as he would like to be; memories of Emer come between his lips and those of Fand. He is not ready to wash out of his eyes "wind-blown dirt" of human memories, even now after all he has learned and suffered since he passed up the waters of immortality. Yet his human love would not be strong enough to "save" him if it were not for Emer's even greater love. She must make up for his deficiency by loving without hope of return for the rest of her life. In spite of the uncompromising antinaturalism of this play, how much more real and powerful her renunciation is than Countess Cathleen's offer to sacrifice her soul!

Yeats's theory of love is of a piece with his whole philosophy. As Heraclitus taught, mortals and immortals die each other's life, live each other's death. Love and beauty are both linked and opposed in the way life is related to art. Beauty is like Keats's "cold pastoral" on the Grecian urn; its unmoving stillness arises out of and inspires turbulence of the blood. The achieved wonder of beauty can astound us into dumbness. Yeats is haunted by that question the musicians sing:

What death? What discipline,
What bonds no man could unbind,
Being imagined within
The labyrinth of the mind,
What pursuing or fleeing,
What wounds, what bloody press,
Dragged into being
This loveliness? [10]

It is unbearable to think that all the creative greatness and the destructive passion should be forgotten in the contemplation of beauty, and equally intolerable that all the ugly agony should be remembered. Cuchulain cannot possess both Emer and Fand, both wife and Muse. He must settle for a compromise—Eithne Inguba, who offers the bloom of youthful beauty and the warmth of human arms. She can give him the joy of temporary forgetfulness but neither lasting freedom from remorse nor complete fulfillment of his desire for loveliness. For the time being she can take pride in the innocent delusion that she has saved Cuchulain. And in a sense she has, though Cuchulain does not even remember her when he is under the spell of Fand. Eithne Inguba makes bearable going back to the rigors of the heroic life, something Emer can no longer do for Cuchulain in spite of the fact that it is the bond of her love that ties him to his humanity. Emer is not jealous of Cuchulain's mistresses, for she knows that she occupies a place in Cuchulain's heart that they can never fill. But Fand is different. If Cuchulain succumbed to her, even his memory of Emer would be lost forever. Better Cuchulain alive in someone else's arms than lost eternally in the Country-under-Wave. Orpheus looked back and lost

[10] *Collected Plays*, p. 282.

his Eurydice. Emer looks unflinchingly ahead and brings Cuchulain safely home to the arms of Eithne Inguba.

In this play, so occupied with beauty and the soul-toil it exacts, Yeats has placed his action on the meeting place between land and sea. The imagery of "white shell" and "white wing," suggestive of delicacy, purity, and freedom from effort, contrasts with the "dark furrows" and "ploughed land," which suggest a rich soil prepared for seed. And the shell is the seed, a gift from the stormy sea. Beauty and the love of beauty connect the worlds of land and sea. We have descended from the bare and lofty heights of *Hawk's Well*; not indeed to indolent meadows but to an arena where the passions of women hold sway. And in contrast to the previous play, here the world of "familiar faces" wins the victory.

Once again we are presented with a stillness against which passion rages, as Emer and Fand play their tug-of-war with the entranced Cuchulain. Love depends on memory, and life being what it is, memories are full of strife and discord. Perfect beauty is a finished thing, however, and therefore can have nothing to do with the erratic fluctuations of love. In the colloquy between Fand and Cuchulain which is the heart of the play, Yeats quickens the pace by using four-stress verse bound by rhyme. The effect is not songlike but intensely immediate—a kind of hypnotic hallucination. Unlike the Guardian of the Well who distracted Cuchulain from his purpose, Fand awakens Cuchulain's soul with a flood of Platonic light: *she* is now the aggressor. He wonders who this apparition of beauty may be, but she counters his question with another: why is he hiding his face on his knees? "Old memories," he says. Fand sets herself to supplant memory with beauty. In the old days Cuchulain's passion was not restrained by "Intricacies of blind remorse," but he is that man no longer. The memory of Emer rises up to prevent the kiss that would release him from "civilized" guilt. Cuchulain's ghost must dream back through the passions of life to arrive at radical innocence, and the task is beyond his powers. The angered Fand, "all woman now," descends to vulgar invective and actually tries to exacerbate the pain of his memories by arguing how inappropriate his scruples are for a hero such as he. Emer, on the other hand, is convinced that Fand, no better than a prostitute, is like those camp-followers who catch vulnerable warriors at their weakest and spoil them for their wives by filling their minds with erotic fantasies. The struggle for Cuchulain's soul is fierce, very human, and not in the least "philosophic."

Nevertheless, as the musician's opening song indicates, this play is both more sensual and more intellectual than *Hawk's Well*. The stillness of beauty, fragile as "a white sea-bird alone/ At daybreak after a stormy night" once it enters the world of time, is almost irresistibly powerful in its ideal state. And man's soul has created that beauty by "toils of measurement" far surpassing the empirical speculations of an Archimedes. Like Plato's idea of the Good, beauty is the product of supersensual mind, but unlike the Good, it involves death, pursuing and fleeing, wounds and blood. Man has proved its authenticity by the struggle and suffering he has been willing to undergo for it. Beauty and love/ hate are in complementary opposition:

without beauty, love could be no more than sexual instinct, and without love, beauty would be mere shadow without substance. Fand promises

> Time shall seem to stay his course;
> When your mouth and my mouth meet
> All my round shall be complete
> Imagining all its circles run;
> And there shall be oblivion
> Even to quench Cuchulain's drouth
> Even to still that heart.

Ghost of Cuchulain.   Your mouth! [11]

What a marvelously paradoxical subtlety there is here! Fand is talking about the oblivion of eternity where there will be no more thirst, and yet she must conceive of it in terms of the meeting of two mouths. Time can only *seem* to stay his course, for passion belongs to time. And yet the passion expressed here is a passion to end passion. Beauty is the artifice created out of man's mental *and* physical aspirations and in turn becomes the desired death of the passion it arouses. Yeats expresses all this with a kind of urgent ease that carries us past logical obstacles with the inevitability of a swift stream running downhill. It is because the naturalness of a kiss between a man and a woman both made for love exerts a stronger pull on our emotions than the (comparatively) superficial intellectual riddles do on our minds. By his repetition of "mouth" and his interlocking rhymes which so perfectly balance the cerebral and the sensual, Yeats exploits the almost unconscious pleasure we take from feeling something more basic and powerful than any rationalizations we can make about

[11] *Ibid.*, pp. 292–293.

it assert its dominance. In prose this combination of effects would be well nigh impossible.

Thus does Yeats wed folklore and the occult philosophy. The Sidhe do not lose their malice toward humans, their internecine jealousies, their power to play illusionary tricks, but Fand nevertheless emerges as a statue—a work of art—exemplifying Yeats's theory of beauty. The dumbfounded musicians bear witness to a beauty which has changed (in their imagery) from shell and sea-bird to statue with a beating heart. In *Hawk's Well* the musicians reacted with dread to the monstrous supernatural spectacle they had seen; here they are no less moved, but their infatuated hearts go out to Fand, thus "objectifying" and universalizing her meaning. But they are powerless to intervene; they can "give but a sigh and a word,/ A passing word." It is Emer who has the bitter duty and reward of intervening.

As Ure says, Emer "is more the heroine of the moral choice than any of Yeats's earlier protagonists," because she fully realizes the consequences of her decision.[12] And Yeats handles the conflict of motivation with great dramatic skill. Both Emer and Fand use a roughness of language about each other that keeps the play safe from airy abstraction: we are reminded of any two women fighting over the man they both love. And Emer's words to Eithne Inguba show the same firm grip on the simple, elemental drama that underlies the subtle and ironic complications Yeats has built into his fable: "We're but two women struggling with the sea." We are reminded of *Riders to the Sea*.

[12] Peter Ure, *Yeats the Playwright* (London, 1963), pp. 74–75.

One of the complications is the "meaning" of Fand. Ure thinks that Yeats has muddled his effect by making Fand seem to promise an appropriate afterlife for the drowned hero. "From what, after all, is [Emer] saving him?" [13] Well, she is saving him to complete his unfulfilled heroic destiny for one thing. Part of Yeats's irony (as in *Hawk's Well* and in earlier plays as well) is that the reward of being a hero is very problematic. Really, there is no answer to the argument that Cuchulain would be better off dead— except to point out that the hero's life in a profound sense is not his own to do with as he pleases. It makes no difference whether *he* would be better off; we humans need him. Emer's gesture of renunciation is made on behalf of all of us. Symbolically, it demonstrates the hero's (and heroine's) implacable doom: love is both curse and blessing. Emer's love proves that Cuchulain is bound to his humanity, and his awaking in the arms of Eithne Inguba proves that Fand has not wholly lost her battle. Even when her beauty is complete (and presumably her heart of longing is stilled at last), "danger [will] not be diminished" for those who remain in the returning world of daylight. Cuchulain, for one, will always be true to the invisible beauty of his moonlit vision and always untrue to living women. The Sidhe or their representatives in these dance plays are guardians of a realm off limits to most humans. They both love and hate the chosen hero who dares penetrate into the forbidden regions where they reign. And they exact a ferocious price for the rare privileges they grant. The hero cannot belong wholly to either world, or he would be *merely* human or *merely* a holy shade. What could be more dramatic than to present these great issues in terms of a battle between love rivals?

[13] *Ibid.*, p. 77.

Whatever the autobiographical implications of the play, and many critics have remarked on them,[14] Yeats would want the play judged on its own merits. (Incidentally, if Fand represents Maud Gonne and Emer stands for Mrs. Yeats, and of course Cuchulain for Yeats himself, the order of events is reversed—Emer comes into Cuchulain's life long before he has met Fand.) Fand has been the stumbling block in interpretations of the play. But critics who want to make her the tragic heroine always seem to realize they are going against the grain of the story as the theater-goer would be expected to understand it. In earlier versions of the play, more space is given to Bricriu and Fand, and the conflict between them tends to overwhelm the "human" story. But in the final version in *Collected Plays*, Yeats has carefully ensured that Emer's renunciation should be the climax of the play. In one version, as Vendler points out, Cuchulain rejects Fand, finding "there's a folly in the deathless Sidhe/ Beyond man's reach." [15] How much better it is to have the "entranced" Cuchulain moved by those powerful principles that lie outside his conscious control!

One of the difficulties in making Fand the heroine of the play is that "she seems more an idol than a human being." Though she wants Cuchulain in order to make herself complete, the condition she offers him, in which human thought and memory are completely blotted out, is certainly "beyond" tragedy. It may be true, as Wilson says, that in the fifteenth phase the spirit suffers intensely from its solitude, but *in the play* Fand does seem complete,

---

[14] See Vendler, *Yeats's "Vision" and the Later Plays* (Cambridge, Mass., 1963), pp. 213–219 and Wilson, *Iconography*, pp. 121–122, for example.

[15] Vendler, p. 229.

despite her disclaimer, and we are given no indication that she suffers anything more than hurt pride at failing to trap Cuchulain. The immortals can never really be tragic—because they are not mortal. The difficulty arises from the fact that Yeats wants to have it both ways: Fand is a beautiful and jealous woman in love with Cuchulain, *and* she is the Muse, the perfect object of desire, the unmoved mover. One thing she is not—merely another woman passing through a series of incarnations. It may be argued that Cuchulain is the tragic figure in the play, that he has missed his chance at union with perfection. From this point of view, Wilson's remark is apt: "It [*Emer*] is the maturest expression in our literature of the hard and demanding religion of Platonic love, not falsified (as Shelley's poetry sometimes is) by a young man's hope, but seen retrospectively and without any form of illusion after the undeviating allegiance of many years." [16] Even this interpretation, however, does not make *Fand* tragic; it is her lover we feel sorry for. But Nathan's argument for considering Emer the central figure of the play is surely convincing.[17] Yeats's revisions result in even greater concentration on Emer's tragic choice.

The closing lyrics, beautiful as they are, are very mysterious indeed. No two commentators seem able to agree on what they mean, and one feels great sympathy for Vendler's remark that they show "Yeats at his most maddening." [18] The pronoun references *are* impenetrably obscure. Yet I cannot agree with Vendler in her ingenious assignment of various lines to Emer and Fand.[19] It seems

[16] Wilson, *Iconography*, p. 120.
[17] Nathan, *The Tragic Drama of William Butler Yeats* (New York, 1965), pp. 236–237.
[18] Vendler, p. 230.   [19] *Ibid.*, pp. 230–236.

more plausible (and certainly much clearer dramatically) to regard the musicians as voicing the "dumb astonishment" of the spectator. Horrified at the phenomenon of a beautiful statue with a beating heart (as the Greek is at Christ's heart in *The Resurrection*), they want to see that beating stilled. Their first question, "Why does your heart beat thus?" may very well refer to their *own* heart, which has been so stirred by what they have just witnessed. And they explain their (and our) excitement by referring to Fand, the power of whose spell is dramatically extended by the way it carries over to the musicians. No man in the "wide world," once having looked at Fand, can resist giving her his love, and that includes the musicians (Yeats refers to the first musician as "he"). It is indeed a bitter thought that apparently even death ("tragic tomb") not only does not bring peace to the restless heart, but actually brings the pangs of love to a new climax. This is astounding because beyond normal human comprehension. Yeats loves nothing better (especially in his later plays) than expressing the shock of the incredible as it suddenly forces itself on the unwilling consciousness. The musicians are powerless (like us) to do more than "give but a sigh and a word,/ A passing word." Even though everything seemed to be in Fand's favor—the door of life was shut and she was irresistible—Cuchulain somehow escaped her, in spite of the fact that he was uniquely endowed as a lover.

> He that has loved the best
> May turn from a statue
> His too human breast.[20]

This is precisely what the play has just shown us. The paradoxes of love continue beyond the grave. What makes

[20] *Collected Plays*, p. 295.

the greatest lover is passion, but beauty, in a sense, is the very opposite of passion and remains imperfect as long as a tincture of human longing still mars it. Fand is inhuman enough to be a statue, but still human enough to have a beating heart. Cuchulain has come very close to shedding his humanity to take on a statuesque perfection, but his "too human breast," the very thing that makes him capable of a love that entices Fand herself, is also what ensures her failure. And the musicians are helpless not to sympathize with her. Nevertheless, they too are human, and they know, so to speak, that Beauty's heart should *not* beat so. Human thought and feeling are alien to an abstraction; when Fand's beauty is complete, she will no longer be bothered by human thought (has she not promised Cuchulain "oblivion"?). But danger will not be diminished for the rest of us in the sublunar world. The cycles of time will continue. It is the *human* heart that has the unhappy right to beat with terror. Once the zenith of subjective temptation has passed ("moon's round is finished"), man will move toward the perils of the objective world and may forget the moon's divine inspiration, and even that of the stars (which also belong to the world of night). The "bitter reward" takes on a further complexity (and the play has shown us this too): it is a real *reward* in the sense that it has brought great revelations and given us proof that Emer with all her "lowly" virtues is capable of genuine heroism, and it is truly *bitter* because the imperfections of human life have been engraved on the hearts of the participants and on ours with a lovely yet harrowing persuasiveness.

In no other play has Yeats achieved this delicate balance of sympathies with such triumphant subtlety as he does in

Emer. The very difficulty critics have in "choosing" between Emer and Fand is a tribute to his skill. Actually,
the tragic *fact* of irreconcilable conflict between different
parts of man's nature, the impossibility of a stasis in which
love and beauty are fused into radiant unity, outweighs
all individual tragedy. Nathan's appealing suggestion that
the final lyric provides an antistrophe to the opening song
is one way of expressing the *aesthetic* unity of opposites
that Yeats has created. "The sorrow of Eithne's frail
beauty," Nathan says, "and the frustration of Fand's superhuman beauty represent opposite extremes of emotion
that widen the range of Emer's suffering as she stands between the two types." [21]

Not the least of Yeats's accomplishments in the opening
and closing verses is their power of generalization. That
first song *does* introduce Eithne Inguba, as Nathan says,
but it does much more—it expresses Yeats's whole feeling
about the necessary relationship of violence to beauty.
The lonely fragility of the "white sea-bird" tossed up out
of the stormy night onto the ploughed land suggests the
pangs of a childbirth both natural and supernatural. The
wavering rhythms and the repetition of key words attune
us appropriately to the mood of expectant calm after a
storm (and we are soon to discover that the "storm" of
Cuchulain's death has only recently occurred). Then we
are informed of the effect, both intellectual and emotional, necessary to "raise" loveliness into being. We are
prepared gently but surely for the new storm that beauty
must raise in this dialectic that has the inevitability of the
tides and of the alternation between day and night. What
irony of understatement there is in calling a woman's

[21] Nathan, p. 239.

beauty "A strange, unserviceable thing"! And yet how perfectly the description of beauty evokes its preciousness. That beauty must be not only "raised," but positively "dragged" into being epitomizes the contradictions at the heart of the play.

The problem of staging *Emer* is as difficult as the task of interpreting it. Obviously it needs to build up a slow and dreamlike power, and yet it must do this with all deliberate speed. Stylization is entirely appropriate, indeed essential, but clumsily used can be just as distracting as an inappropriate naturalism. We know something of Yeats's reaction to performances of the later plays (beginning with *At the Hawk's Well*) from his notes and letters,[22] but other records of performances given during his lifetime are very sparse. It is recorded, however, that a young Dutch actor, Albert Van Dalsum, read the *Four Plays for Dancers* when it was first published (1921) and produced *The Only Jealousy of Emer* the following year.

He saw this as, before anything else, an experiment in the use of the mask (he was familiar with Gordon Craig's writings) and the style of acting that this imposed, the slow, grave, extended gestures and movements; he saw the adoption of the mask as an attempt to rediscover style, and as an "act of self-liberation," relevant in an age which realised the profound power of the irrational, the mystery behind the mask.[23]

---

[22] See, for instance, the note in *Plays and Controversies* (London, 1923), pp. 415–419, 212–215, and *Letters* (London, 1954), pp. 612, 639, 645, and (on *Fighting the Waves*) p. 767.

[23] D. J. Gordon (with contributions by Ian Fletcher, Frank Kermode, and Robin Skelton), *W. B. Yeats: Images of a Poet* (Manchester, 1961), p. 64.

The sculptor Hildo Krop made the masks ("of papier-mâché, with woollen hair, painted basically in ivory, with deep shadows") and the costumes were "severely stylized in deep pure colours . . . with very simple geometrical patterns, in sharp contrast." [24] The play was revived for a single performance in Amsterdam in 1926 and photographs were taken. When Yeats was shown pictures of Krop's "bronzes" he was "immensely impressed" and had the photographs of the production sent to him. Yeats rewrote his play in prose as *Fighting the Waves*, and when it was produced at the Peacock in 1929 Krop's masks were used.

As might be expected, when the Abbey opened the Peacock Theatre in 1928 as a "small experimental playhouse" there was grumbling that the money (£4,094) was simply being thrown away. "The Abbey, it was repeatedly argued, was an experimental theatre in the best sense and should remain so, while the Peacock was an insult to Dublin writers." [25] Yeats, of course, welcomed it as a training school for actors and dancers. Its comparative intimacy—it seated one hundred—made it a much better place for the production of his dance plays. Kavanagh says concisely of the performance of *Fighting the Waves* that "it puzzled the people who came to see it." [26] And though he believed Yeats's later plays "were exactly the kind of strong purgative needed for an audience which was coming to believe that the plays of Shiels were the highest kind of drama," he had to admit that the response to these experimental plays was negative. "Many were so sickened by the first

[24] *Ibid.*, pp. 64–65.
[25] Kavanagh, *The Story of the Abbey Theatre* (New York, 1950), p. 149.
[26] *Ibid.*, p. 151.

dose that they made certain not to get another, and they carefully avoided in future all plays by Yeats." [27] In 1948 Austin Clarke's Lyric Theatre Company went back, finally, to the original *Only Jealousy of Emer* and used the masks designed by Edmund Dulac. This was apparently the first performance given in Ireland! [28]

The Dreaming of the Bones

But Yeats was taken up with his new experiments. He wanted the good opinion of the old friends he respected, and he no longer worried about the others. Nevertheless, Ireland was, as always, continually in his thoughts. And especially the events of Easter week, 1916. In *The Dreaming of the Bones* he was able to combine his interest in the Noh technique, his thoughts on patriotism, and his theories on love and death.

Character is reduced further than ever before. The Young Man who is the protagonist of the play is, as a matter of fact, *negatively* characterized. He is an automatic hero because he was at the Dublin Post Office and has had to flee for his life, but he tells us nothing of his part in the stirring event he has so recently witnessed, nor does he say or do anything to set him apart from many another fugitive from justice. The circumstances of his isolation, however, are special. He is in a lonely coastal region in the west of Ireland, hoping to make contact with his rescuers, who if all goes well will whisk him to the

[27] *Ibid.*, p. 152.
[28] A. William Becker, "Yeats as a Playwright" (unpublished Ph.D. dissertation, Wadham College, Oxford, 1953), the appendix of first performances.

Aran Islands by boat. We can imagine his distraught state
of mind. Nothing would be more likely than night visions
on top of a lonely mountain.

The musicians create the proper scary feeling in their
opening lyric, reminding us how "old writers" (who
should know) have said "That dizzy dreams can spring/
From the dry bones of the dead." And in the unerring way
we have become accustomed to, Yeats indicates in the
few opening lines the subject of his play: the passion of a
shade. From dry bones a very flood of dreams can "over-
flow the hills" as wine fills a jade or agate cup. The passion
of two bloodless, fleshless shades is made to seem all the
more living for its disembodied state. The meeting of the
Young Man, the Stranger, and the Young Girl takes place
"Somewhere among great rocks on the scarce grass" an
hour before dawn. With the blowing out of the Young
Man's lantern, he is left completely at the mercy of two
strangers who know very well a country *he* knows not at
all. They are in County Clare, the barest of Irish counties.
And there are human ruins to add to the desolation of the
scene. The First Musician describes the progress of the little party as they pass a well fouled by the cattle and a
narrow lane down which corpses have been carried to
burial for five centuries. An owl cries out above their
heads. But this night that sets the heart thumping is not
merely horrifying; it has a "bitter sweetness." As the
climbers ascend, the musicians feel a kind of exultation:

> My heart is in a cloud;
> I'll let the whole world go;
> My rascal heart is proud
> Remembering and remembering

> Red bird of March, begin to crow!
> Up with the neck and clap the wing,
> Red cock, and crow! [29]

On a windy night like this when the moon is blotted out "Calamity can have its fling." What the musicians are remembering is not specified, but we take it to be all the centuries of heroism, suffering, and loneliness connected with this "holy" ground. And now the living and the dead meet on what might be an historical occasion: if this young man, escaped from the Dublin Post Office and under sentence of death, can be brought to forgive the crime of seven centuries ago, the unforgetting lips of Diarmuid and Devorgilla, those lovers who betrayed Ireland to the Normans, might touch again.

The Young Girl is forced to tell the story of these accursed lovers, though she allows her identity to dawn on the Young Man only gradually. She explains that these two shades "have no thought but love" and yet "their lips can never meet." One might imagine this was neither the time nor place to indulge in metaphysical discussion, but she must enlighten the Young Man if she is to gain his forgiveness. He must understand that the absence of blood and nerves and warmth is no barrier to desire. Though dead, these shades live a fully human torment and have no power to overcome the guilt that "flows up between" and keeps their lips apart. Of the first man (ghost or living) they have spoken to since their death, they are asking a mighty reprieve. In the beginning the Stranger does the talking, explaining the purgatorial idea of reliving one's life again and giving an account of the history of the re-

[29] *Collected Plays*, p. 438.

gion to the Young Man, but after the Young Man curses those rebels who have weakened Ireland by dividing it, the Stranger speaks no more and the Young Girl (appropriately) is left with the harder task of expounding and pleading the specific case of the lovers. The Young Man's immediate, involuntary response to the news that this "accursed pair" would have their misery mitigated if only one of their race should finally say, "I have forgiven them," is to say

> O, never, never
> Shall Diarmuid and Devorgilla be forgiven.[30]

And he repeats this a moment later. As the horizon grows brighter, the Young Man recognizes the Aran Islands, the Connemara hills, and Galway stretched out before him. And the sight strengthens his resolution for the climax, which is still to come. The ruin of noble houses is the fault of those traitors. "Our country, if that crime were uncommitted,/ Had been most beautiful." Now the ghostly lovers begin their dance. In the ecstasy of that moment, all the ruin they have wrought is as though it had never been "Because their eyes have met." Then they themselves cover their eyes—they cannot forgive themselves and, heartbroken, they drift away, reaching for a sleep that always evades them. When they have gone out the Young Man "awakes," so to speak, and verifies how close their appeal had come to success.

> I had almost yielded and forgiven it all—
> Terrible the temptation and the place! [31]

The Young Man has "done the right thing," the only possible thing, and yet he has, as the closing lyric puts it,

---

[30] *Ibid.*, p. 442.   [31] *Ibid.*, p. 444.

heard the "Music of a lost kingdom." Morning has come and the red cocks crow, and with a little luck the Young Man will escape in a coracle, but he has felt the brush of a supernatural wing, and he has had an ineffable experience of both the glory and the horror of a deathless love.

All Yeats's dance plays deal with transactions between the living and the dead in one sense or another, but *Dreaming* is unlike the two earlier Cuchulain plays in its purely human theme. No otherworld divinities intervene in human affairs; the dance expresses a love between two equal lovers who suffer in the same way for a shared crime. It might be said that such a love indeed has something heroic about it, but the mood Yeats induces is rather one of passive and tender longing. Against this mood is counterpointed the arduous forward movement of a Young Man very much alive and determined to continue so. He belongs to the morning world of lusty crowing cocks; he is anxious to get *through* the night, not to get stuck *in* it. And the morning does save him. What he can see in the dawning light is what ties him to the rest of humanity, for in this play love is not an assertion of humanity but of antihumanity. Perhaps without intending to, Yeats is demonstrating the awesome difficulties of love in Ireland. (And how many of his plays deal with the frustrations of love!)

The Young Man represents a kind of character Yeats is to make great use of from now on: the learner who is less a hero in his own right than a transmitter of racial experience. He has the choral function of guiding the audience to the proper dramatic response to the epiphany offered by a critical moment in myth or history; what he learns is what the audience also learns. Yet he is also necessary to the action. Like the other dance plays, *Dreaming* is full of irony. Here the Young Man's action might be described as "To reject the temptation to forgive lovers and thereby release them from a centuries-old agony." How harsh that virtue should demand such a rejection! And the shades, who seem to have the Young Man at their mercy when they blow out his "candles," turn out to be completely at his mercy. The red cocks do bring in the March dawn, and a bitter cold dawn it is. The day may come when it is possible to extend charity to these loving traitors (seven centuries hence?), but the day is not yet. *Dreaming* must be one of the strangest "political" plays ever written, but it is political in a much profounder sense than, say, *Cathleen ni Houlihan*, For the ecstasy of love which the Young Man must reject has an undying sweetness and perfection which mankind can ill afford to lose. This Young Man, however, cannot allow himself the pity that caused Dante to swoon at the fate of Paolo and Francesca. It is a final irony that Diarmuid and Devorgilla must appeal to the latest victim of their policy, which brought the foreign invader in.

To several critics Yeats's attempt to combine politics and purgatory does not seem a complete success. The poet himself, though he thought it his best play for years, was afraid it was "only too powerful politically." [32] It was not publicly performed until 1931, when the Abbey did it to Yeats's great satisfaction. And he added, in a letter to Olivia Shakespear, "It was enthusiastically received." [33] Curtis Bradford, praising the dance plays as "the first successful poetic drama since the seventeenth century," says that "Dubliners still talk of a production of *The Dreaming*

[32] *Letters*, p. 626.   [33] *Ibid.*, p. 788.

of the Bones in Yeats's drawing room at 82 Merrion
Square." [34] Most commentators agree that the play is closer
to the Noh models Yeats used than any other of his plays.

In the *Nishikigi*, for instance, a priest wandering north
comes to a town where a couple peculiarly dressed offer
him merchandise famous in the area, a certain kind of cloth
and little wands (Nishikigi). He wants to know why these
things are so renowned, and this leads the couple to tell
him their story, though at first they conceal the fact that
they are the lovers of the story. For one thousand nights
the man had wooed the lady, planting a wand each night,
but she had gone on weaving inside her house and paid
no attention. The man died of grief. Then the lady re-
pented and died also. They have never consummated their
love, and their story has become famous. The priest, eager
to bring back a good tale, goes to the woods with them,
and after night falls is vouchsafed a vision of the two
lovers finally united.[35]

In spite of the iterative imagery, the feeling for natural
setting, and the theme of a stranger provoking lovers into
telling their sad story—all resemblances—the impression
left by the Noh play (at least by the bare text) is very
different from the effect of Yeats's play. *Nishikigi* com-
memorates old custom and, in the second part, plays openly
with the idea of illusion and reality. The play ends with
the chorus begging the priest not to wake up because "We
all will wither away." He has no essential interest in their
fate but is a sort of spiritual tourist sufficiently "un-

[34] Curtis B. Bradford, *Yeats at Work* (Carbondale and Edwardsville, 1965), p. 216.
[35] See *The Translations of Ezra Pound* (New York, n.d.),
pp. 286–298.

worldly" to make these ghosts ambiguously live again. The charm of "A dreambridge over wild grass" which the priest makes possible for the lovers is very sophisticated; it seems a kind of metaphysical conceit which we are to admire for the ingenuity with which anecdote merges into mystical speculation and legend heightens into art. By comparison, *Dreaming of the Bones* is immediate and passionate. Tragic fates and a desperate life hang in the balance and illusion is, and needs to be, something that is broken. Whatever the faults of Yeats's play, it is timely and urgent in a way deliberately avoided by the Noh play.

The doubts about the effectiveness of Yeats's play often seem to focus on the role of the Young Man. Ure, for instance, finds it inconsistent that the young soldier, fleeing from the consequence of the lovers' treachery, should also be a potential mediator between the lovers and the audience. Up until the end he is preoccupied with his own concerns and "neither experiences nor transmits to the audience anything resembling pity or horror at the ghosts' fate." [36] But this has its own irony, an irony entirely appropriate to the play. Yeats, to be sure, is determined to give the audience enough of his theory about the "dreaming back" of the dead to make the play intelligible without footnotes, and the Young Man is the "provoker" of this necessary information. It is left to the musicians to create the emotional atmosphere of the night scene, and we may imagine them as, at least in part, speaking for the Young Man. Besides, there is really nothing, except perhaps fear, for the Young Man to react to until he discovers the shades he has been talking to are in fact the lovers of the

[36] Ure, p. 96.

preceding theoretical discussion. Vendler, who believes that the Young Man, "like the shades," is "dreaming back," concludes that he rejects the vision that has been vouchsafed him. "The main difficulty with *The Dreaming of the Bones*," she says, "is that there is no necessary connection between the lovers and the Young Man." [37] If we interpret the characters as mere "principles of the mind" this is true, but for an audience with the events of 1916 still fresh in their hearts, the connection would not be far-fetched.

Certainly *Dreaming* does not have the tragic resonance of *Emer*, but it is essentially a different kind of play. The conjunction of the famous lovers and the unknown soldier is "in their stars" and not in their characters. In a way this makes Yeats's point about the unity of history, at least of Irish history, all the more powerful. Whether the Young Man forgives or does not forgive Diarmuid and Devorgilla, he cannot, he *has* not, escaped being involved in their tragedy. If he did forgive them, he would indeed take on a stature for which Yeats had not prepared us; the play would be merely sentimental. But he is no Cuchulain; he is a hot-blooded young Irish patriot on the run for his life. Caught up in a moment of cloudy vision, he is compelled to admit the wild sweetness of a side of existence he had never previously imagined. Under the circumstances, to forgive the lovers would seem the dizzy weakness of an exhausted man's confused judgment, not an act involving the making or unmaking of his own soul.

Considering the subject of the play to be "the spiritual life of Ireland as a nation," Nathan describes the theme as "the protagonist's refusal or incapacity to assume the tragic mask." [38] This would be the proper way to regard

[37] Vendler, pp. 191, 194.   [38] Nathan, pp. 210, 211.

the work if the Young Man were presented as a hero, but it seems to me too much of a spiritual burden to put on this anonymous young man's back to make him symbolic of modern Ireland in such a large way. The lack of connection between lovers and young soldier that Vendler objected to is relevant here. If the Young Man is really in a position to bring about Unity of Being, by joining subjective and objective modes of experience, then we should feel that his decision comes from the center of his own vitality, that it has heroic dimension—and we do not. The play seems much more satisfying and successful if we do not try to make a hero of the Young Man. He *is* representative of a modern Irish dilemma, a dilemma heroes of the old kind can no longer solve. What is needed is charity, not the martial virtues of courage and self-sacrifice. The Young Man is too much of a "March cock" himself to be reasonably expected to become a night bird too.

Calvary

Calvary is a study in types of loneliness. In his note to the play, Yeats has explained the contrasts he had in mind. "I have surrounded Him with the images of those he cannot save, not only with the birds, who have served neither God nor Caesar, and await for none or for a different saviour, but with Lazarus and Judas and the Roman soldiers for whom He has died in vain." [39] The subjective kind of loneliness means an absorption in self to the exclusion of the outside world; the objective man may be physically separated from others but is never alone in his thought because he defines himself in relation to them. Christ came out of pity for the suffering of mankind, but

[39] *Plays and Controversies*, pp. 459–460.

especially for the sake of the poor, "who are most subject
to exterior vicissitude." He can help only those who lack
what somebody else can give them. For the self-sufficient
His gifts are meaningless or worse—a positive tribulation.
Christ's calvary consists in the discovery of the limits of
His power, even when that power is conceived as universal love. The Savior is impotent to impose his unity on
the recalcitrant duality of the world.

With the narcissistic image of the white heron "dumbfounded" by his own wavering reflection in the stream,
Yeats introduces us to his theme. The bird is an emblem
of unique being attempting to fix its identity in the distorting mirror of time. The outside world provides the
occasion for subjective experience and for nothing else—
the bird would not even be able to feel his physical reality
except that the condition of subjective trance cannot be
maintained. With the passing of the full moon a measure
of objectivity will return, hopefully enough to prevent
the unnatural occurrence of the fishes eating the one who
is supposed to eat them.[40] "God has not died for the white
heron" because, presumably, nothing that Christ could do
would make any difference to him. What went on before
Christ came will continue exactly the same after He is
gone.

Now it is Good Friday—any Good Friday—and seated
on an "ancient stone" the First Musician is privileged to
witness Christ dreaming His passion. Our Savior is in the
midst of a mocking crowd that challenges Him to give an

[40] Helen Vendler sees the heron as waiting for his (subjective)
cycle to come around with the new moon. Perhaps so, but there is
a sense in which the subjective type must be "self-reliant" and
lonely, no matter what the historic phase. See Vendler, p. 173.

exhibition of His saving power. The Musician, sympathetic with Christ, is made fearful,

> As though a flute of bone
> Taken from a heron's thigh
> A heron crazed by the moon,
> Were cleverly, softly played.[41]

It is the *leit-motif*, so to speak, of Christ's impotence. And immediately an example appears—Lazarus raised from the dead and still retaining his deathly face, though "he moves/ Like a young foal that sees the hunt go by/ And races in the field." Surely Lazarus will not mock Christ, since raising him from the dead was one of the most impressive examples of Christ's power. But Lazarus had hoped to escape God's love in the peace of death, and now he has come to demand back the death Christ took away from him. The idea that Christ has conquered death is a deprivation hardly to be borne. Christ's only answer is, "I do my Father's will," to which Lazarus retorts, "And not your own." As Lazarus sees it, he is condemned to eternal life, not released into it.

In a counter-movement, we see Christ protectively surrounded by Martha and the three Marys and the others who "live but in His love." They have so given themselves to Christ that almost nothing of themselves remains. Without His love, their own is as insubstantial and subject to the elements as

> Tossed hither and thither
> A drowned heron's feather
> Upon the bitter spray
> And the moon at the full.[42]

[41] *Collected Plays*, p. 451.   [42] *Ibid.*, p. 453.

Just as Christ has sacrificed Himself for them, so have they sacrificed their independent "souls" to Him. From the subjective standpoint (the full moon) they are completely at the mercy of passionate forces outside themselves. Again Christ has no effective answer. Exactly because Judas believed in Him, it was necessary to betray Him. There *must* be some escape from such absolute determinism, such all-encompassing power. Though it was decreed "When the foundations of the world were laid" that someone must betray Christ, Judas himself determined who that specific person was and how he should perform the deed. Now he mocks Christ with His inability to save him from damnation. All Christ can say is "Begone from me." Yeats never forgets theatrical effect, and here he has the happy inspiration of having Judas hold up the cross upon which Christ stretches His arms.

The three Roman soldiers are good fellows. They keep the crowds back so that Christ can die in peace. But they are gamblers and ask nothing of God. They accept whatever comes, preferring that it be "unexpected." Their existence is the final irony; they are further out of Christ's reach than any of the others. Glad to do anything they can for the dying god, they offer to perform their pantomimic dance around the cross, representing quarrel and reconciliation. They feel that after all His difficulties it must be a comfort "To know that he has nothing that we need." Christ's objective loneliness is finally complete; the only thing to do is return to His father, Who seems to have forsaken Him. We return in the closing lyrics to kinds of loneliness unaffected by the coming and going of Christ: the sea-bird completely at one with nature, now blown about and now seeking its prey; the ger-eagle soaring in upper air, quite content to rely on his own "savage heart"; and finally the swans, most aspiring of all, who have left the lake behind and flown off leaving a question behind them, but not one addressed to the Christian God.

> Why do they fling
> White wing out beside white wing?
> What can a swan need but a swan? [43]

The musicians cannot answer their own question, but its effect is to suggest the incompleteness of either subjectivity or objectivity without the other.

Though Yeats intends a contrast between types of loneliness, the hypothesis is that we are watching Christ dream his own passion through, and thus His loneliness is completely subjective. He is reliving a more famous agony than that of the lovers in *The Dreaming of the Bones*, but like them He is caught in a dream where forgiveness fails. If only objective natures can surrender themselves to Him, as He apparently has surrendered His own will to His Father's, He is, nevertheless, in His curiously cold and pure asceticism, something of a solitary heron Himself.[44] He seems to have had the ambition of swallowing the whole of humanity into His dream; his subjectivity is so vast it would force objectivity on all true believers. But his journey to the cross is self-fulfillment for *Him*. In his note Yeats tells us, in the words of Robartes, that Christ "pitied those whose suffering is rooted in death, in poverty, or in sickness, or in sin, in some shape of the common lot." [45] But in the play there is no representation of this

[43] *Ibid.*, p. 457.
[44] Cf. Ure, p. 119. "The songs are finally seen to be *about* Christ as well as about the birds."
[45] *Plays and Controversies*, p. 460.

side of Christ's nature, except negatively. The figure in the play is withdrawn and remote. His impressiveness, which might be considerable in a good performance, must come from the reaction of others to Him. And, as always, Yeats imagines a dramatically powerful ending for his play. The implication is that Christ has been sent on a fool's errand. He has learned that He is not all-knowing, all-powerful, or all-good, and He has learned it the hardest way.

In spite of Yeats's clear bias in favor of the subjective personality and his satisfaction in showing Christ's limitations, Vendler is surely right in pointing to Yeats's ambiguous attitude toward Christ.[46] Sometimes Yeats did identify, in a Blakean sense, Christ with the creative imagination, and the idea of salvation for all mankind though the sacrifice of One is a breathtaking example of imaginative audacity; yet it is hard to see *Calvary* as being "about the creative imagination," unless we say that *all* art is. It is about the impossibility of comprehending the variety of the universe within Christianity (and by implication within any theistic dogma). Undoubtedly, it "is concerned with the interaction of objective and subjective life, the double interlocking gyres," but only in an ambiguous and ironic sense can it be said that Christ has made Lazarus and Judas what they are.[47] True, He has forced them to realize that their natures are opposed to His; and that is the very reason He has not been able to make them what He wished. Unlike His Father, Christ is not able to feel that whatever is, is a manifestation of the Son's power. The indifference of the Roman soldiers, who worship the god of Chance, is the final proof of the distance between Father and Son. The soldiers' dance, unlike the dances in

[46] Vendler, pp. 169–171.   [47] *Ibid.*, p. 173.

the other dance plays, is not a showing forth of some subjective beauty and temptation, but a dumb show, made all
the more ironic by its good-natured intent, of the mean-
inglessness of purpose (and specifically of Christ's purpose) in a universe "governed" by chance. Wilson sees the
dance as a "mime of the divine bestowal of variety upon
the world," and as typifying the reconciliation of *all* psychological types, all contributing to "the Buddhist Great
Wheel, . . . each of them an integer in the many-spoked
wheel of reincarnation." [48] This appealing notion, however, strikes me as being *too* hard on Christ. In the context
of the play, the dance evokes from Christ His most de-
spairing words. Are we to take the dance as God's mocking
at His own Son, Who *alone* is left out of the reconciliation?
It is better, I think, (and kinder), to interpret the soldiers
as lost souls from the Christian standpoint, too primitive
mentally and spiritually to respond to any "otherworldly"
message.

Although there seems to be no record of English or Irish
performances of *Calvary*, Earl Miner notes that the play
has been performed at Hamline University in St. Paul.[49]
Since the play is a "negative" action—describing Christ's
failure to do good where He meant to—and the protagonist is passive, the dramatic energy of the piece must come
from our participation in the conflict of sympathies

[48] Wilson, *Iconography*, p. 203.

[49] Earl Miner, *The Japanese Tradition in British and American
Literature* (Princeton, 1958), p. 256. It has come to my attention
that the Lyric Players Theatre in Belfast, under the direction of
Mary O'Malley, has presented *Calvary* very successfully on several occasions. For a list of their productions see *Threshold*, No. 19
(Autumn, 1965), pp. 63–65. The whole issue has much of interest
for the student of Yeats's drama.

aroused by this suffering servant's predicament. We must be made to feel both the arrogance and the shock of those crucial words, "God has not died for the white heron." And the play does have an oddly haunting power, created in part by the conflict between man and nature. This could be brought out by effective contrast between the lyrics and the action they enclose. Yeats has already indicated in his greater than usual difference in language between the songs and the dialogue how this might be done. By turns dry, vehement, or jocular, Christ's opponents are very much engaged with their roles in the world; by contrast the birds have an isolation that in no way interferes with their freedom to be themselves, unconcerned with what others may do or think. It is a mistake to deprive them of their "birdness" in order to reduce them entirely to symbols of human psychology, though it would be a greater mistake to read them as mere emblems of nature. They do, however, suggest the inviolability of nature by any ideas whatsoever; it is as though ideas, even with the grandeur of Christ's egoism, were but a spume that plays on a solider nature quite independent of any thoughts we may have about it.

In Oscar Wilde's story, which had so much struck Yeats when he heard an actor's account of it, Christ is a victim of paradox.[50] The leper He had cured, the blind man whose sight He had restored, the woman whose sins He had forgiven, all have misused His priceless gifts to fulfill their own sinful natures. In saving them He has assured their damnation. Finally He meets a young man weeping outside the walls of the city of sinful pleasure. "But I was dead once and you raised me from the dead. What else

---

[50] "The Doer of Good," conveniently reprinted in *The Works of Oscar Wilde* (London and Glasgow, 1948), pp. 843–844.

should I do but weep?" The Doer of Good has confounded Himself with a perilous neatness. Yeats gives this anecdote greater philosophic depth and more dramatic meaning. Lazarus and Judas are intellectual rebels, not sybarites, and even the Roman soldiers, furthest from the birds in Yeats's symbolic scheme, yet share with them a kind of natural stoicism. And Christ "shivers in a dumbfounded dream" as surely as does the white heron for whom He has not died.

The Cat and the Moon

Yeats makes merry with the moon in this "afterpiece" to his four serious dance plays.[51] The humor is Yeatsian enough, though the blend of delicacy and farce is unusual. The relationship between the cat and the moon is playful; the toy moon that spins round "like a top" fascinates the "creeping cat" and excites him. Change is speeded up. The kinship of moon and cat depends on their shared rhythm of periodic alternation between crescent and full. On the face of it, this kinship has nothing to do with primary and antithetical tinctures. It rather suggests the yowling of the tom cat for its mate under the influence (according to folklore) of the bright moon. Minnaloushe, black and sexy, feels an unease that he can only wail about. And yet the ideal coldness and the animal heat that energize all the dance plays are expressed:

> The pure cold light in the sky
> Troubled his animal blood.[52]

---

[51] It was not the last written, since it appeared in 1917. See Saul, *Prolegomena to the Study of Yeats's Plays* (Philadelphia, 1958), p. 76.
[52] *Collected Plays*, p. 461.

In some way the cat is to the moon as the white heron is to its stream in *Calvary*—nature provides a mirror image for the soul to contemplate, and the soul is entranced at the spectacle. But it is a question (and remains one) whether or not Minnaloushe can think with anything subtler than his blood. And the moon is pretty close to being an inert disc of light in the sky.

Nevertheless, by the end of the play the moon has become "sacred" and the cat, though still creeping, appears to be "alone, important and wise." The objective cat may have become subjective, but he couldn't care less. Meanwhile we have seen a little parable of the mixed nature of humanity. Blind Man and Lame Man, bound together in a symbiotic relationship like body and soul, have discovered their irreconcilable differences and gone their separate ways. St. Colman has allowed them to fulfill themselves by giving them the power of realizing their inmost desires. The Blind Man chooses to be cured (and thereby surrenders the inner vision he has had) and the Lame Man chooses to be blessed (which means giving up his physical lameness). As men, both beggars are scalawags willing to take what they can get wherever they can find it. By combining their abilities they have succeeded in compensating for their disabilities, and their forty-year companionship has been tolerable enough.

Like the protagonists of many a Noh play, the two beggars are on a journey. They quarrel about the uncertainty of the world. How will they know when they have reached the saint's well? As they resume their journey the musician sings a question about Minnaloushe. Is he dancing? What could be more appropriate than a dance when "close kindred meet"?

> Maybe the moon may learn,
> Tired of that courtly fashion,
> A new dance turn.[53]

It is as though Yeats were saying, now for a satyr-piece parodying the whole dance-play conception and setting it in a new perspective: the aristocrats have had their turn, now let's give the beggars their innings. Instead of the moon majestically presiding over the destinies of man, let us imagine it adapting itself to the ways of the world.

Yeats cannot help thinking (and feeling) dialectically, so the "low" argument imitates the "higher," and the Blind Man and the Lame Man are continually pointing out to each other what the other one lacks. They discuss the *pros* and *cons* of being cured by the saint. The Lame Man argues that the Blind Man will be better off when he can see and keep people from stealing his hard-won goods. On the other hand, the Lame Beggar, accustomed to riding through the world on the Blind Beggar's back, has "flighty" thoughts and even ventures to imagine that to see the saint might be a "grander thing" than to have the use of his legs. The Blind Beggar is something of a wise fool who has "been hearing and remembering the knowledge of the world" since he was ten. To his companion's astonishment, he explains why saints prefer a sinful man to the innocent: it gives them something to talk about. It's like the case of the holy man of Laban and the old lecher from Mayo (those in the know would catch the reference to Edward Martyn and George Moore). The lecher keeps telling his sins, real or imaginary, and the holy man keeps trying to shush him. And yet neither would have the situa-

[53] *Ibid.*, p. 463.

tion different; they complement each other perfectly. The attraction of opposites is irresistible.

When it comes to the choice, naturally the Blind Beggar, who has had enough of "spiritual" insight, will choose earthly vision; equally naturally, the Lame Beggar, who had quite enough of worldly wisdom, will choose the unearthly wisdom the saint has to offer. In a dim way, these two beggars foreshadow Beckett's "tramps" both in attitude and tone of voice. After their interesting discussion of saint and sinner, the Lame Beggar says, "We have great wisdom between us, that's certain." This is like those brief resting places of satisfaction that punctuate the storm and stress of Gogo and Didi's companionship. But Yeats's beggars *have* their Godot. The saint, indeed, requests the pleasure of their company. The Blind Beggar, though apologetic, is firm in asking to have the use of his eyes back. The Lame Beggar, though hesitant, decides in favor of the "grander thing." This means a parting of the way for the old companions. The Blind Beggar, his eyes opened to the viciousness of the world, beats his lame brother and exploiter for stealing his sheepskin and lying about it. To be blessed, the Lame Beggar finds, means to become scapegoat and take a beating from the world; it is also fitting purgation for one on his way upward to a better state. The Lame Beggar thinks he'd better get going before his erstwhile friend has aroused the whole countryside against him. He confides to the saint,

And I have it in mind not to even myself again with the martyrs, and the holy confessors, till I am more used to being blessed.[54]

[54] *Ibid.*, p. 470.

But now the time for miracle has come. Not only must the Lame Beggar take the saint upon his back, he must dance too. The dance quickens in comic celebration of his blessed soul's salvation, and the joyful beggar exits triumphantly, the invisible and weightless saint upon his back.

We may not know whether Minnaloushe is "alone, important, and wise" in a merely instinctive or in a higher spiritual sense, but we have seen a manifestation of a change of phase enacted before our eyes. The motivations of both beggars never belie their "peasant" characters; what Wilson happily calls the Lame Man's "spiritual cupidity" is just as evident as the Blind Man's greed for possession.[55] Nevertheless, when Wilson unveils for us the esoteric meaning of the play, he sees the Blind Man as representative of the toiling masses who have an intuitive wisdom but are incapable of realizing, as the Lame Man, representative of aristocracy and intellect, does, that "the goal of human existence is sanctity." [56] The journey to the well is a journey to Unity of Being. The result, however, of the saint's gift is a separation: the Blind Man awakens to the fact that he has been exploited by his guide and master; "the masses discover the idea that they and not their masters are in fact God's chosen people." [57] The age of democratic enlightenment begins. The Lame Man's enlightenment is different. Taking advantage of the supernatural descent at this moment in history, he has the choice of the artist "between integration into the community and momentary sanctity." [58] When the saint mounts on his

[55] Wilson, *Iconography*, p. 143.   [56] *Ibid.*, p. 154.
[57] *Ibid.*, p. 155.   [58] *Ibid.*, p. 155.

back, mystic and artist are fused into one, and the Lame Man, his deformity miraculously removed, has his "dance of beatitude." [59] Perhaps Yeats intended, as Wilson speculates, to have the Lame Man, his moment of glory past revert to his lameness and pick up the Blind Man's deserted staff, thus symbolizing the tyranny of the elite over the masses in the years to come.

In the closing lyric, Yeats gathers together all his meanings—the lunar symbolism refers to individual body and soul, the parallel movements of history and biography, the interplay of subjective and objective oppositions, and the single unifying principle that controls the cyclic repetition in both macrocosm and microcosm. Minnaloushe comes from real life, but the symbolic kinship and antagonism of cat and moon come from ceremonial magic. [60] This very Blakean play can be summed up in one of his aphorisms "without contraries is no progression." It is also true that the progression is endless. It is a "pathetic fallacy," as Wilson says, that man can bring the dance to a halt and escape from the wheel of eternal recurrence. But he can, and does, combine in himself the alternative possibilities of deformity and harmony. "He was Minnaloushe, the creature of mystery, as much as the maimed beggar." [61] I think Wilson is right in seeing a rare combination of simple humaneness and concentrated symbolic richness in this play. But it is unnecessary to make it a political or spiritual allegory in order to respond to the pleasant wit which links the moonstruck cat and the saintstruck beggar.

[59] *Ibid.*, p. 156.   [60] *Ibid.*, p. 159.   [61] *Ibid.*, p. 162.

[11]

Two Ideological Plays:
The Resurrection and
Words Upon the Window-Pane

The Resurrection

Yeats was a man who wanted to believe many things. In *Calvary* his ambivalence toward Christianity took the form of an enactment of Christ's limitations in both knowledge and spiritual authority; in *The Resurrection* the tables are turned, and Christ persuades the doubters of a reality beyond their previous comprehension. And whereas in the earlier play Christ depended, at least by implication, on the simple logic of His position (I saved your life, you ought to be grateful; I offered you salvation, how could you betray me), in this later play He remains silent and lets the paradoxical fact of His being speak for him.

The idea of the resurrection—that mortality is an illusion—can only properly be put to the test when a mortal transcends his death. A true god never dies and a true man never escapes death. The Hebrew in *The Resurrection* believes that Christ "was nothing more than a man, the best who ever lived." The Greek believes "No god has ever been buried; no god has ever suffered." [1] Neither can accept the idea of a man-god. Nevertheless, both believe in

[1] *Collected Plays* (London, 1952), p. 583.

Christ enough to be willing to defend the apostles to the death against the hostile mob. In this play Christ's power extends far beyond what later would become orthodox Christianity.

Part of the meaning of the lyric for the folding and unfolding of the curtain is surely that those divine and cataclysmic events that usher in a new age also represent a larger continuity. When a "staring virgin" tears the heart out of holy Dionysus and thereby causes "all the Muses" to sing the spring of the great year, she is playing her part in maintaining the eternal round of life. Troy, the Roman Empire, and therefore Christianity as well, all pass away, but only to return again. The Muses sing "As though God's death were but a play," and so it is in the sense that it can be performed many times. However opposed the new dispensation may be to the last, it is the same God who manifests himself in varied forms to the human imagination, just as "*another* Troy must rise and set" [2] and there must be a new golden fleece which is only a "flashier bauble" than the last.[3] As in "Lapis Lazuli," all things must be rebuilt again. And in Western mythology, fierce virgins and sacrificed gods have a lot to do with keeping the wheel turning.

The lyric at the end of the play continues the theme Christ pitied man's "darkening thought" and yet contributed to it: "Odour of blood" at His crucifixion died away with "Platonic tolerance" and "Doric discipline." The winding of one gyre is only the unwinding of another; each new vision, by fulfilling itself, destroys the creative impulse from which it originated; and through it all the interdependence of the divine and the human is continually reaffirmed. Lover, artist, warrior all exhaust

[2] My italics.   [3] *Collected Plays*, p. 580.

themselves the more the harder they burn, but their efforts
do flame out against the background of primeval darkness,
and

> Whatever flames upon the night
> Man's own resinous heart has fed.[4]

The image of the heart gathers the separate themes of
Dionysus and the beating heart of Christ into a still greater
theme—the "resinous heart" of all mankind. The spirit
feeds on the heart, the heart is consumed by fire, and fire
reinvigorates the heart.

The three young men are committed to guard with their
lives what they do not comprehend with their minds, yet
they feel an overwhelming need to understand. At the
risk of all their lives, including the eleven Apostles, the
Greek has sent the Syrian to investigate Christ's tomb. The
Greek knows (but he must *prove* it) that there will be no
body there because Christ, being God, only put on the appearance of flesh. The Hebrew is shocked that at a time
of such great danger the Greek should be willing to
weaken the guard. But to the Greek, knowledge is more
important than life. For both young men the Christian
doctrine (which of course has not had time to become
that) goes against the grain, though both are loyal to the
figure of Christ. The insane idea that a man could think
himself the Messiah mortally offends the law of logical
categories as the Greek conceives them.

The Greek. To say that a god can be born of a woman, carried in her womb, fed upon her breast, washed as children
are washed, is the most terrible blasphemy.

The Hebrew. If the Messiah were not born of a woman he

4 *Ibid.,* p. 594.

could not take away the sins of man. Every sin starts a
stream of suffering, but the Messiah takes it all away.

The Greek.   Every man's sins are his property. Nobody else
has a right to them.

The Hebrew.   The Messiah is able to exhaust human suffering
as though it were all gathered together in the spot of a
burning-glass.

The Greek.   That makes me shudder. The utmost possible
suffering as an object of worship! You are morbid because
your nation has no statues.[5]

This is marvelously dramatic in its philosophic concision. To the sophisticated mind of the Greek, the idea of
worshipping a divine scapegoat is repulsive. And the idea
of surrendering one's individualism—and what is more a
part of a man than his own sins?—is an invasion of privacy
that would take away a man's reason for being along with
his suffering. God has no business confusing himself with
the humans. The Greek, be it noted, has the same sort of
objection to the cult of Dionysus: he cannot believe, despite the name of the god, that such "self-abasement" is
Greek. "When the Goddess came to Achilles in the battle
she did not interfere with his soul, she took him by his
yellow hair." [6] The true gods "can be discovered by contemplation, in their faces a high keen joy like the cry of a
bat, and the man who lives heroically gives them the only
earthly body that they covet. He, as it were, copies their
gestures and their acts. What seems their [the gods'] indifference is but their eternal possession of themselves." [7]
For the divine to descend to the human is as incongruous
as stones that fell upward would be. The gods should represent an unsullied perfection toward which man can aspire.
No true god would offer himself as the victim of a mob.

[5] *Ibid.,* p. 584.   [6] *Ibid.,* p. 587.   [7] *Ibid.,* pp. 586–587.

Such a morbid idea, in the Greek's witty words, could only arise in a nation that had no statues. A developed aesthetic sense would rebel at the thought of divine beauty disfigured by human ugliness. Even more important, man himself would be degraded by such self-surrender of the will. The self-possession which distinguishes the hero, who in a sense must challenge divinity in order to prove his own worth, would become meaningless or worse. Like Judas in *Calvary*, the Greek abhors the principle of intellectual and spiritual tyranny. Man's greatest achievements have come from a free and enlightened use of his individual reason. Only if Christ can be regarded as a manifestation of divinity with no real human vulnerability, can he be an object of rational worship for the Greeks.

The Hebrew presents, essentially, the Christian point of view in his argument with the Greek, but the Hebrew has already abandoned it. "What I have described is what I thought until three days ago." When Christ actually died on the cross and then his body was removed and placed in the tomb, the Hebrew was convinced He was not the Messiah, but "merely" a very good man. In spite of their opposed positions, the two young antagonists have quite similar objections to Christianity. The Hebrew confesses his relief that Christ was *not* the Messiah; like the Greek, he is not ready to sacrifice this world for the next.

One had to give up all worldly knowledge, all ambition, do nothing of one's own will. Only the divine could have any reality. God had to take complete possession. It must be a terrible thing when one is old, and the tomb round the corner, to think of all the ambitions one has put aside; to think, perhaps, a great deal about women. I want to marry and have children.[8]

[8] *Ibid.*, p. 585.

For the Greek, statues and all they stand for; to the Hebrew, a wife and children. Neither the sacrifice of mind and its achievements nor the sacrifice of body and the solace of physical creation is acceptable. The cost of Christianity is too high. Then what are they to make of the news the Syrian brings?

The Greek is still able to believe that his case is proved; the Hebrew refuses to accept "the dreams of women." But they agree that the Syrian should not be permitted to disturb the Eleven with his news until all [three?] of them are convinced the news is true. "Though we are so much younger we know more of the world than they do," says the Greek, with unconscious *hubris*. (The remark is another example of the ironical wit operating in this play.) Besides, the Greek is convinced that the phantom will appear to tell his own story. The Syrian laughs, as the Greek had laughed when he looked out on Calvary through the window. His laughter dramatically represents the loss of self-control, the return of the irrational. A moment later he denies that he has been laughing and says the noise comes from the Dionysian revelers outside. Their orgiastic rites are a constant reminder of the barbarism that the Greek is depending upon "human knowledge" to protect civilization from. Ominously, it is from outside that the cry comes, "God has arisen! God has arisen!" And as God has drawn nearer the sanctuary of the apostles, the crowd has become silent. The phantom has entered the room. The Hebrew kneels, but the Greek, confident in his knowledge, advances unafraid to demonstrate that this is no thing of flesh and blood. He screams as he feels the beating heart, and Christ passes on into the next room (where the apostles are). Doubting Thomas, we are told, also tests the wound—but, of course, with quite opposite results. One faith is destroyed and another renewed. Even so, the Greek is able to fit what has happened into a Greek context which ironically shares the Christian belief in miracle but interprets it not in a redemptive but in a cataclysmic sense.

O Athens, Alexandria, Rome, something has come to destroy you. The heart of a phantom is beating. Man has begun to die. Your words are clear at last, O Heraclitus. God and man die each other's life, live each other's death.[9]

Yeats apparently began work on *The Resurrection* in 1925 or 1926.[10] He first conceived it as a dance play in which a musician describes the rolling away of the stone revealing the figure of Christ. Women come forward and unwind His grave clothes. Gradually Christ recollects who He is—He has died to take away the sins of men. He is questioned by others who also died for man. In reply to a question, Buddha says, "No, I died of eating too much pork." Another made the worst sacrifice—he gave up dying and going to heaven in order to stay with suffering mankind forever. The others go out and Christ is left with the three Maries at His feet. He says, "I am the way and the life." [11]

There are obvious analogies here to *Calvary;* in fact it is a weaker version of the same idea. Yeats soon abandoned the idea of the dance play, though he did make a slightly fuller version of the above scenario. When he starts again

[9] *Ibid.*, p. 594.
[10] Bradford, *Yeats at Work* (Carbondale and Edwardsville, 1965), p. 239.
[11] *Ibid.*, pp. 239–240.

he has conceived the idea of dramatizing the theological argument about the nature of Christ as a discussion between a Greek and a Hebrew who are guarding the Apostles. They consider the question why Judas hanged himself. "He betrayed Christ because he doubted Christ's divinity, and because he had expected Christ to found a temporal kingdom." The Hebrew is happy the whole thing is finished: " 'I know a wine shop where there are girls.' " [12] The Dionysian revels are going on outside. The Syrian brings the news that Christ's tomb is empty. He is not permitted to take his news to the Apostles. The end of the play is in substance very close to that of the final version, but the language is vastly inferior. Here is the end as quoted in Bradford:

Hitherto we have had the quick or the dead, now we have the dead and the quick. Never before did the heart of a phantom beat. It is very terrible. (*Then with a loud* [*voice*]) Here, all you men of Jerusalem, know now all men whether men of Rome, of Alexander, or of Athens. The heart of a phantom is beating.[13]

It was not until he had completed four manuscript versions that Yeats was ready to give us the play as it appears in *Collected Plays*. He eliminated discussion of Judas, added the lyrics, greatly expanded and then greatly contracted the illustrative material, and always worked toward a more intense dramatization of his idea. His capacity to improve his work laboriously but surely in the process of revision is awe-inspiring.

What he had achieved in *The Resurrection* was a means of combining the strength to be drawn from a realistic

[12] *Ibid.*, p. 242.   [13] *Ibid.*, p. 245.

presentation of motive and feeling with the enlightenment to be gained from a shocking juxtaposition of ideas. If his theme is Unity of Being and his action a dialectical groping toward the human significance of this unity, he could hardly have devised a more effective vehicle. As Helen Vendler has said, "resurrection" has multiple meanings for Yeats, and the Blakean contrast of a "fall into Divisions" and a "Resurrection to Unity" may be particularly applicable to this play. "Resurrection and rebirth always imply for Yeats the restoration of a Unity of Being which has been damaged through an inevitable attrition, and they imply as well a corresponding courage in acceptance of the revelation." [14] To the three young men struggling to understand the phenomenon of Christ, ideas have an almost physical immediacy; what they think will determine their whole life attitudes. They give us, in a very condensed way, the sensation of what it would have been like to experience the greatest of Christ's miracles. Like so many of the young men in Yeats's later plays, they learn by living through a strange and shattering metamorphosis, previously undreamt of in their philosophies, how to bear witness to supernatural reality. They are less the actors than the acted upon, but without the wit and courage and enterprise to explore truth in exotic places, they would never have been candidates for the wisdom that befalls them.

As for the revelatory moment, who has ever thought of a more daring way of dramatizing the Incarnation than Yeats thought of here? Even the worshippers of Dionysus are suddenly struck dumb by the appearance of Christ as

[14] Vendler, *Yeats's "Vision"* (Cambridge, Mass., 1963), pp. 183–184.

He makes His way toward the house where His apostles are gathered. They dance a step unlike anything the Greek has ever seen in Alexandria. The irony of the Greek's conclusion is turned on him; these crude barbarians are "converted" before he is. Nathan remarks on Yeats's successful use of a device practiced by the Elizabethans—"characters in the play, suddenly confronted by the supernatural, are forced not merely to accept it; in the very intensity of their reaction to its presence they reinforce the sense of its reality. Marlowe in *Doctor Faustus* and Shakespeare in *Macbeth* used the same means to bring the supernatural into the drama." [15] Perhaps they could count on a more primitive, visceral reaction than Yeats can (which may be one reason Yeats kept his serious plays short); nevertheless, Yeats himself was able to feel when he read Sir William Crookes' account of touching a materialized form and finding a heart beating (*Studies in Psychical Research*) a terror which he compares to Job's. "I felt, though my intellect rejected what I read, the terror of the supernatural described by Job." [16] The very conflict of intellect and of ancestral belief that lies beyond the reach of rational persuasion may produce an emotion subtler but no less troubling than the panic of a child lost in a ghostly wood.

The Words Upon the Window-Pane

In *Words Upon the Window-Pane* Yeats writes, for the only time in his career, a play with middle-class characters set not in a fisherman's hut or a palace or a primitive dwelling but in a civilized house. In a sense, civilization and its discontents are the theme of the play. And this theme re-

[15] Nathan, *The Tragic Drama* (New York, 1965), p. 209.
[16] *Wheels and Butterflies* (New York, 1935), p. 98.

lates it to the other plays. Swift, the symbolic champion of man's intellectual powers, struggles in the toils of a purgatorial passion to which he can find no rational solution. Those people gathered at the séance hoping to hear a word from their own friends and relatives are forced instead to listen to the ravings of a madman who is no better than an unidentified evil spirit to most of them and who is unknown as a person to the medium who gives him voice. Among them, however, is a young graduate student from Cambridge, John Corbet, who is writing his doctoral essay on Swift. Corbet provides the link between the living and the dead in an intellectual sense just as Mrs. Henderson the medium does in an occult sense. She is a modern priestess of the oracle who quite definitely does not put on knowledge with her power. And though the versions of Swift offered by the young scholar and the aging medium support each other, the ultimate mystery of Swift escapes them both.

As in *The Resurrection,* intellect is confronted with an irrational perplexity beyond its powers of comprehension. The Greek confronted the living reality of Christ, but Swift is himself a phantom with a beating heart. He relives in agony of spirit the problem of the denial of the body in a love relationship between members of the opposite sex. We catch him in the midst of his passion against Vanessa because she has inquired of Stella whether she and Swift are married. No matter how much he insists on the greater nobility of an intellectual love free of physical complication, Swift cannot convince himself any more than he convinces Vanessa. And her love for him is entirely generous—she wants to protect him from the loneliness of old age. He tells her his blood is tainted, but she is not put off by that. Even if he could have a healthy child, he would not. "Am I to add another to the healthy rascaldom and knavery of the world?" He would "leave to posterity nothing but his intellect that came to him from Heaven." But he is tortured by the responsibility he has taken for another's happiness, who has loved him all her life, by denying her children, lover, and husband. For when Stella replaces Vanessa in his thoughts, Swift imagines the other side of the question: by what right did he persuade Stella that the only true love was that transcendent love which she has celebrated in the poem she wrote for his fifty-fourth birthday? Swift clings to intellect with all the passion of a man who finds the surrounding darkness of irrationality unbearable to contemplate. He knows his own sanity is corrupt and precarious, and he knows that without Stella his reason could do little more than expose with ruthless candor the madness that lies ahead.

After the séance, the disappointed customers nevertheless insist on paying, and John Corbet gives a pound. He is very satisfied to have his own theories about Swift's celibacy borne out, though he is just as sceptical as before about "spirits." He wants Mrs. Henderson to clear up one question: Did Swift refuse to have children because he dreaded the historical future—"Democracy, Rousseau, the French Revolution"—or because he himself was mad? But the poor woman has never heard of Swift. She has only the horrible image of an old man in dirty clothes, his face covered with boils, and one eye starting out of its socket like a hen's egg. She can show forth Swift but she cannot explain him. Nor can Corbet. And in this play Yeats does not attempt to dramatize the ideology of *A Vision*[17] but instead speculates on the fate and character of a unique mind. Swift has, in the play, no interest in communicating with those who came after him, yet the commanding passion of his spirit silences all lesser spirits in this house which he truly haunts. Mrs. Henderson cannot choose whether or no she will be "possessed" by him. Reduced to the despair of a Job but with no expectation that God may answer out of a whirlwind or otherwise, Swift speaks through the lips of Mrs. Henderson his final passion: "Perish the day on which I was born!"

Unlike the Greek of *Resurrection* or the young attendant in the later *Full Moon in March*, the young learner of *Words* is granted no revelation. For his climax Yeats dismisses all the others and leaves the stage to the body of Mrs. Henderson and the spirit of Swift. Corbet has served the function of verifying historical facts about Swift and has shown us how far purely intellectual investigation can carry us. For a certain distance reason and faith run on parallel tracks. But past a certain point intellect can only confound itself: if Corbet were there to hear Mrs. Henderson speak Swift's last words, how could he be sure that she was not putting on an act for his benefit? Such are the credulities of scepticism. It is the audience alone who receives the revelation when the "god" speaks. Dramatically, it is the guileless Mrs. Henderson who convinces us of Swift's authenticity.

What Swift says, however, is of no avail in helping us

[17] But see David R. Clark, *W. B. Yeats and the Theatre of Desolate Reality* (Dublin, 1965), pp. 63ff., for the variety of mythologies worked into the texture of the play.

penetrate the mystery of his great refusal. Having outlived all the particular individuals to whom he could give his love and friendship, Swift ironically (and horribly) experiences the triumph of body and disease over mind and sanity. He can no longer think his life was worth living. Was he mistaken, then, in teaching that a knowledge of right and wrong could keep the body youthful? Stella had written out of her conversion that hymn of praise asserting the power of mind over matter.

> 'You taught how I might youth prolong
> By knowing what is right and wrong,
> How from my heart to bring supplies
> Of lustre to my fading eyes.' [18]

Swift's terrible old age seemed to prove the opposite. Perhaps his moments of lucidity assured his collapse into madness! At any rate his soul must relive over and over again those agonizing moments of decision when the rational knowledge of right and wrong was put to its most critical test. "Was Swift mad? Or was it the intellect itself that was mad?" Corbet's unanswered question has the subtlety of an oracular riddle. Does the irrationality of history defeat the rationality of man? Or is man's pride of intellect a mistake ruthlessly punished by God? Never was there crueler variation on the theme of Yeats's famous lines:

> The intellect of man is forced to choose
> Perfection of the life, or of the work,
> And if it takes the second must refuse
> A heavenly mansion, raging in the dark.[19]

In spite of its admixture of humorous realism, *Words* is the most pessimistic of Yeats's plays, with the possible ex-

[18] *Collected Plays*, p. 601.   [19] *Variorum Poems*, p. 495.

ception of *Purgatory*. There is no tragic gaiety here, no implication that the sacrifices of heroism are compensated by its rewards. Yet Swift's prayer that he leave no posterity but the intellect that came to him from Heaven is granted.

From the beginning, to judge by the scenario reprinted in Bradford's book,[20] Yeats had conceived the idea of making Swift the center of a drama in which eighteenth century Ireland would confront modern Ireland through the device of a séance, and he had thought out action, characters, and even a good deal of the dialogue. An old man and a young man talk about Swift, and the lines of Stella's poem are in Yeats's mind but are not quoted or discussed, merely referred to. The medium's control is a little American Indian girl called Silver Cloud who says of Swift's spirit, "Bad old man. Big chief once. Bad old man, [does not] know he is dead."[21] The scene with Vanessa is roughly worked out, but Stella's part is merely outlined. The climax, ending the play with Job's words, is in place. From too little explanation Yeats goes to too much and then finds the happy medium in successive drafts. He greatly improves the sharpness of characterization. The distance between early and late versions is great, but not nearly so great as in most of the previous plays.

As Clark points out, the house, "a shrine sacred to the spirit of Swift," is considerably more than that; "it is also a symbol of Swift's life, having decayed like him, having the same memory cut into it." Beyond that, "it is a symbol of Ireland."[22] The very names of places and characters

[20] Bradford, pp. 219–225.   [21] *Ibid.*, p. 223.
[22] Clark, p. 61.

reflect the patterns of meaning and the conflicts of value. "A pattern of classical ideals, of traditional religion, of traditional literature and of Irish patriotism is allied against a pattern of commonness, of commercialism and of abstract fanaticism: Cato, Chrysostom, Crashaw and Curran are allied against Democracy, Folkestone, Moody, and Sankey: Ireland and ancient Rome against England and Belfast." [23] The outer, historical conflict is symbolized by the opposed ideologies attributed to Swift and Rousseau; the inner drama, reflecting the outer, is the ordeal of Swift as he relives the maddening dissociation of sensibility brought on by the impossibility of reconciling his chaste intellect and his passionate heart. Ironically, the suffering of Swift is no more than an ugly and incomprehensible impediment to those attending the séance, with the exception of Corbet. If Swift's final words show "external reality shattered by the reality of the soul," [24] these words nevertheless fall on empty air. Perhaps, as Clark suggests, we can regard the séance as a simulacrum of an unsuccessful Yeats play: "they [the audience] do not hear what they came for. They cannot understand the voice of an influence hostile to their abstractions, the argument of genius with itself." [25]

Among those on whom Yeats's image of Swift left a profound impress was T. S. Eliot, whose "familiar compound ghost" in Little Gidding suffers the same impotent rage as Swift at human folly and also re-enacts his own guilt, realizing that what he once took for virtue may have wrought irreparable human harm.[26] The words upon the

[23] Ibid., p. 65.   [24] Ibid., p. 74.   [25] Ibid., p. 76.
[26] Torchiana, W. B. Yeats and Georgian Ireland (Evanston, Ill., 1966), pp. 120–121.

window-pane of Stella's poem (and we must remember that her spirit never speaks in the play) express not only the private idealism to which Swift has committed his deepest faith but also Swift's own importance as a "culture hero." No individual can prevent the forward movement of history, but he can do something to sustain achieved greatness for a little longer than its natural course. So Stella's tribute to the power of virtue to prolong beauty has historical reverberations. As Torchiana puts it, "In their way, then, Stella's words pay the tribute to Swift that Yeats pays him for his hopes to prolong the epoch of that civilization." [27] In Swift the image of a man caught between his rage at the folly of the world and his guilt for having savaged innocent humanity fixes itself in the minds of Yeats, and then Eliot, as an extreme and, so to speak, pure example of a too-lucid idealism maddened by its vision of evil.

In the play Vanessa becomes the embodiment of that evil despite the "humanity" of her arguments; in fact her very distance from any conscious villainy contributes to the irony of the situation—the kind of irony apparently built in to the constitution of the world and finally intolerable to such a mind as Swift's. For he was capable of loving many imperfect individuals, or perhaps more exactly, incapable of *not* loving them, no matter how great his hatred for humanity in the abstract. Thus Swift's rejection of Vanessa in the play is in effect a rejection of the age to come. "Both Swift and the intellect of his age," says Torchiana, "react in revulsion—on grounds of blood and excellence—to Vanessa's visions of maternity." [28] Swift's efforts to raise Vanessa to his level have failed. ("How

---

[27] *Ibid.*, p. 135.   [28] *Ibid.*, p. 138.

very closely she must also resemble the new Ireland that Yeats would educate. And how attractive the beastly wench was to both men.") [29] Torchiana remarks on the similarities between their rejection scene and the scene near the end of *Gulliver's Travels* where Gulliver swoons at the embrace of his loving wife. Opposed to this reductive force which would drag Swift down into the mire of humanity is Stella, for whom, oddly, Swift has served as Muse. She has learned to perfection the lesson Swift had to teach. And she could offer to the now independent Ireland a model of the only kind of chastity in which Yeats believed.[30]

In spite of Yeats's brilliant foray into Ibsen's territory, *Words Upon the Window-Pane* is not as atypical of Yeats's usual dramatic procedure as it seems on the surface. Swift becomes a mythical hero who has a vision of a transcendent order of reality. In the name of that vision he sacrifices his ordinary humanity. One female figure represents the claims of the ideal, another the claims of womanly love. The obsessive problem of generation reappears. How can heroism be passed on from one generation to the next? Certainly it is not handed on from father to son. It can have only the kind of immortality that Swift desired, the passing on of the intellect that comes from heaven.

[29] *Ibid.*, p. 138.

[30] Yeats was well aware of Irish folklore about Swift and his sexual exploits. He cites in a footnote an anecdote explaining the dismissal of a servant. "I had always known that stories of Swift and his serving-man were folk-lore all over Ireland and now I learned from country friends why the man was once dismissed. Swift sent him out to fetch a woman, and when Swift woke in the morning he found that she was a negress." *Explorations* (London, 1962), p. 282.

And yet man cannot dwell in a timeless world of ideas. The attempt to do so is always in some sense a betrayal of humanity. The hero is caught in an impossible position, owing as he does allegiance to opposed realms of being. Whether he wishes he had never been born when the final reckoning comes, or whether he finds courage and joy in the fact that his severed head sings, he discovers that it is not given to man, even heroic man, to achieve unity of being. Even at his most mythical, reality is always a part of Yeats's myth; and even at his most realistic, myth is a part of his reality.

12

A Full Moon in March and
The King of the Great Clock Tower

A Full Moon in March

To turn from the Swiftian passion and Swift's highly civilized dilemmas to the excremental passions of a swineherd may seem a more violent shift of focus than it really is. *A Full Moon in March* is all fable and song; the irrelevant humors of the outside world are strictly excluded. Everything is mythical; nothing historical or "real." Nevertheless, the basic dilemma is the same as in *Words:* how is man's desire for intellectual and aesthetic immortality to be reconciled with his instinct for biological immortality? Swift succeeded in ravishing the soul of his Stella but left unresolved the body's perplexity and his own human guilt. To think may be perfect bliss for a god, but it means suffering for a human, for he is caught in the embarrassing position of being unable to think without his body and incapable of acting according to his animal nature without thinking about what he is doing.

In *Full Moon* man's body and soul are artificially separated. The Swineherd has the freedom of an animal because he accepts destiny unconditionally. He obeys instinct with mindless serenity. The Queen has, apparently, complete freedom of choice, but she is more complicated than the Swineherd. She cannot permit body's gross insult to the soul; she must show the power of mind over matter. Insofar as she is pure soul, her moral sense is no more involved in her actions than the Swineherd's is in his. He approaches with the measured certainty of an automaton set on its course by an unseen hand. Secure in her power, the Queen is not in the least intimidated. When the situation has been made crystal clear—that her strange suitor has no tincture in him of love for goodness or truth or beauty or power, in other words that civilized values mean nothing to him—she orders, we might say, the "machine dismantled." This is attended to with no fuss at all and no hard feelings on either side. It is clear that Swineherd and Queen are complete opposites and have no common ground whatsoever.

But this is far from being the end of the matter. Superimposed on this paradigm of irreconcilable duality is a legend of true lovers. From this standpoint the Swineherd is the lucky and innocent rustic who has the magic to outdo his high born rivals and win the hand of the queen. He is like the third son in fairy tales who does right what his two elder brothers do wrong. His weapons are honesty, courage, and a naive and therefore invincible resolution. The Queen, so far disappointed in her hopes of finding a champion worthy of her, is won over by the utter and selfless integrity of a lover who wants her for herself alone (and not her yellow hair). For the first time she feels the stirring of love, both maternal and amorous. She would help and have this audacious but vulnerable creature. Their very lack of compatibility in all other ways becomes a proof of the authenticity of their need for each other. Yet her virginity *is* her soul just as his singing head *is* his virility. Body and soul must equally be bruised to pleasure each other. Perfection, especially that bodiless perfection of the fifteenth phase whose emblem is the moon, *does* lack something—"desecration and the lover's night." Love is both a giving and a possessing. To sacrifice all is to gain all.

The dialogue between Queen and Swineherd is a "comedy of misunderstandings" that abruptly ends in what would be tragedy if this play were realistic instead of mythical. The two are playing with chance and choice, which in the event turn out to be the same thing. What is absurd from one point of view (and the Queen points this out with great concision: it is outrageous that this savage should be "courting" her at all) is both inevitable and necessary from another. It is the very nature of existence that we should die each other's life, live each other's death (in a sense distinct from but related to the meaning of those words in *The Resurrection*). Such love must be cruel in order to be kind. The Queen's role compels her to play a part against her natural instincts. And the songs insist on the exoneration of the woman from the misdeeds of the goddess within her. Unlike those girls who have been able to let themselves go, who have given their love with no sense of self-sacrifice, the Queen is committed to upholding value. Those girls

> Gave their bodies, emptied purses
> For praise of clown or king,
> Gave all the love that women know!
> O they had their fling,
> But never stood before a stake
> And heard the dead lips sing.[1]

[1] *Collected Plays* (London, 1952), p. 627.

Those happy lovers who lived all for the moment had no need or use of miracle. But the Swineherd and Queen assert the mortal longing for immortality. Once the Swineherd has given all, the Queen knows she has found her match. He is worthy of receiving all, but he is "dead." The absolute is incompatible with the relativity of life. On the other hand, desecration depends on holiness for its meaning: crowns of gold can be insulted by the dung of swine precisely because there is a hierarchy of values. But the Swineherd is right in ignoring those values, in trampling on all "class distinctions," because he thereby reveals a more ancient, primitive value that underlies them. *A Full Moon* triumphantly demonstrates the interdependence of love and death.

From *At the Hawk's Well* on, Yeats is careful to give us the "human" protest to the exigencies of myth; *A Full Moon* is no exception. The Second Attendant (the young man with a bass voice) is horrified at seeing the sacred descend to the profane. Very reasonably, he had asked, "How can she laugh,/ Loving the dead?" He is heartbroken to see Beauty (the imagery suggests a statue) destroyed by Sex. (It is as though Plato's Idea of the Good should consent to be mastered by the appetitive part of the soul.) Yet (like the Yeats of "The Man and the Echo") he must understand, if he can, what seems a monstrous evil: the mandatory linking of perfection with flesh and blood. The First Attendant (an elderly woman with a soprano voice) is the wise counselor who instructs him: perfection without love is sterile; the human use of beauty demands its desecration. And never was there an apter student! At the first repetition of the lesson, the young man has forgotten the awe that made his legs give way at facing the faultless "emblem of the moon" and asks that his heart be delighted "yet again" by a repetition of the lesson. He now understands that *both* the swineherd and the queen are bearers of "all time's completed treasure"; he asks us to look upon "the pitchers that *they* carry." The queen's desecration, in the final version of the lesson, has become "*their* desecration." It is an added subtlety that the Second Attendant, who sang as the swineherd's head, has in a sense *become* the swineherd—at least he has learned the glory of the lover's courage, what it is that "can make the loutish wise."

Though the swineherd is more the embodiment of a poetic principle than a moral agent, we do get a sense of his character. He is absolute for love. From this spring his gay acceptance of chance, his self-confidence in his destiny, his contempt for danger, and his transparent candor. The queen is equally absolute for love; this is what ensures the marriage. As a queen she must demand the death penalty for the swineherd's radically subversive insolence; as an incomplete human being she knows she has found fulfillment in this unsavory suitor. His love has the blind strength of a biological instinct and the ruthlessness that allows the species to survive at the expense of the individual life. Though the play dramatizes two attractions—raising the low through the power of the ideal to immortality and pulling the high down into the mortal but reproductive world of nature—the latter has the more shocking force, as Yeats has insisted through his "reflector," the scared young man with the "savage, sunlit heart." The swineherd obstinately refuses to become a renaissance prince or lady's *sirvente*, and the queen, far from being the pedestaled beauty the Second Attendant takes her for, leads the swineherd on to sing his passion with a purposefulness that balances the swineherd's audacious declaration of his Caliban-like foulness.

It is a strange wooing. The swineherd warns the queen:

> But when I look into a stream, the face
> That trembles upon the surface makes me think
> My origin more foul than rag or flesh.[2]

He presents himself as a filthy, crazed, ignoble savage beyond redemption. Nevertheless, he is the only man who has come on this full moon in March, and that is the decisive fact. Still, the queen issues a counter-warning: she is crueller than the solitudes from which she has come; her beauty goes with the wintry cruelty of virginity; yet for some reason beyond her comprehension she would not harm him; let him go before it is too late. Of course it is already too late. Their coming together has the inevitability of a conjunction of the stars. Yeats deftly underlines this fatality by evoking the grotesque and natural repulsion which the greater attraction must overcome. The swineherd, completely fearless of danger, thinks only of their marriage night, "Imagining all from the first touch and kiss." The queen has to remind him, mockingly, of the song required by decree: such songs praising her beauty have never moved her in the past. But, obviously, she will get no such song from this clownish fellow who merely rolled in the dung of his swine and laughed when he first heard her name, who cares for nothing and can offer her nothing but "the night of love,/ An ignorant forest and

[2] *Ibid.*, p. 623.

the dung of swine." All the subterfuges which disguise the object of love have been swept away, all the decorum that gives love its distinctively human meaning has been despatched, and the queen knows the alternative offered if she leaves "these corridors, this ancient house,/ A famous throne, the reverence of servants." She can do no other than reject this intolerable bestiality; yet she must hear the song and have her lover. Such is the bitter paradox civilization imposes on that creature man, divided between angel and beast.

The play moves in a no-man's land between extremes outside the bounds that define, or enclose, rational human conduct. Yet nowhere else in Yeats's work do we get a stronger sense of the tension the precious fabric of civilization must withstand, of the necessity of instinct and the equal necessity of its control. The queen must drop her veil and the swineherd must lose his head. Interpreted as a parable of the fate of love circumscribed by human conventions, the play is as grim as a Lawrencian jeremiad against "mental love," but such an interpretation would distort the thematic balance of the play and falsify the implications of its highly sophisticated formality. Yeats has invented a form here (to be further developed in the last plays) which allows him to be ironical at the expense of "literary" rationalizations of love and at the same time to exploit the Romantic conventions for his own purposes. The lovers are endowed with an invincible innocence, proof against any rational or worldly compromise, but the strength of this innocence comes from the experience it embodies. The queen has never been moved by a lover's song before because she knows the singer's art has concealed desires for fame, power, beauty. These are not the essence of love but its enemies. And the swineherd has a complementary wisdom: he knows he cannot win the queen by being other than he is. What the queen needs is to lose her virginity, and he is the very quintessence of unchastity.

Needless to say, the story is far removed from the "realistic" pattern of the stableboy winning the countess's hand. (For an interesting contrast, compare this play with Strindberg's *Countess Julie* in which "desecration" wins a total victory.) The queen and the swineherd do not change; they have nothing to learn from experience. They are, rather, the constants of experience. They merely highlight in a condensed, symbolic way the oppositions that are fused in the universal of human love. Cleverly, Yeats is able to suggest a puncturing of illusion that gives access to a profound truth without sacrificing his supreme fiction: love can make man whole by joining the impure with the pure, the mortal with the immortal parts of him —and thus give poets their ultimate theme for song.

The King of the Great Clock Tower

March is the month of victims and saviors. Wilson has collected an impressive list of myths related to the god of the dying year and argues that Dionysus is central to Yeats's thought as it appears in *The King of the Great Clock Tower* and in *A Full Moon*.[3] He sees an "exact symbolic relation" between Zeus, Cybele, and Attis-Dionysus and the King, Queen, and Stroller in *Clock Tower*.[4] But Yeats has deliberately pared away such as-

[3] Wilson, *W. B. Yeats and Tradition* (New York, 1958), especially pp. 63–68.
[4] *Ibid.*, p. 70.

sociations in order to get at something both more immediate and more primitive. If we must have an archetype for *Clock Tower*, perhaps the "family romance" of Freud will fit as well as any. The stroller then can be imagined as a long lost son who challenges the dominance of the father, overcomes the intuitive repugnance of the mother, and effects an unspeakable union, only to pay the price of emasculation and transformation into a spirit. In the timeless realm of fantasy the one true love—of mother and son—is consummated without the actual source of the desecration ever being revealed. Certainly in their stylized way the three characters of the play suggest stock attitudes associated with father, mother, and son in the classic Oedipal situation. Projected into fantasy, family relations are dissolved in order to give free rein to instinctive desires. The king is a figure of absolute authority in the time-bound world but ultimately powerless either to command the love of his queen or prevent the love of the stroller. It doesn't matter (though it should to a poet) that the queen is not "so red, nor white, nor full in the breast" as he had expected; he will inevitably replace the king "when the old year dies." The king is there to protect the values of conscience, of respectability. The queen will not answer his question whether the stroller was her lover in the place she came from, but in spite of her dread she does not refuse to dance for the severed head. When she surrenders with a kiss, the king draws his sword as though to strike but is himself unmanned. He lays his sword at the queen's feet. Generations pass, but the old pattern remains.

Such a reading, of course, distorts Yeats's theme and is too reductive to do justice to his sense of the power of imagination to conceive immortality, but it may shed light on one source of Yeats's dissatisfaction with the play. The king stands as a shield between his queen and the stroller, thereby preventing the queen from giving expression to the rich ambiguity of her feelings. Too much emphasis is given to the irritated mystification of the king at the expense of the "real" drama—the relationship between stroller and queen. And yet, as we have seen, Yeats returns again and again to the eternal triangle in which one member is confronted with a fateful choice of love and loyalty. To be true to one demand on his or her need is to sacrifice the other. In *Clock Tower* the king is so uninvolved with either queen or stroller that he becomes a dramatic abstraction, and yet his language lacks the dignity or mystery to give him symbolic resonance. In a way, he is the figure upon whom revelation breaks when the dead lips *do* actually sing and his queen kisses them, but he is deprived of a dramatically effective response, and not only because he is reduced to gesture. He is a father-figure who, in spite of all the lines assigned to him, is condemned to remain mute about the only passions that could give him magnitude. He knows his queen no better than he knows the stroller. They know instinctively that they belong to a world beyond time; the king as locked in his time-bound world. This division could be dramatic—in fact, in the lyrics it *is* dramatic—but so far as the king is concerned, it is not. He is too uncomprehending to know or desire what he lacks and is thus denied any significant feelings at all.

By eliminating the king, Yeats was able to give full expression to his central theme, the violent contraries which love must comprehend if it is to be both ideal and real. In *Clock Tower* both stroller and queen act as though the king didn't, in any sense that matters, exist. The king is caught in an absurd situation; he is the superfluous man. Ionesco could have made grand farce of this tyrant's attempt to *prove* that he exists, and there are signs in the play that Yeats was tempted to exploit the humor implicit in the situation he had invented. The king is a god or demon stripped of his supernatural powers and denied divine (or even human) insight. Yeats can make the role of fatherly authority grotesque and sinister, even pathetic, but never (intentionally) merely funny. But that is what he should have done here. Instead, he scrapped the notion of an external force (a kind of "time machine") interposing itself between immortal lovers and incorporated the conflict of time and eternity in the lovers themselves. Thus both queen and swineherd in *A Full Moon* feel (and express) an inner ambivalence. The god is within. The choral role of astonished spectator (learner of the lesson and explicator of the moral) is transferred to its appropriate place, the second attendant.

By making these changes, Yeats lost one opportunity and seized another. He could (at least in theory) have revised *Clock Tower* in such a way as to make a tragic farce out of it and brought all three of his characters into dramatic conflict with each other. He proved in *Player Queen* and *Herne's Egg* that this mode was not uncongenial to him. As it is, he left in *Clock Tower* a play which is neither flesh nor fowl in spite of its fine songs. When the play was presented with maximum emphasis on song, pantomime, and dance, as it apparently was at the Abbey Theatre with Ninette de Valois in the part of the queen as dancer, it was effective enough so that Yeats could write Olivia Shakespear:

I think I read you and Dorothy *The King of the Great Clock Tower*. It has proved most effective—it was magnificently acted and danced. It is more original than I thought it, for when I looked up *Salome* I found that Wilde's dancer never danced with the head in her hands—her dance came before the decapitation of the saint and is a mere uncovering of nakedness. My dance is a long expression of horror and fascination. She first bows before the head (it is on a seat), then in her dance lays it on the ground and dances before it, then holds it in her hands. Send the enclosed cutting from Dorothy [from the *Sunday Times*] to Ezra that I may confound him.[5]

As a *dance* play, then, we must admit that *Clock Tower* has considerable possibilities.

To say, as Vendler does, that the last plays "are dramatic neither in conception nor in end, but are rather devices within which to embody lyrics," [6] is to confuse Yeats's way of working with the end product of his method. Until we have a theater that can give them a fair test, we cannot be sure of their theatrical viability, but from everything we know of the workings of Yeats's imagination (and that is a great deal), we can say that he conceived both life and art dramatically. In the last plays, and above all in *Full Moon*, Yeats is experimenting with a kind of drama that "purifies" character into symbol, transforms scene into emblem, and condenses action into epiphany. This attempt to push drama to its ultimate degree of poetic lucidity may unfit it for the public stage but certainly does not alter either the conception or end Yeats had in view from his first play to his last: to show

[5] *Letters* (London, 1954), pp. 826–827.
[6] Vendler, *Yeats's Vision* (Cambridge, Mass., 1963), p. 141.

man's deepest passions in conflict, and to show how from that conflict a soul travels, through shock and catastrophe, to a new and greater understanding of its essential condition.

The lyrics, even when, as often, they can stand alone, gain in precision and impact from their dramatic contexts, just as they in turn help clarify and universalize the destinies of particular heroes or heroines. A case in point is the song sung by the two attendants at the end of *Clock Tower*. The "rambling, shambling travelling-man" sees lovely ladies dancing in the ruins of Castle Dargan and is told by the "wicked, crooked, hawthorn tree" that those days and dancers are dead and gone. The travelling-man retorts, "O, what is life but a mouthful of air?"

> Yet all the lovely things that were
> Live, for I saw them dancing there.[7]

This is an assertion that lovely things, and especially the dancing of lovely ladies and gallant men, cannot die while there is still an imagination to *see* them. They are the Idea of Beauty made visible to that inner eye that can never be blurred by the corruption of time. The tree's answer, that it has "stood so long by *a gap in the wall*" (my italics) that maybe it will keep on living forever, as though by a kind of inertia, shows a "wicked" incomprehension of the vital distinction between a continual and unending progress (or at least succession of moments) in time and the true meaning of eternity, which is deathless because only the perfection of a pattern wrought out of a living desire and belief in the absolute dwells there. Like the king in the play, the tree (a tree of sterility and death) would

[7] *Collected Plays*, p. 640.

deny any reality outside time. By taking a queen and executing a stroller, the king deludes himself that he is a master of life. But the event shows that he is in fact powerless to *see* what lies beyond the gap in the wall. Thus immortal love eludes him.

At the moment when the severed head sings in both these plays we can see how the Queen, "first an aloof and solitary object of worship," has become united with the poet, causing "him to sing through her inspiration, and at this point [she] may rightly be named the Muse." [8] But the relation of poet and Muse which Vendler sees fits *Clock Tower* better than it does *Full Moon*. The Swineherd in the latter play is of the earth, earthy; he rejects an aesthetic stance in order to affirm something more cosmically fundamental. As Wilson remarks of the ending of *Full Moon*, "to our surprise we see that in this resurrection it is the Queen who descends." [9] The Swineherd never swerves from his end; it is the Queen who bends to accommodate him. As a parable of art, *Full Moon* suggests the inadequacy of any theory of "art for art's sake" and the sterility of any art that tries to live in the world of Platonic forms. The Muse must be "desecrated" by the poet. In spite of the similarity between *Clock Tower* and *Full Moon*, their respective conclusions point to opposite emphases; in the first, the world outside time is the home of the true and beautiful, and the King stands for an inferior, and ultimately illusory, order of reality; in the second, the sacredness of the body is the necessary condition for immortality, and the Swineherd must die in order that eternity may exist. The two views are complementary.

[8] Vendler, p. 145. [9] Wilson, p. 91.

Eternity is in love with the products of time, and those products give life to eternity.

Pound's famous rejection of his friend's *Clock Tower* when Yeats showed it to him in Rapallo in June, 1934, worried Yeats, who had "written little prose for three years." Was he losing his grip? Pound had said he wrote "nobody's language." But to a manuscript book Yeats confided, "But 'nobody's language' is something I can remedy. I must write in verse, but first in prose to set structure." [10] Naturally Yeats was pleased when the play was produced the following month to see its stage success. Yet this didn't satisfy him for long, and he set to work to write *Full Moon*. In the first (prose) scenario as it appears in Bradford's book we are struck by the new air of brutality. For instance, the Stroller and Queen seem to engage in an agon with no holds barred. When the Queen tells the Captain of the Guard to cut off the Stroller's head, she says, "When I [have] bathed my hands in his blood, you can take him to the top of the great tower. Put his head upon a stake and leave it." Later she calls out, "The axe, the axe. I will listen to his insults no longer." [11] The description of the dance in the second manuscript emphasizes its sensuality. "The marriage night. His blood has poured upon her at the first coupling; she conceives of his blood. After that the bridal sleep." [12] In the third manuscript the attendants appear, and though it is entitled "The Severed Head," the theme of the full moon in March becomes a focal image. In manuscript four experiments with verse, including the use of the shorter line than blank verse,

[10] Bradford, *Yeats at Work* (Carbondale and Edwardsville, 1965), p. 268.
[11] *Ibid.*, p. 270.   [12] *Ibid.*, p. 273.

show Yeats still a considerable distance from the finished product. In "The Swineherd," Yeats's fifth extant manuscript, he combines elements from the earlier versions. He is now within sight of his goal. The description of the dance is still more candid than in the printed versions, as Bradford points out. He also speaks of Yeats's resolution in the play (final version) of the Romantic theme of the severed head, mentioning instances from Blake, Stendhal, and Wilde. The "emblematic situation at its simplest . . . appears to say that part of the Romantic ethos was a desire by some women—and some men—to be loved without responding to the brutal demands of their lover's bodies." [13] Yeats has made this theme "clear and deeply moving in *A Full Moon in March*" by raising it to the "level of myth." He has cleared it of morbidity. Certainly we may say that the effect of classic balance Yeats has achieved here creates, despite the violence of the subject, a final repose rare in his drama.

[13] *Ibid.,* p. 292.

The Herne's Egg

Yeats wrote to Ethel Mannin in December, 1935, that he was working on a new play, "the strangest wildest thing I have ever written." [1] He thought that if it was ever played it would provide a full evening's entertainment. Reading *The Herne's Egg*, one is immediately struck by the wildness but equally reassured by familiar Yeatsian landmarks. The rite of the hero has merely entered a new phase. The old-fashioned pattern of romance has been squeezed dry of all sentiment, and the hero's quarrel with deity is enveloped in a shimmer of grotesque illusion. Having fled to Mallorca to escape the busyness of Dublin, Yeats worked on his play, staying in bed till noon. Later Shri Purohit Swami came over, and Yeats spent the afternoon helping the Swami with his translations of the *Upanishads*. Yeats described *Herne's Egg* as the Swami's "philosophy in a fable." The Swami's opinion of the play is not recorded.

In *The Herne's Egg* we see the same action regarded from a "tough," pragmatic standpoint and then from a "noble," transcendent one. Both views are reduced to logical absurdity by deflation. Congal, the hero of the play, ludicrously straddles the two realms, being both the

[1] *Letters* (London, 1954), p. 845.

old soldier who will put up with no nonsense and the chosen victim of divinity. Attracta, the priestess-bride of the Great Herne, is a lunatic because of sexual repression; melt the snows of her virginity and she will be perfectly normal. So Congal thinks until supernatural thunder brings him to his knees and he accepts the heroic curse: to die on the holy mountain at the full of the moon by the hands of a Fool. The familiar components of Yeats's hero myth are here once more, but they are combined in strange, expressionist patterns and treated with a new rhythmic energy.

The first scene serves the same function as a musical overture: the ritual battle between the two kings presents a perfect balance of action and reaction, each mirroring the other in word and gesture as though the world were timeless except for the mathematically exact repetitions of a rigidly circumscribed action (all their battles have been perfect ones). But, says Aedh, there is a story of two rich fleas going around—they were so rich they retired and bought a dog, "A fat, square, lazy dog,/ No sort of scratching dog." Our two heroes "hop like fleas, but war/ Has taken all [their] riches." Rich fleas dominate this phlegmatic dog of a world; the heroes have been left behind by history to dance their old roles, no longer significant to anyone but themselves. The humor is double-edged. The two kings may laugh at the world, but the world can laugh right back. In the play that follows, each action can be interpreted as cancelling another. We start (in Scene II) with a donkey and end with a donkey-to-be.

The donkey Corney wheels in is "like a child's toy, but life-size." He emphasizes the artificiality of the adult games we are about to witness. He is described as tough and strong (like an old campaigner), but all his good points are spoiled by his "rapscallion Clareman's eye"; he may have been a thief and breaker of hearts in a previous existence, but if so he is paying for it now, being but a "chattel, a taker of blows, not a giver of blows." Congal is bent on a little thieving himself and has come with his men to get herne's eggs as a special delicacy for his feast of reconciliation with Aedh. Mike, a "wise fool" whose telegraphic and ambiguous messages Congal interprets in his own downright fashion, has to remind his king to mind his manners. And Corney, the man with the donkey, instructs the hero how to call the priestess by playing on a flute carved out of a herne's thigh (obviously related to the Great Herne who, being one-legged, is self-sufficient and yet incomplete).

Congal, unlike the young Cuchulain of *At the Hawk's Well*, is a baffled and ignorant man badly in need of instruction if he is ever to rejuvenate the ritualism that has become mechanical and therefore sterile. Ironically, he is full of a misplaced self-confidence based on his experience as a battle-scarred veteran. Is he to be denied "Because a woman thinks that she/ Is promised or married to a bird?" He does not blame Attracta for her mystic lunacy; it comes from mere inexperience of the flesh—a matter the literal-minded Ovid failed to understand when he told the stories of Danae and Leda. But this old campaigner knows the cure for all women's dreams. If he had but time he would take care of the matter himself. There is no meeting of minds, however.

Attracta.   There is no happiness but the Great Herne.
Congal.   It may be that life is suffering,

But youth that has not yet known pleasure
Has not the right to say so; pick
Or be picked by seven men,
And we shall talk it out again.

Attracta.   Being betrothed to the Great Herne
I know what may be known: I burn
Not in the flesh but in the mind;
Chosen out of all my kind
That I may lie in a blazing bed
And a bird take my maidenhead,
To the unbegotten I return,
All a womb and a funeral urn.[2]

The familiar confrontation of principles is here again—
the timebound and the timeless. Neither can comprehend
the other; divine innocence and fallen experience, each has
its wisdom but lacks the knowledge of the other and so is
unfulfilled. Unlike the swineherd of *A Full Moon*, Congal
is a product of civilization and so has none of the former's
instinctive certainty; in fact he dismisses what is *outside*
his experience as mere ignorance or abnormality simply
due to *lack* of experience. The "unbegotten," whose vestal
virgin encloses life as a "womb" and a "funeral urn," is
the other side of the moon to Congal, who understands
quite well what lies between the womb and the funeral
urn, but not at all what lies between death and *re*birth.

Corney, forced to return with the donkey whose creel
is now loaded with Herne's eggs, in his indignation at the
sacrilege wants Attracta to go into her trance, that the god
may be brought out of her "gut" and make these rascals
"Wiggle upon his beak like eels," but she knows the time
for vengeance is not at her command, and still less at that

---

[2] *Collected Plays* (London, 1952), p. 650.

of this underling who, she says, "must obey/ All big men who can say their say." This is Yeats's roughest treatment of that always violent god who seems at least as eager to be the enemy and destroyer of man as to offer him the extra dimension that will save him from the otherwise flat and finally meaningless existence that pure "history" affords. The sexual metaphor that underlies the communion of man and god in virtually all the plays, and that becomes so explicit in the later plays, is here made deliberately grotesque and "unpoetical." It is as though Yeats challenged the reader to pass Tertullian's test: I believe *because* it is absurd. But perhaps only in Ireland would this fantasy be taken seriously enough to cause religious dissension among prospective producers. (At Yeats's death the play had not been staged.) [3]

Scepticism has infected even Attracta's faithful servant, Corney, who thinks that the ancient curse supposedly pronounced by the Great Herne on anyone who should presume to steal a herne's egg may have been a trick.

> I think it was the Great Herne made it,
> Pretending that he had but the one leg
> To fool us all; but Great Herne or another
> It has not failed these thousand years.[4]

However uncertain or obscure the "theological" tradition may be, Corney does not doubt the spiritual fact: sacrilege brings down catastrophe from heaven. Congal is not discomfited; he has a sensible and soldierly rejoinder.

[3] It was produced by Austin Clarke at the Peacock Theatre in the 1940's and has been done since in Belfast and in New York.
[4] *Collected Plays*, p. 651.

That I shall live and die a fool
And die upon some battlefield
At some fool's hand, is but natural,
And needs no curse to bring it.[5]

This masculine and aggressive scene, in which nothing is resolved, is followed by a quiet, feminine scene in which three girls, assured the fierce men have gone, offer presents (of cream, butter, and eggs) to Attracta as though she were a goddess. She gently rebukes them for fearing "A woman but little older" than they are and promises that they will all have good husbands when she herself is married. Thus is divine marriage linked with ordinary marriage. But no matter how like one of themselves Attracta may try to appear, the girls know that she is destined to be the bride of no human, but of some god-like bird. Their questions combine awe with a strong childish curiosity. They want to know if this bird whom they imagine with terrible beak and terrible claws, will "Do all that a man does." Attracta's answer implies, Yes, and so much more that it will be entirely different. She imagines (and prays) that all foliage of the flesh stripped away, she will "shoot into [her] joy." It is an extraordinary image in its paradoxical use of the physical (and specifically phallic) to suggest a disembodied experience. Appropriately enough comes the sound of the flute, and Attracta goes into her trance. Her humanity is gone and she is like a "doll upon a wire." Her devotees, the three girls, serve as chorus to describe her "long loop like a dancer" and to speculate on the mystic marriage that awaits her. Their uncomprehend-

[5] *Ibid.*, p. 652.

ing but complete faith in Attracta (like that of the disciples in Jesus) provides a dramatic contrast to the tough scepticism of Congal.

Though the Great Herne "in a red rage" has flown over their heads, and Congal and his men have unavailingly tried to kill him with stones and swords, the eggs have been brought safely to Tara for the royal feast. Now we see the banqueting hall deserted and a drunken Congal enters, crying out his rage and betrayal—he alone has been given an ordinary hen's egg at the banquet. Aedh, equally drunk, blames Congal for the mishap and a riot breaks out, with tablelegs and candlesticks being used as weapons. The ritual battle of the first scene has been degraded into worldly farce—let the Irish take it as a parody of their political history if they will. It is no more ridiculous, perhaps, than some of the quarrel scenes Homer gives his Olympians, and here too the source of the trouble is false pride. The egg of discord has upset the old equilibrium between the two kings, and Aedh dies accusing Congal of cheating by "secretly practising with a table-leg."

Even in Congal's speeches the ludicrous and the dignified jostle each other. In one breath Congal finds everything all right because he has taken the kingdom and throne and therefore can afford to weep at his old opponent's funeral; in the next he declares Aedh "should have been immortal" but that "a new leader will be found/ And everything begin again." But it will be different; "Much bloodier," as Mike says, because the fighting will no longer be for the disinterested joy of battle but for possession and survival. Congal begins to believe in the Great Herne's curse: loss of the spiritual vision that can raise the struggle for existence above the level of the beast.

The hero is gaining insight, as he shows in interpreting Mike's remark, "Horror henceforth":

> This wise man means
> We fought so long like gentlemen
> That we grew blind.[6]

Only the shock of degradation has made Congal face the fact that the ritual code he has taken such pride in sustaining has become an empty form—a mere hen's egg and no herne's egg.

Immediately Attracta enters carrying a herne's egg (and we remember that when she went into her trance Kate had remarked on her taking a hen's egg from the girl's basket). Still walking in her sleep, Attracta holds the precious egg out towards the throne. Congal is about to take the egg when Mike stops him. Pat and James, representing his men, say she must die because she is responsible for all the bloodshed. And Congal accepts this "democratic" decision because he sees a chance of getting revenge on the Great Herne through his bride. The king decrees that seven men, including himself, shall rape her. They will melt her "virgin snow."

> And that snow image, the Great Herne;
> For nothing less than seven men
> Can melt that snow, but when it melts
> She may, being free from all obsession,
> Live as every woman should.
> I am the Court, judgement has been given.[7]

If Yeats were writing an "anti-myth" play, Attracta would be cured, the Great Herne would be put in a zoo,

[6] *Ibid.*, p. 660.   [7] *Ibid.*, p. 662.

Congal would marry her, and her "girls" would be appropriately paired off with the boys. Perhaps they would dance a jig played on the flute supposedly made from a herne's thigh. But no such enlightened happiness is in store for these benighted men. They are scared and offer comic excuses: "people say that she is holy/ And carries a great devil in her gut," says Mathias; Malachi promised his mother to keep away from women; John's wife is jealous if he but looks "the moon in the face"; James is promised to an educated girl of a most particular family. Congal must advise them that whoever refuses to rape in the name of the law "Is an unmannerly, disloyal lout,/ And no good citizen."

Thus Yeats, with sardonic relish, focusses on the paradoxes of Law at the thematic heart of the play. Law is a necessary regulator of men's lives, and lawlessness means not freedom but chaos. But what does man do when he is caught between opposing principles of law? These men superstitiously and instinctively shrink from what old custom tells them must be an act of desecration. Though they have themselves, figuratively speaking, called for the execution of the old religion, they must become drunk to go through with it. Only Congal, the old aristocrat and soldier, can express with any intellectual dignity the rational basis on which he acts:

> A Court of Law is a blessed thing,
> Logic, mathematics, ground in one,
> And everything out of balance accursed.[8]

And yet, in perfect keeping with the technique of incongruity Yeats has devised for this play, the logic and mathe-

8 *Ibid.,* p. 663.

matics Congal has just praised so judiciously are reduced
to absurdity in application: the order of rape is to be
decided by having the men throw their skullcaps to see
who is nearest the mark. Significantly enough, the Herne's
egg is used as the mark. Attracta concludes this part of
the play by singing a song affirming her faith in her immortal bridegroom and in his power to guarantee her
purity against any "lesser life, man, bird or beast." The
mystery of what we might call divine "inviolation" leaves
certain questions unanswered, however; specifically the
kind of question asked in "Leda and the Swan."

> When beak and claw their work begin
> Shall horror stir in the roots of my hair?
> *Sang the bride of the Herne, and the Great Herne's bride*
> And who lie there in the cold dawn
> When all that terror has come and gone?
> Shall I be the woman lying there? [9]

Intercourse with a god seems to threaten a rapture surpassing in brutality anything that "lesser life" could offer.
Can the chosen victim ever be "the same" after such an
experience?

That is something we cannot answer dogmatically, but
there is no doubt of the change in the hero in the next
scene; we see him being bent to the Great Herne's purpose
before our eyes. It is dawn before the Gate of Tara and
Corney has just aroused his donkey. As before, the familiar and the grotesque, the direct and the cryptic jostle
each other. Attracta is collecting all the uneaten or unbroken herne's eggs as though she were collecting the
remnants of her own virginity. Congal congratulates her

[9] *Ibid.*, pp. 664–665.

on behaving like a good housewife and sensible woman;
she has apparently been cured by lying with seven men.
But she insists that she is the pure bride of her husband,
the Herne, and prays to him that the heavens may vouch
for her, which they promptly do with thunder. All Congal's men kneel and repent, but Congal remains upright.
Attracta foretells the animalistic degradation awaiting the
men in their next incarnation as a result of their impious
behavior; only Congal's fate remains uncertain. The thunder speaks again, confirming her words, and even Congal
is brought to his knees, though whether terror, awe, or
love for Attracta plays the main part in his decision is
something that he himself could not say.

Equally indeterminate is the degree of his freedom.
Though Attracta says his "fate is not yet settled," he himself accepts the inevitability of the curse pronounced
upon him. Like Yeats's Cuchulain who challenges fate in
At the Hawk's Well, Congal is out to subdue the feminine
divine as well as devote himself to it, only Congal goes
further than previous Yeats heroes. He fights against admitting the divine element at all. Even after he has knelt
in obeisance he, unlike his men, sticks to his version of
what happened the night before, and in answer to Attracta's question, "Why did you stand up so long?" he
answers, "I held you in my arms last night,/ We seven
held you in our arms." In accepting his assignation with
superhuman mystery—to meet his death on the holy
mountain when the moon is full—he reaffirms his loyalty
to human experience, and it is this very loyalty that makes
him paradoxically worthy of *as*cending instead of *de*scend-
ing like his lesser companions. Attracta holds out the offer:

One man will I have among the gods.
Congal.   I know the place and I will come,

Although it be my death I will come.
Because I am terrified I will come.[10]

Terror makes the ordinary man shrink, but the hero discovers in it his true stature.

The last scene on the mountain accentuates the thematic contrasts the play has developed. Congal approaches the adventure with the wary reasonableness we have gradually come to expect from him. How can he outwit the Great Herne? Congal makes a good companion of the fool who has come to kill him with a kitchen spit, allows himself to be wounded, and then wounds himself, thinking thus to falsify the curse (that he must die at the hands of a fool) laid upon him. Attracta appears with Corney and the donkey and sings the last stanza of her "bridal" song to the Great Herne again, but Congal and Attracta do not meet until he is dying of his self-inflicted wound. Here desecration and the lover's night have become ambiguous indeed. Congal calls out to Attracta, and she answers:

> I called you to this place,
> You came, and now the story is finished.
> *Congal.*   You have great powers, even the thunder
> Does whatever you bid it do.
> Protect me, I have won my bout,
> But I am afraid of what the Herne
> May do with me when I am dead.
> I am afraid that he may put me
> Into the shape of a brute beast.
> *Attracta.*   I will protect you if, as I think,
> Your shape is not yet fixed upon.[11]

Attracta's power has won over the sceptical Congal, but *his* power has won her over too. He admits her superiority

---

[10] *Ibid.*, p. 670.   [11] *Ibid.*, pp. 676–677.

in knowledge and control of "reality," but he defies the authority behind her, of which she *seems* the mere instrument. And yet she herself has become an ally of Congal and would protect him against the wrath of her immortal bridegroom. Congal dies declaring he has beaten the Great Herne—"In spite of your kitchen spit—seven men"—and Attracta exhorts Corney to lie with her at once, trying to allay his fears by assuring him that if she is doing the Great Herne's will, "You are his instrument or himself." The work at hand requires not a self-mirroring spiritual image but "The imperfection of a man." Too late. The donkey has slipped his knot and, during this moment of human hesitation, has fulfilled his animal need with another donkey. Like his six companions, Congal must descend the chain of being. The abominable snow of Attracta's virginity is preserved against her will by the god; the Great Herne gets the last laugh. Nevertheless, Attracta's will and desire had turned to Congal and the "imperfection of a man." Perhaps the answer to the question of her song, "Was I the woman lying there?" is that the Great Herne made a woman of her capable of attracting Congal to his fate.

The play offers Yeats's most complex analysis of the heroic dilemma. The first scene suggests that Congal is a hero born, not made; he is a man who responds naturally to the aesthetic principles of soldierly combat, understanding that formal pattern, playing the game according to the rules, is the important thing and not any ulterior motive, such as riches or power. Yet this purity of masculine play has become barren. The herne's eggs that Congal seeks as a delicacy for his banquet symbolize the fertile reinvigoration required if heroic artifice is to be restored to life again. Congal, isolated in his aristocratic solipsism, has no awareness of the significance of the eggs or of Attracta or of the Great Herne. Through a series of "accidents" he learns. He is never allowed to understand completely (presumably he never knows that he will be reborn a donkey).

It is hard to say whether he is more fool than hero, but there is no doubt that in his own eyes he wins the battle to retain his human dignity. The play suggests, however, that the self-reliance of a hero is illusory; even Law and Justice degenerate into mechanical principles inadequate to their purpose when they are not informed by some spirit of divinity. As frequently in Yeats, the hero's access to divinity is through the "medium" of a woman. Congal is actually god's rival for the sexual favors of Attracta. In trying to save her humanity (make a normal woman of her), Congal sacrifices his life, and even his next life to come. Attracta fails to raise him to the company of the gods, though she has clearly chosen him. Woman is both the hero's blessing and his curse. Attracta is responsible for ending the ideal friendship of Aedh and Congal. She brings out the worst in men, reducing them to bestiality. Yet she beckons toward the highest. Or is it all the work of the Great Herne? At any rate, the hero is the man most acutely aware of the difficulties of being human—of avoiding the mindlessness of the animal on the one hand and the superstitious subservience to irrational authority on the other. Though the play remains securely within its mythical framework—it does not ask us to doubt the Great Herne's ultimate reality—it does present a view of the supernatural at once so austere and so fantastic that we may well honor Congal for his unrelenting struggle against a holiness which apparently denies the value of specifically human virtues—rationality, generosity, self-respect, and love. From this standpoint, Yeats has gone further than ever before in offering us a deity that invites negative criticism: an old bird arbitrary, vengeful, terrifying, cruel, and absurd.

Before our eyes, "high up on a backcloth," is the commanding image of the play—a great herne standing on a "rock, its base hidden in mist." The rock is the very egg of the world, and most of the play's action takes place in that mist of illusion where men try to seize on certainties only to have them melt like snow in their hands. In no other play has Yeats insisted on artifice with such intensity as in this one. From the first scene, where the men dance their fight like puppets in a ballet, through the description of Attracta's "long loops like a dancer" when she is possessed by divinity, to Congal's ritual death wound on a spit, everything suggests a shadow dancer imitating mystic rites of worship. At the same time the staccato rhythms of the generally four-stress lines and the homely, sometimes vulgar diction forcefully present the bumptious immediacies of earthy experience. Downright "common sense" is always being played off against exalted nonsense. Against the images of moon, black midnight, holy mountain top, snow, swords, and the Great Herne himself stand in equal prominence the images of ordinary domesticity—hen's eggs, butter, cream—a toy donkey, a doll-like Attracta, a "fat, square, lazy dog," tablelegs and spits and pots for weapons; and drunkenness offsets the thunderous manifestations of deity.

In the brilliant first scene the tone of this masculine, warlike play is set. Aedh and Congal act as their own chorus, distancing themselves from ordinary humanity with every equation they complete. They can go from daybreak until morn without eating or drinking because they are men of spirit in a double sense. Caring nothing about material riches, they have let the world go to the "fleas," who have made it into a dog of their liking. Yeats's fantastic conceit expresses a theme conventional enough with him: the proper order of the world has been subverted when the crafty ones, the merchants, all the fools and blind men take charge of things. But the hero of this play has so far abstracted his code of life from any living reality, either natural or supernatural, that he might be said to be committed to nothing except pure form. He must be dragged back into the natural world in order to have access to the supernatural. And what more natural than that the hunt for eggs should lead him into his destiny?

Congal has no interest in Attracta; he has simply heard that he can get a rare delicacy for the dinner to celebrate his fiftieth battle with Aedh in the territory where she happens to preside. He wants to steal the eggs without more ado—for he only stands on ceremony where his "vital" interests are concerned. When Corney tells him how the priestess may be summoned, Congal's only comment is "That's a queer way of summoning." What custom permits or forbids seems ridiculous if it stands in the way of the culinary fancy of an old veteran, and especially if he is denied his pleasure "Because a woman thinks that she/ Is promised or married to a bird." Not understanding women very well, Congal is irritated by Attracta's foolish

obsession and is sure a little healthy sex will cure her neu-
rotic hallucinations. Mike, who has reduced what might be
choral song to one-or-two-word reminders of Congal's
own thought, drives home for us the soldierly resolution
of a man's world with no time for female hysterics. Thus
Congal stumbles in over his depth. The Great Herne's
curse almost seems to amount to the disturbance caused
by allowing women into a man's world.

Corney's description of the life-size donkey on wheels
foreshadows Congal's fate, and it shows Yeats's technique
in this play of modulating in and out of rhyme. Here the
rhyme does not elevate the level of discourse but emphasizes the physical appearance of the donkey; when Corney
scoldingly addresses him the rhyme disappears and the
donkey's subservient position in his present condition is
vigorously affirmed. Why Corney has brought him is
never made clear. He is in Attracta's service and yet he
helps Congal and his men in the sacrilegious tasks for
which he is soon upbraiding them. In violent terms he
asks Attracta to "Bring the god out of your gut." True,
Attracta finally stops his flow of invective and rebukes
him for forgetting his place—but where else is a priestess's
helper allowed such insolence? The same lack of decorum
that the characters frequently exhibit is reflected in Yeats's
own rough and ready shifts in language. Nothing is "beautiful" in this play; there is no repose. But in compensation
we get a brilliant pungency of expression and swift modulations of tone that show a startling power of condensation.

One of these modulations occurs when the men go out,
leaving Attracta with the three timid virgins. Their childlike questions and her frank and friendly answers give us

a charming though momentary glimpse of the "human" side of that virginity which elsewhere is mystical or humorous or "abominable." The girls are allowed little time for questioning Attracta about their own hopes and fears because the god calls her and they assume the choral function of describing their entranced patroness. Mary doesn't know whether or not Attracta becomes a "puppet" when she stiffens in rapture, but she has obviously observed attentively and thought curiously about these seizures.

> How do I know? And yet
> Twice have I seen her so,
> She will move for certain minutes
> As though her god were there
> Thinking how best to move
> A doll upon a wire.
> Then she will move away
> In long leaps as though
> He had remembered his skill.
> She has still my little egg.[12]

Here Yeats has tightened his verse to three stresses a line and made his diction both natural and simple. What Mary describes suggests in a very innocent way a certain scepticism about this god so powerful, mysterious, and peculiar. It is as though his skill had grown rusty from disuse and he had to *think* to remember how he had managed this delicate operation in the past. But Mary is no philosopher and does not try to puzzle things out. The present moment is what is important to her, and so she ends by observing that "She has still my little egg." Attracta will, hopefully, not fail to provide "the lad that is in

[12] *Ibid.*, p. 654.

[Mary's] mind." This is comedy of a sort, but much softer than any provided by the men.

If, in one sense, the action of *Herne's Egg* is to end virginity one way or another—and we might extend this to include virginity of mind as well as body—there is also a counter-action to preserve godhead from contamination by the lesser breeds without the law. Reincarnation becomes less a way for humans to work their way toward Nirvana than a device for sardonic deity to remind humans of their *animal* pretensions. During the drunken fight between Connacht and Tara that breaks up the banquet, Pat enters alone and drunk. He philosophizes.

> Herne's egg, hen's egg, great difference.
> There's insult in that difference.
> What do hens eat? Hens live upon mash,
> Upon slop, upon kitchen odds and ends.
> What do hernes eat? Hernes live on eels,
> On things that must always run about.
> Man's a high animal and runs about,
> But mash is low, O, very low.
> Or, to speak like a philosopher,
> When a man expects the movable
> But gets the immovable, he is insulted.[13]

Such strategically placed drunken speeches always merit close attention. Pat is not at all sure of the difference between herne's egg and hen's egg, but the fact that he is drunk and has been fighting about the difference must be rationalized somehow. He knows that an insult to honor is involved. Why? He starts at the source—hernes and hens. We are what we eat (as Sir Thomas Browne pointed out long ago). And hens are "low" because they eat mash and

---

[13] *Ibid.*, p. 659.

slops, the pap that is provided for them. Hernes are more enterprising—they are hunters and catch things on the move. "Man's a high animal and runs about," so naturally he would prefer eggs from an animal that is more like himself. So far so good. But now Pat takes a flying leap into abstraction. Eggs themselves are not "movable" or "immovable"; it must be what they stand for that counts. Congal and his men have been confronted by the immovable (actually the manifestation of the supernatural curse), and it is "higher" than the movable, the world of flux they are accustomed to. Everything is topsy-turvy. But insult remains. It is clear that hen's eggs are "low" and demeaning. Unwittingly, though, Pat has succeeded in voicing a "higher" truth: natural man is upset when confronted by the supernatural.

This speech has the choppy association of ideas characteristic of the intoxicated and conveys the effort of a drunken man "to walk the line" with admirable clarity and directness. It entirely lacks the romantic posturing of the drunken Septimus's speeches in *The Player Queen*. Yeats has arrived at a style strongly accentuated and yet capable of an irregularity that borders on "free" verse; his rhythmic freedom is matched by his hospitality to a diction that easily accommodates such words as "slop," "mash," "odds and ends"; and his irony can be simultaneously abrupt, even crude, while it works in subtler, more meditative ways. Congal has enough "character" to suit Yeats's purposes, as does Attracta, but the dramatic focus is all on the dance of ideas so thoroughly incarnated in image and gesture that we are more apt to be shocked into laughter at Yeats's "daring" wedding of high and low than moved to dismay by the grim analysis of the world that his play implies.

The episodic structure of the play is designed to exhibit Congal in a series of symbolic "poses" that lead him in a circle from one form of empty ritual through a round of challenges of the Great Herne to a final empty ritual. But with a difference. No longer the complacent warrior fighting his "perfect" battles, Congal has become a lover, imperfect and foolish but inextricably bound to the human race. Without wishing or intending it, he has had the heroic role thrust upon him and thereby become the champion of everyone doomed to suffer reincarnation. As he describes himself to the Fool, he is "King Congal of Connacht and of Tara,/ That wise, victorious, voluble, unlucky,/ Blasphemous, famous, infamous man." His steadily growing insight may be painfully acquired, but it has not reconciled him to the world's order; on the contrary he has become a hardened rebel and dies asserting *his* truth, shaking his fist, so to speak, in the Great Herne's face.

A psychological analysis might say that the Oedipal conflict has been transposed into a new key. The hero denies his divine father in order to affirm his own identity and is reduced to a donkey for his presumption in trying to steal Attracta from his father. Like the queen in *A Full Moon*, Attracta has motherly qualities (the scene with the three maidens helps emphasize this) in spite of her virginity. But in *A Full Moon* the issue of godhead is not raised, at least not directly. Humanity is seen as a product of the union between the ideal and the natural. *The Herne's Egg* risks bringing what is above humanity and what is below into closer conjunction: it is as though Yeats were saying that natural and supernatural are ultimately one; the humanity in between is the alien and disruptive element. Thus Congal is not part hero and part fool; being a hero *necessarily* involves being a fool—the two aspects are inseparable, and which we stress depends on where our sympathies lie. Sex (and certainly there is no "love interest" in this play), as often before, is the instrument of divine communion, but never before has the hero's fate hung on the speed of another's copulation! Only for humans is sex such a complicated thing: ridiculous and shameful, mysterious and liberating, the cause of tragic conflict and the excuse for raucous laughter. Yeats exploits all these potentialities in *The Herne's Egg*.

What Wilson calls Yeats's "focal point" in *Herne's Egg* "is always the squalor of the material world" rather than the vision of Eden.[14] Perhaps it would be more precise to say that degradation comes from the interanimation of nature and spirit. From one standpoint Congal's sustained effort to "cure" Attracta of her neurosis—though his shock therapy is admittedly harsh—is surely motivated by a humane desire to undo the vile mischief that the Great Herne has let loose in the world. As Congal sees it, that bird is, like Blake's Nobodaddy, a tyrant of the imagination, and it is the warping of nature by repression that accounts for the transformation of innocent joy into shameful obscenity. Wilson himself puts this very well, though in somewhat different terms, when he describes Congal's arguments "to dissuade Attracta from her mystic marriage." He says, "They are the arguments of experience against ignorance, of energy against spirituality, of life against the absolute."[15] And Wilson (rightly) insists that Yeats wants us to sympathize with Congal. He is the

[14] Wilson, *W. B. Yeats and Tradition* (New York, 1958), p. 131.
[15] *Ibid.*, p. 119.

"same" hero Yeats has so often shown us, only more so: both his aggressiveness and his vulnerability are greater than ever before. Like Cuchulain in many ways, he is "dumber" because less aware of his true vocation. Earlier heroes vent their scorn on the ways of *this* world; Congal dares, like Satan, to defy the ugly dictatorship of the deity himself. The whole painful and funny spectacle of puny man trying to assert the divinity within at the expense of the divinity outside his reach creates an oddly moving effect.

To put it schematically, what we are watching is the will asserting its freedom within a completely determined system. Ure sees the play this way [16] but is bothered by the ending because Congal's fate—to be reborn a donkey —suggests that "the Great Wheel, like other kinds of machinery, can be halted by the most trivial forms of accident." [17] This is to fall into Congal's own trap. To be sure, the Great Herne is an arbitrary old bird—when has he not been?—but there is no reason to suppose that what looks like accident to the innocent bystander and to an all-too-human Attracta—who is obviously doing her best to betray her lord and master—is in fact any less determined than anything else that befalls the accursed Congal. From the Herne's point of view, nothing could be more fitting than that Congal should start all over again as a donkey. It is Congal's vocation to be a fool in taking on an opponent too big for him, and he must face the consequences. Nevertheless, he has almost succeeded in making divinity stoop to him—indeed he *has* succeeded, if we regard Attracta as representing the merciful aspect of divinity. To

[16] Ure, *Yeats the Playwright* (London, 1963), p. 151.
[17] *Ibid.*, p. 156.

have a success greater than this, to ascend to heaven as the immortal paramour of Attracta, would be a triumph of sentimentality at the cost of tragic dignity. It would undercut the grim premises of the play, both depriving the Great Herne of his inscrutable majesty and making a romantic prince out of the doughty hero. And the next life *is* the issue, since for Congal to make Attracta his bride he must first die in this life.

If *Herne's Egg* has natural affinities with *The Player Queen* in its relatively large-scale exhibition of the follies of the lapsarian world, a pandemonium badly in need of redemption (and it does), its close thematic affiliations with *Clock Tower* and *Full Moon* are equally evident. The fiercely opposed parties are locked in a struggle to the death, each seeking to establish absolute dominion over the other. And the Queen or Muse or Priestess, half compelled and half willing to consummate an "impossible" union with a savior-victim-lover, precipitates the crisis. Being comedy, *Herne's Egg* gives us character as well as personality; Congal is a seasoned veteran of life's wars who has earned the right to tell the girlish Attracta the facts of life which her father, presumably, has kept hidden from her. Certainly we feel that Congal is old enough to be Attracta's father (though still virile enough, of course, to be a more than adequate lover). His various attempts to lay down the law and her virginal imperviousness to all his noble wickedness, however profound the symbolic overtones, have an irresistibly comic absurdity. The agon between Swineherd and Queen in *Full Moon* has the seed of comedy in it too, but there Yeats firmly excludes the comic perspective, mainly by the use he puts his lyrics to but also by the concentrated formality of his structure, especially his conception of the attendants. The Queen in *Full Moon* demonstrates her instinctive maternal feeling for the Swineherd, whom we assume to be a young man. In *Herne's Egg* Attracta offers Congal the herne's egg, as though inviting him to fertilize it—a gesture that would be brazen if she did not make it "unconsciously" (she is still in her trance).

The egg itself—what Melchiori calls (after Blake) "the mundane egg" [18]—is an image that had been accumulating significance in Yeats's mind for a very long time. In the beginning was the egg, or rather the "ever invisible, mysterious Bird that dropped an Egg into Chaos, which Egg became the Universe," as Madame Blavatsky wrote in *Secret Doctrine*.[19] Gradually the egg becomes Yeats's key symbol for the inauguration of each new historical cycle. Yeats gathered ideas from Blake, Aristophanes, Plato, the occult tradition and the lore of alchemy. From Leda's egg came Love and War, which make the world go round, but Yeats felt the need for a symbol that would *include* the world and go beyond his whirling gyres. Such a symbol is the sphere. In "Among School Children" Leda, the sphere, and the egg are "strictly associated." According to Wilson, "The Herne's egg represents the egg of Brahma, 'boundless infinity,' and it is also in a sense forbidden fruit, since Yeats has connected it with the 'circle pass not' of theosophy. Infinity is the province of the mystic, Attracta and her kind, and Congal's crime is that he tries to arrogate the egg to himself; that he claims for himself what is god's, and what man can come to share only through the medita-

[18] Melchiori, *The Whole Mystery of Art* (London, 1960), pp. 164–200.
[19] *Ibid.*, p. 165.

ive life." [20] And so we can compare Congal's theft, as Wilson does, with the eating of the forbidden fruit in the garden of Eden.[21] Such is the progress of the egg. Unlike Adam and Eve, however, Congal does not eat his stolen fruit. And Yeats leaves us with the puzzle of whether the role of Satan the tempter belongs more to Congal or to Attracta—or to the Great Herne himself.

[20] Wilson, *W. B. Yeats and Tradition*, p. 121.   [21] *Ibid.*

14

Two Views of the Hero's Fate: *Purgatory* and *The Death of Cuchulain*

Purgatory

Purgatory goes further than any other Yeats play in the direction of unredeemed and apparently unredeemable blackness. Symbols that elsewhere have an at least hopeful ambiguity here lead only to a dead end. To "study that tree" is to recognize that its glistening purity is not of the soul but of life reduced to a sterile stick. What was once the tree of life has now proved itself to be the tree of death. (Beckett is, at least in this respect, more hopeful in *Waiting for Godot*, where the tree has a few green leaves in the second act.) The ruined house is ironically related to more spiritually elevating sanctuaries which commemorate brilliant moments forever rescued from time (how far it is from the Castle Dargan extolled in *Clock Tower!*) The passion of those hoofbeats whose pounding will not cease in the Old Man's brain is a dirty passion. And though the Old Man's love-hate for his mother spurs him on, she herself can neither speak to him nor hear him. Insofar as the Old Man is given to know it, supernatural reality is a wholly dismal thing. No muse or priestess or beloved offers the Old Man a glimpse of mystic fulfillment. His

mother is not even cruel except involuntarily and inad-
vertently. There is no inspiring bird—only that predator,
the jackdaw, who has left no wholesome egg behind, nor
any egg at all—merely bits of eggshell thrown out of the
nest. A boy being lectured to by an old man hears a lesson
in history that ends with his own death.

In this tale of three generations that (in some sense) meet
at the fatal crossroads of this play, the woman is *literally*
the mother of the protagonist, though she appears to the
Old Man as a young girl, the way she was before he ever
knew her—in fact he sees her reenact the night of his conception. And her thoughts (unfortunately) are not on moth-
erhood at all. It was weak and wrong of her to give in to the
groom who was so far beneath her, but as the Old Man
watches her he has a moment of insight and sympathy—
his father was better-looking sixteen years before his son,
the Old Man, grew up to murder him. Yet she should have
known better, and *her* mother was quite right never to
speak to her again after the marriage. Nevertheless, whatever dignity and self-respect the Old Man has he owes to
his mother. He is the product of sin, and the sin consisted
in a mismating of bodies for which the Old Man holds his
father responsible.

The father proved his plebeian vulgarity by squandering
his wife's fortune to pay for his drinking and gambling—
luckily she never knew the worst because she died in giving birth to the Old Man. When he reached the age of sixteen he killed his father on the night when, being drunk,
the father set the house on fire, burning it and the great
library of books "modern and ancient" that were "made
fine/ By eighteenth-century French binding" and thereby
killing the precious continuity of aristocratic and learned

tradition. Though the Old Man loves the purified image of
his mother, he can no longer *see* it. His father has blasted
it. And the Old Man has continued the downward direction inaugurated by his father; his own sixteen-year-old
son is beside him as living proof of the fact. Now man and
boy have returned to the scene of the crime. Perhaps the
Old Man can force his son to see *his* vision of things. And
in a way he succeeds, though when the boy *does* see, all
he sees is the incomprehensible horror of "A dead, living
murdered man!" [1]

Essentially, the Old Man is utterly alone. He kills his
son almost, it seems, to prove that there is no contact between the worlds of the living and the dead.

> That beast there would know nothing, being nothing,
> If I should kill a man under the window
> He would not even turn his head.[2]

Once both his father and his son are dead, the Old Man
hopes that the way has been cleared for a guiltless communion with his mother, but the Old Man has no right to
a priestly office, and what he has done to his son turns out
to be simple murder, not a proper sacrifice. The beastly
taint in the blood cannot be exorcized, even though one
murder with the best will in the world, and the Old Man's
pathetic moment of illusion when he lullabies his dead son
as the baby of a knight and his lady bright quickly gives
way to the rationalization of his deed. He tries to see the
poor ruined tree as an image of his mother's liberated soul
and explains to her how he has ended all the evil consequences of her original mistake. But he has failed to break
the purgatorial cycle, as the returning hoofbeats remind

[1] *Collected Plays* (London, 1952), p. 687.   [2] *Ibid.*, p. 688.

him. Whatever the condition of his mother's soul may be, there is no doubt that the Old Man is suffering the fires of hell in *this* life. And at the end of the play he may well be damned, unless his cry to God from the depths of his misery shows that he has suddenly learned the meaning of true repentance. At any rate God is silent.

In *Purgatory* the squalor of material reality has descended from the stilts of myth that still made it loom fantastic in *Herne's Egg* and treads the familiar ground of lowly poverty and desolation. The Boy constantly reminds us of the real meanness of spirit that a life of begging entails. For him the stop in front of the ruined house is merely a meaningless interruption in a life of monotonous mobility that leads nowhere but from one door to the next. For the Old Man, of course, it is a cyclical return to the place of his origin. Throughout the play we have two time schemes: the Boy lives in an endless but immediate present that shades off into a blur at either end; the Old Man lives, or tries to, in the past of his memory and the future of his hope and dread. His imagination circles around obsessive events and he thinks in terms of repetitions, of anniversaries. The Boy glimpses this kind of significance when his father mentions that he was sixteen when the house burned down, for that is the boy's own age "at the Puck Fair," but the son has no inkling of what this is going to mean for him. The very idea of the intersections of times is horrifying to him—one might almost say that the shock of his discovery when he *sees* that he is related to a grandfather who still "lives" in the ruined house of time is enough to kill him. At least he cannot bear to look at what he has seen. By killing his son the Old Man hopes to escape from the cage of "mythical" time in which he is trapped, to awake from the nightmare of history, and to return to the normal world of eating and sleeping, of making a living and telling jokes. The climactic revelation of the play is that there is no escape from the greater reality once the inner eye has had a vision of it. Like Swift and Job, the Old Man could well say, "Perish the day on which I was born."

So in spite of its greater sense of reality in the everyday meaning of the word, *Purgatory* insists as much as its more obviously mythical companion pieces on a unity of existence larger than time, on a perspective from which, so to speak, time can be seen bending back to form the circle of eternity. But no promise of song from queen or saint, from bird or severed head, hangs in the expectant air. Only the return and the dying away simply to return again of hoofbeats signifying an ever-renewed fall into creation in the mind of a mad old man. For no less a myth than the Fall of Man is at the bottom of Yeats's naughty parable on eugenic breeding.

After the lowborn father has once again committed the act of lust with the mother, the Old Man sees him hunting for a glass to put his whiskey in. He leans at the window "like some tired beast." In the Old Man's memory springs up a line from Rossetti's *Eden Bower:* "Then the bride-sleep fell upon Adam." The first act of human procreation links itself ironically in the Old Man's mind with his own begetting. Irish history, romantic poetry, odd bits of philosophical erudition reach out from the Old Man's now confused memory toward some resolving synthesis that evades him. What he does not and cannot forget is the ideal for which his virginal mother stands: the ceremony and "innocence" of the aristocratic tradition. Knowing

himself to be a product of degradation, an Oedipus in rags
who loves his mother with an ambiguous purity but who
lacks entirely the ancient hero's kingly power to rid his
land of plague, the Old Man speaks all the more passionately because of his insider's knowledge of the decadent
life. Probably the oldest of Yeats's heroes, certainly past his
prime though still capable of murder, the Old Man retains the good of his intellect but has lost the key to heroic
action. Quite incapable of challenging God after the manner of Congal in *Herne's Egg*, the Old Man at last must
throw himself on His mercy.[3] The Yeatsian hero always
finds himself isolated, but the Old Man's isolation is the
cruellest of all. The play proves that, suspended between
a mother who *should* be too good for him and a son who
must be too bad for him, the Old Man has literally no one
to talk to.

Clark puts very well one effect of the severe compres-
sion of the play, the "effect of simultaneity," when he
says,

It is almost as if, at the moment of the knife thrust, one might
view all these actions happening together in a timeless instant:
the conception of the child who would grow to be the old
pedlar, the death of his mother in childbirth, the "killing" of
the house, the murder of the father, the conception of the
pedlar's son, and the murder of that son by his father.[4]

But if we are thus enabled to see history under the aspect
of eternity (i.e., to see it mythically), we are equally made

[3] Ure comments: "Yeats—can it be said?—has at last found a
use for God" (*Yeats the Playwright* [London, 1963], p. 107).
[4] Clark, *W. B. Yeats and the Theatre of Desolate Reality* (Dublin, 1965), p. 88.

aware of the agony of existing in time. In spite of its
Shakespearean echoes—particularly of *King Lear*—Yeats's
play is more like a compacted Greek tragedy in which the
curse on an ancient house brought about by an involuntary
act of guilt works itself out from generation to generation.
The Old Man cannot reconcile himself to the facts of life
nor can he escape them. To give up the furies that haunt
him would be to exchange his human condition (however
degraded) for the life of a mere beast. So he clings to a
memory that assures his moral identity at the expense of
keeping alive the fire of guilt that threatens to burn away
his mind entirely. Lacking knowledge of *A Vision*, though
he partly understands the lore of that book, he cannot take
satisfaction in a new age to come; and he has none of the
laughing serenity of a Chinese sage. Yet he does have clear
and absolute standards and stubbornly resists sinking to
the level of his cynically pragmatic son. One pleasure is
left him: the joy of a savage and scornful moral indignation.

In Wilson's opinion, "*Purgatory* is particularly concerned with the condition of humanity at a reversal of the
gyres, and Yeats's conclusion is that as a cycle nears its
end, brutality, violence, and terror are to be expected." [5]
Wilson shows with a wealth of detail the thought and
reading that lie behind the play, and he admits the relevance of understanding it as a commentary on recent Irish
history, though he rejects any allegorical reading of it in
favor of a symbolist one.[6] The difference between *Purgatory* and the other later plays is not a matter of theme or
idea primarily—it has obvious similarities to *Dreaming of
the Bones* in its use of the ghost theme, and the Old Man's

[5] Wilson, *Yeats and Tradition* (New York, 1958), p. 149.
[6] *Ibid.*, p. 156.

ideas have a good deal in common with those of Swift in *Words Upon the Window-Pane*—but of structure and language. And however striking and integral its use of the supernatural is, the brutality and terror are specifically modern and Irish in their background and meaning.

When interviewed about the play after the Abbey production in 1938, Yeats said in answer to a reporter from the *Irish Independent* who put the question of the play's symbolic meaning, previously raised by a Father Connolly, who had received no answer at a lecture by F. R. Higgins on Yeats the evening before:

Father Connolly said my plot is perfectly clear but that he does not understand my meaning. My plot is my meaning. I think the dead suffer remorse and re-create their old lives just as I have described. There are medieval Japanese plays about it, and much in the folklore of all countries.

In my play, a spirit suffers because of its share, when alive, in the destruction of an honoured house; that destruction is taking place all over Ireland today. Sometimes it is the result of poverty, but more often because a new individualistic generation has lost interest in the ancient sanctities.

I know of old houses, old pictures, old furniture that have been sold without apparent regret. In some few cases a house has been destroyed by a mesalliance. I have founded my play on this exceptional case, partly because of my interest in certain problems of eugenics, partly because it enables me to depict more vividly than would otherwise be possible the tragedy of the house.

In Germany there is special legislation to enable old families to go on living where their fathers lived. The problem is not Irish, but European, though it is perhaps more acute here than elsewhere.[7]

[7] Quoted in Torchiana, *Yeats and Georgian Ireland* (Evanston, Ill., 1966), pp. 357–358.

What Yeats insists on here is the relevance of his play to the Ireland of his immediate theater audience. And this comes through in the play itself. An actor who played the part of the Old Man told me in Sligo that he could imagine such an event taking place somewhere in the west of Ireland. Perhaps the scholar is at a disadvantage in knowing too much about Yeats's occult theories (which, of course, *are* there in the play); certainly this is so if his concern about symbolic meaning makes him miss the force of its grip on contemporary historical fact. Torchiana has worked out in ingenious detail the significance of dates in the play. Thus the destruction of the house, when the Old Man was sixteen, would have occurred about the time of Parnell's death in 1891. The Boy would have been born in August of 1922. The Saturnalian Puck Fair takes place in August. "The Fair, the beginning of the Free State, and the opening day of the play, August 10, 1938, all seem tied together." [8] The characters symbolize critical periods in Irish history as Yeats conceived them, according to Torchiana.[9] And Yeats's pressing concerns in *On the Boiler*, to which he intended *Purgatory* to form a conclusion, help re-enforce Torchiana's thesis.

What distinguishes *Purgatory* among Yeats's plays is the way it brings together archetypal family drama and specific cultural analysis. The Old Man, a more complicated figure than he first seems, is a link between past and present, between a visionary excellence and a darkling mediocrity, between parents and children. He not only knows both sides, he embodies them. And yet, old as he is, he has come to no settlement with life. His attempt to make a fresh start fails. Half learned and half ignorant, half hero

[8] *Ibid.*, p. 360.   [9] *Ibid.*, pp. 360–365.

and half silly old man, half speculative thinker and half violent man of action, he has attained an uneasy and ungolden mean.

The language Yeats has devised as a vehicle for this extraordinary creation is as subtle as—is indeed inseparable from—the creation itself. Of this language Clark has made the fullest technical analysis known to me. He shows how the rhythms of the irregular four-stress line imitate the action of a restless traveling "back and forth," "up and down," "in and out," "over and over," "time after time." [10] The diction accommodates itself to the speaking voice, though it draws on philosophy, the language of prayer, slang, and folk idiom for its terms. The syntax, sometimes distorted for effect, never gives the impression of being wrenched for some special artificial purpose. "In other words, Yeats is giving us not common speech but the qualities of actual speech in phrases which are new-created, archaic, or distorted, and therefore, have some of the purposeful difficulty of poetry." [11] By contrast with the language of *Purgatory*, the speech in the other plays is less unified; in them we are aware of a greater deliberateness in the intent, whether the language is jocular and colloquial or elevated and lyrical (which is not to say, of course, that this greater stratification and stylization is inappropriate; it often brilliantly justifies itself). In *Purgatory* the nervous urgency is so great that there is not time, so it seems, for ceremonious play with words. Paradoxically, a play which focusses on a horrible fixity in things and in which the two speaking characters hardly move from their appointed "spots" is, in its poetic rhythms, bursting with staccato energy. Surely something of its un-

[10] Clark, pp. 95ff.   [11] *Ibid.*, p. 95.

canny power comes from the tension between an outraged and frustrated potentiality for high thought and noble action and a stillness at the center, immovable, inexorable, malevolent and at the same time haunted by a poignant (though lost) sweetness and purity.

The Old Man has brought the Boy back to "study" the meaning of a once blessed but now accursed spot. He has called a temporary halt to the endless begging from the half-doors of the peasantry to the hall doors of the gentry. And the Boy realizes his father has "come this path before." The father is already wrapped in contemplations that mean nothing to his son—or so the Boy thinks—and the crazy tiresome talk has begun.

> The moonlight falls upon the path,
> The shadow of a cloud upon the house,
> And that's symbolical; study that tree,
> What is it like?

Boy.   A silly old man.[12]

This is a new kind of symbolical style. We feel the force of the Old Man's symbol-making power—for him the things of this world are symbolical not because he has a "poetic" imagination but because the subjective reality of memory will not let him see them otherwise. The Boy feels this compulsive quality in his father as lunacy. There is nothing difficult or obscure about the symbols themselves—a house under a cloud, a barren tree that was once a green tree—until the Old Man puts them under his nightmare magnifying glass. Then healthy foliage becomes "Green leaves, ripe leaves, leaves thick as butter,/ Fat,

[12] *Collected Plays*, p. 681.

greasy life." The leaves have become grotesque because
they have to take on the burden of meaning a once-rich
life in woeful contrast to the present lean and shabby existence of the Old Man. As this studious play reveals, the
Old Man is tormented not only by the decline of a noble
life to decay and ruin but by his effort to comprehend the
meaning of it all. (One might have expected him to
acquire wisdom with old age, but Yeats was very sceptical
of ancient wisdom in *that* sense.) The Boy sees history—if
he can be said to see it at all—as a junk heap not worth
investigating. His retort about the tree is very much in
order from his point of view. As a pupil, the Boy intends
to respond to his pedantic teacher with impudent (and deflating) common sense. He wants "what we all want"—
money, drink, sex. The rest is nonsense.

By the time the Old Man has reached the eloquence of
the passage about the house—"Great people lived and died
in this house"—he is essentially talking to himself. He declares his father to have been guilty of a "capital offense"
and thus retrospectively passes judgment on the criminal
for whom he long since served as executioner. His "Cherry
Orchard" mood is entirely lost on the Boy, but the Old
Man here, nevertheless, finally kindles his son's imagination. "My God, but you had luck! Grand clothes,/ And
maybe a grand horse to ride." And now the tension between father and son grows as the Boy is led to compare
his "luck" with his father's. When the father is ready to
reveal the dreadful family secret, for the first time the Boy
addresses him as "Father." The father's description of the
bloody deed and its consequences is swift, direct, and cir-
cumstantial; it is as unsentimental and unsymbolical as the
Boy could wish. And it is ominous. "I stuck him with a

knife,/ That knife that cuts my dinner now,/ And after that I left him in the fire." The Old Man has saved the knife as though it were a holy relic or a hero's magic sword, but it equally serves the "profane" purpose of a butcher knife. And no matter how high-minded the Old Man's defense of his deed, he still appears—and knows himself to be—a murderer. The trade of pedlar was good enough for him, as he says,

> Because I am my father's son,
> Because of what I did or may do.[13]

The Boy has been fairly warned, if warning were needed. And Yeats has exhibited the range of stylistic prowess with which he has endowed the Old Man, from introspective pedant to eloquent defender of the past to scornful chronicler of his own career.

The next step is into the haunted world of the Old Man's ghost-ridden imagination, and here the Boy cannot yet follow him. The Boy does not hear the hoofbeats or see the young girl in the lit-up window. But Yeats has steadily raised the temperature of expectancy and kept us off balance by making the Old Man seem shrewd as well as crazy, pious as well as savage. We don't yet know what to make of him. But with "Do not let him touch you!" we are plunged into a peculiar realm of speculation. The Old Man is quite aware that the spirits of his father and mother would not hear him if he threw a "stick or a stone" and considers this "a proof my wits are out"; yet the problem of whether his parents renew pleasure as well as remorse in the act of conceiving him is not only *real* but pressing.

[13] *Ibid.*, p. 685.

> I lack schooling.
> Go fetch Tertullian; he and I
> Will ravel all that problem out
> Whilst those two lie upon the mattress
> Begetting me.
>   Come back! Come back!
> And so you thought to slip away,
> My bag of money between your fingers
> And that I could not talk and see! [14]

The magisterial tone of the Old Man's "I lack schooling," his ridiculous command (apparently) to the Boy to fetch Tertullian in this godforsaken spot, his associating himself as a colleague of the philosopher, and his cool acceptance of the idea that all this is taking place while he himself is being conceived—this is a truly breathtaking example of extravagant condensation. Nothing in the crazed King Lear's imagination is handled more audaciously. It would be hilarious if Yeats (or the Old Man) did not have such firm control of the dramatic context. But this is not all. The Old Man does not allow the brilliance of his inner sight to obscure the sharpness of his outer vision. The Boy is not going to be allowed to get away with anything. The Old Man's spiritual treasure may be locked in the past—or in eternity—but he never forgets that he is living in the dirty present. Father and son are of the same blood and have more in common than either would care to admit. By such rapid juxtapositions does Yeats create the effect of vast reaches of mental and physical consequence contracted into a little space.

This Old Man (perhaps unfortunately for him) is no dreamer withdrawn from the grim realities of life. He may

[14] *Ibid.*, p. 686.

—he does—have too many things on his mind at once, but the forces of distintegration are matched by a savage energy of mind and will. His half-lost learning and distorted piety cannot prevent his iron determination to cast out "evil consequence." Over and over he demonstrates the power of mind to inhabit physical places, as when he says of the image of his drunken father at the window,

> And yet
> There's nothing leaning in the window
> But the impression upon my mother's mind;
> Being dead she is alone in her remorse.[15]

Even the Boy is compelled to see this bestial image because it corresponds to the level of his own imagination, though he lacks his father's power to distinguish "impressions." The horror the Boy sees leads to his death, for he covers his eyes (which is as good as offering himself for sacrifice). Seeing his father in the window is too much for the Old Man—he cannot get at this mere "impression," but neither can the impression get at him—and seeing the likeness (perhaps even identity) of his father and his son, he does what he can: he stabs the Boy. The Old Man should now be safe with his own mother. At any rate the window darkens, and we have the nearest we get to song in this play.

> 'Hush-a-bye baby, thy father's a knight,
> Thy mother a lady, lovely and bright.'

Typically, the Old Man is not permitted to luxuriate in pleasurable illusion even long enough to complete a stanza before his merciless intellect returns to the task of analysis.

---

[15] *Ibid.*, pp. 687–688.

No, that is something that I read in a book,
And if I sing it must be to my mother,
And I lack rhyme.[16]

The Old Man is a fool with a style to mock philosophers
as well as knights of romance. But he is an absolutely serious fool. He is the very opposite of a sceptic; he is the hero
as believer whose beliefs lead only to the most dreadful
parody of the heroic action of old. And yet he would not
establish the grip on us that he does if in addition to his
erudition and passion he did not have the grimy aspect of
a pedlar wandering the roads of the *present*.

Yeats, of course, did not arrive at such a destination
without some of the usual toil. In an eight-page scenario
he imagines the scene more fully than it appears in the
finished version of the play. The ruined home is provided
with a large window, a door, and a garden walk or hedge,
and "the characters are to be well-lighted by a stream of
moonlight falling on the front of the stage." [17] We learn
that "the boy's grandparents will relive a crime committed
sixty-three years before." The main events are outlined
much as they appear in the play, but the killing of the Boy
is more directly related to the vision he has just seen—he
obeys his father's commands as though hypnotized. As
Bradford transcribes it, the scenario ends this way:

Come, come, come, I say, that I may kill, and my mother find
rest now that the evil is finished. (BOY *rises and comes slowly
to* OLD [MAN], *who stabs him. The vision fades. As it fades*

[16] *Ibid.*, p. 688.
[17] Bradford, *Yeats at Work* (Carbondale and Edwardsville,
1965), pp. 295ff.

the hoof beats are heard again.) O my God, she does not understand—her agony, her agonized joy, or her remorse begin
all over again. Even when mother sees all [her soul] does not
understand that the evil set in motion is finished. O my God,
what is man? Are they never ending, the misery of the living
and the remorse of the dead? [18]

This is a considerable distance from the final ending.
Events and explanation are huddled together with a rapidity that has its own excitement but that would hardly
allow an audience time to catch its breath. But this passage
does make clear one meaning of the Boy's seeing of the
vision which he had earlier "refused" to see. Deprived of
his cynical, common sense view of the world by the over-
mastering power of the ancestral imagination, the Boy
unconsciously (?) admits his guilty membership in his accursed family and half voluntarily offers himself as an ex-
piatory sacrifice to put an end to the horror. Ure points
out that in the play the Boy sees the grandfather but not
the grandmother, and suggests as a reason that the Boy's
"evil nature cannot 'dramatize' it [apparition of the grand-
mother]." [19] Perhaps so. Maybe the Boy's "revelation" is
so unendurably horrible that it completely unmans him,
leaving him as evil and ignorant as he ever was. On the
other hand, Torchiana suggests that "only before his death
does he [the Boy] begin to see the light of his grandmother's purgatorial dream. Does Yeats hope that the sixteen-year-old Eire will also see its light?" [20] So we might
consider the boy's shock of recognition as a horror that
suddenly invests him with a previously unknown re-

---

[18] *Ibid.*, pp. 296–297.   [19] Ure, p. 104, footnote.
[20] Torchiana, p. 363.

morse.* In any event, we can agree with Nathan that Yeats allows us to think that the "presences" the Old Man sees may be his private illusions. "Wishing to preserve this ambiguity, Yeats withheld until the play's climax the Boy's shocked confirmation that the Old Man does, in fact, see actual ghosts." [21] Unless we choose a transcendent ambiguity, and say that the Old Man has succeeded in imposing his "illusions" on his son as he imposes his knife on the Boy's body!

To return to Bradford's account of Yeats's working out of the play, we remark the long struggle Yeats had to put it into verse. Nevertheless, he wrote it more speedily than such plays as *The Resurrection* or *A Full Moon in March*.[22] His dramatic conception is unusually fully worked out to begin with, and we feel a personal urgency behind the play exceptional even for Yeats. The structure of his fable, it seems to me, might be diagrammed as a circle which, winding around its center, contracts until it becomes a single point. On opposite sides of the circle are father and son, each trying to wind the circle in a different direction. They are engaged in a struggle for power to see whose view of reality shall prevail. Presiding over their agon are the ruined house and the blasted tree, ominous symbols of temple and garden turned into tomb and desert. Unknown to the agonists, this is a place and time of final reckoning. The father wins (as he did long ago, but how differently, in *On Baile's Strand*) by "converting" his son.

---

* Though Torchiana does not mention this, might not the play's harping on "sixteen" also be intended to set up an ironic echo of Easter, 1916, in the minds of the audience?

[21] Nathan, *The Tragic Drama* (New York, 1965), p. 247.

[22] Bradford, p. 301.

It is as though the malevolent deity of *The Herne's Egg* had been incorporated in the Old Man, who in a mocking parody of the story of the Prodigal Son sentences his child to death to pay for a crime committed by the Boy's grandfather—and, to be sure, the Boy might be a reincarnation of his grandfather, judging by his behavior. At the center of the play looms the Old Man's mother, a burning light that refuses to be extinguished. Neither goddess nor priestess nor muse, she yet occupies the place "vacated" by them. One of Yeats's most powerful characters, she says nothing and appears only to the mind's eye.

The Death of Cuchulain

Yeats had written in 1927 to Olivia Shakespear, after giving a humorous account of a mysterious kiss a woman claimed to have seen his wife giving him at a performance of *Oedipus* (but she was shocked to find when George came in that George was *not* the woman) and of a mysterious ghostly dog who had barked in the middle of a performance of *Colonus*, that he was "still of opinion that only two topics can be of the least interest to a serious and studious mind—sex and the dead." [23] In *The Death of Cuchulain* these two topics are intertwined, as so often before, to spin the fate of the hero. One effect of the dramatic summary of Cuchulain's career in this play is to remind us how much more important women are than men in the hero's life. Encircled by Eithne, Aoife, Maeve, the Morrigu, and Emer, Cuchulain is the darling and victim of the adoration he inspires.

In contrast to the tense concentration into which *Purgatory* almost immediately plunges us, the bold, arrogant, and gaily self-deprecating prologue of *Death* offers us a

[23] *Letters* (London, 1954), p. 730.

frank entertainment. Speaking for Yeats, the Old Man compliments his audience by comparing them with the select few who attended the first performance of Milton's *Comus*. And he heightens the flattery by contrasting them with the "pick-pockets and opinionated bitches" who think they are cultured but who, we may be sure, don't know "the old epics and Mr. Yeats' plays about them." Then he explains his aesthetic. The dance play we are about to witness will celebrate the mythology to which the Old Man "belongs," there will be severed heads for Emer to dance before, and there will be "the music of the beggar-man, Homer's music." The Old Man spits upon "the dancers painted by Degas" because they represent, to him, not timeless passion, "love and loathing, life and death," but a mechanical and meaningless submission to "that old maid history." The play will be a proud assertion of the *permanence* of myth in defiance of what the ravages of time can do.

The play dispenses with "theological" explanations; everything is reduced to plot, and the plot lays before us the essential *vita* of Cuchulain. A lover of women, a master of fate, a high and lonely spirit, a victim of fools and yet an immortal ideal, he is in the process of drawing up his will (in a double sense), of disengaging himself from life. And there are those who are ready to help him on his way. Eithne comes bearing a message, ostensibly from Emer, that he must "out and fight" at once. His house is burning and there is no time to lose. But she carries a letter in her hand which says the opposite—on no account must he move, for he would face overwhelming odds; tomorrow Conall Caernach will arrive with re-enforcements. Maeve has cast her enchantment over the girl, putting lying words on Eithne's tongue. Jokingly, Cuchulain says that what makes it certain he will not stir till morning is Eithne's arrival to be his bedfellow, but he immediately proceeds to reassure her that it is his choice to fight, despite Emer's letter.

The Morrigu, the war goddess, is suddenly standing between them, unseen by either but clearly manifest to Eithne, who has felt the touch of a black wing on her shoulder. Now she understands that Maeve, no longer the pretty creature she was when she slept with the boyish Cuchulain but a monster with "an eye in the middle of her forehead," had put her in a trance. Cuchulain scoffs at these superstitious explanations and analyzes the problem "realistically." He is too old; Eithne needs a younger man; she fears Cuchulain's violence but really wishes him dead. Eithne rises to the challenge by saying that Maeve's strategy makes perfectly good sense—whose word would Cuchulain be more likely to trust than Eithne's? Cuchulain reminds her that it was Emer who brought him back from the sea after his maddened fight with the waves. And Eithne counters, "but 'twas to me you turned." This Cuchulain cannot deny, nor can she deny the implication he draws from it: only her youthful beauty and the warmth of her arms can comfort Cuchulain, and she is in mortal terror lest he kill her when, as it must, her bodily attraction begins to wither. This is the fate of all sublunary things, and if Cuchulain has not changed, "that goes to prove/ That I am monstrous." Stung by his coldblooded acceptance of time's callousness, Eithne flings out that indeed he *has* changed.

Like Deirdre trying to play chess with Naoise while they wait for death, Eithne breaks down. Her outcry is a protest against losing the Cuchulain she has loved, against

the accusations she will go to any lengths to prove are un-
just, and ultimately against that greatest murderer of precious things, time itself. She promises to condemn herself of
treachery and invite whatever horrible death Cuchulain's
avengers wish to inflict on her, if only in the end "my
shade can stand among the shades/ And greet your shade
and prove it is no traitor." Unlike Dido, she would gladly
embrace her lover's shade in that other world forever deprived of the sun. But already she and Cuchulain belong to
different kingdoms. There is nothing more for them to say
to each other. Yet Cuchulain must provide for her and
protect her against herself. Telling a servant how she has
accused herself of treachery, he asks how she can be kept
from harm. To the servant's question, "Is her confession
true?" Cuchulain imperiously declares,

> I make the truth!
> I say she brings a message from my wife.[24]

In the event of his death, he directs the servant to see that
she is given to Conall Caernach "because the women/
Have called him a good lover." Eithne must be content
that the Morrigu is an unimpeachable witness in her defense. Cuchulain, with the detached insight of a man with
one foot already in eternity, understands Eithne better
than she understands herself. He loves her, but he will not
mar his leavetaking by an unseemly show of emotion. His
passion is within and must be detached from the temporal
pains and pleasures he is about to abandon forever.

So ends the first part of the play. It is a masterly evocation of heroic fortitude that might be mistaken for a dry
and cruel arrogance if it were not so clear that both lovers,

[24] *Collected Plays*, p. 698.

in their different ways, are fearfully concerned about each other's future. Their defiance is not so much directed at each other as at the fatal Morrigu that stands between them, unassailable and inexorable. Cuchulain, old in experience but still in the vigorous prime of life, is doomed; yet he has deliberately chosen his destiny even as it was thrust upon him. Eithne flutters like a netted bird, wildly beating its wings to escape when there is no escape. Cuchulain is "monstrous" in his heroism exactly because he does not yield to external pressure but remains his own steady center of action. Three fates conspire against him: Maeve, who in her supernatural monstrosity has become a symbol of the world's hatred for what is greater and stronger than a worldling has any right to be (and who, more specifically, is a rejected love of Cuchulain's youth); Eithne, who against her own will is on the same side as Maeve, being but a passing fancy Cuchulain must also leave behind when destiny beckons; and the Morrigu, at once the most abstract and the most powerful shaper of Cuchulain's end, who calls him to his warrior's vocation and, as a figure of death, rapes him from life (we might say) in order to possess him wholly for herself. But their combined efforts to eject Cuchulain from mortality are made to seem feeble beside the hero's own self-possessed, almost serene, mastery of circumstance. He is in command, he chooses, he "makes the truth." And sees it too. By choosing his role long ago, he determined his fate; and now his fate determines him. And one aspect of the lot he has chosen—a compensation for all he has given up—is that he will ride to his end as a horseman rides into battle, disposing his fortune as *he* wills, neither hurried nor delayed by the world pressing in about him. If his last scene with Eithne has the poignancy of

Age saying farewell to Youth, it also has the astringency of an unmoved mover turning his back on life.

In the second part, the necessity to act is past and Cuchulain can let death come as it will—except for one final action, fastening himself by his belt to the pillar-stone so he may die upright. Aoife, a "white-haired woman," at least as much older than Cuchulain as Eithne is younger, has come to kill him. Cuchulain does not know where he is, or why. Aoife explains and helps him fasten the belt. They recall the events in the story of *On Baile's Strand*, and Cuchulain admits her right to kill him. She wraps her veil around him despite Cuchulain's remonstrance against soiling it with his blood. ("Your veils are beautiful, some with threads of gold.") But she is "too old to care for such things now." The gesture is eloquent of the love that still binds them together. Conquered in battle, she had given her virginity to Cuchulain though she had intended to kill him in his sleep. And their son had grown up to die at his father's hands. Cuchulain, now distant from such passions, cannot understand hers.

But a "just" death from her motherly hands is not to be his. They are interrupted by another relic from the past, the Blind Man from *On Baile's Strand*, and Aoife withdraws, planning to complete her mission later. Like the fool in *Herne's Egg*, he hopes to get pennies for delivering a hero's head to those who wish the great man's death. Ironically, it adds to a hero's dignity to be killed by a small man; it proves no big man is great enough to do the job. (Compare Achilles, shot in the heel by Paris's poisoned arrow.) Cuchulain's sardonic comment—"Twelve pennies! What better reason for killing a man?"—is lost on the "good sense" of this human scavenger. The Blind Man

gets at his knife and begins feeling his way up to Cuchulain's neck. The hero sees floating "out there" the shape
waiting to receive his soul, "a soft feathery shape," odd
for "a great fighting-man." Uninterested in what Cuchulain sees or does not see, the Blind Man goes about his
work. In answer to the question whether he is ready
Cuchulain replies, "I say it is about to sing."

When the curtain rises on a bare stage, we see the Morrigu with her crow's head holding "a black parallelogram
the size of a man's head." Near the backcloth are six other
parallelograms. She addresses the dead (and us), explaining who the owners of the six heads, the men responsible
for Cuchulain's six mortal wounds, were. She has "ar-
ranged the dance." She yields the stage to Emer, who
dances her rage against Cuchulain's foes and her adoration
of him. She seems to hear something and stands motionless,
and then we hear it—"in the silence a few faint bird
notes." Yes, Cuchulain's soul has taken its new shape. But
his head sings no song we can understand. The stage darkens, and the past is swallowed up in the present. The
music of "some Irish Fair of our day" strikes our ears;
Emer and the heads have vanished from the brightened
stage. In their place are three ragged musicians. One of
them sings the song "the harlot sang to the beggar-man."
The memory of the heroic tradition is in their keeping.
The song tells a story and asks a question: "Are those
things that men adore and loathe/ Their sole reality?" At
least for an old man (and it seems as though a second singer
is answering the first, though Yeats does not have it this
way) a hero's bodily prowess means little. The living
reality comes from spirit, unimpaired by the passing of
time.

> What stood in the Post Office
> With Pearse and Connolly?
> What comes out of the mountain
> Where men first shed their blood?
> Who thought Cuchulain till it seemed
> He stood where they had stood? [25]

Aoife's confrontation with Cuchulain recalls a past both more distant and more crucial than his life with Eithne. A teacher who had inducted him into the mysteries of heroism, Aoife wishes to exercise that exclusive claim over him that all his lovers desire. As Cuchulain himself had recognized in *On Baile's Strand*, love for him is like the lion's tooth, as it is for Crazy Jane. He is destined never to know love

> but as a kiss
> In the mid-battle, and a difficult truce
> Of oil and water, candles and dark night,
> Hillside and hollow, the hot-footed sun
> And the cold, sliding, slippery-footed moon—
> A brief forgiveness between opposites. [26]

Love is not love unless it resists the hero's impetuous onward course through the thick and thin of battle to his predestined end. Nor is Cuchulain Cuchulain unless he rips himself free from love's entanglements. For love is the demand that the sun stand still, that time give way to eternity, if only for a precious moment. True lovers never surrender their right to the impossible, even though time mocks them to their faces—and thereby they may achieve a miracle, but only at the cost of leaving the flesh behind.

[25] *Ibid.*, p. 705.   [26] *Ibid.*, p. 259.

Aoife has been the patron goddess of her hero. In a sense she gave birth to him and has a right to lay him out.

She has come to seek a just revenge—as Cuchulain acknowledges—for his disloyalty to her, but even more her coming is an act of piety—to perform the last rites due to an authentic hero. She combines a mother's proud curiosity to learn all she can about the son whom Cuchulain killed and whom she will avenge with a lover's determination to see that Cuchulain's death does not lack the dignity he deserves. But as his life has shown, Cuchulain does not belong to her any more than he belongs to Eithne. His death at the hands of the Blind Man not only shows how indifferent the "low" are to heroic merit; it also shows that Cuchulain, whatever his superhuman attainments, belongs to mankind. Which, of course, does not mean that the Blind Man has the power to put an end to heroism. With his dying words Cuchulain asserts his faith in his own survival. And Emer's dance proves he has "come through." It is *her* love, first and last, that is the greatest, for as *The Only Jealousy of Emer* bore witness, she alone is able to love Cuchulain without possessing him. She asks only that her love may safeguard and preserve him, not that it bend him to her will. Among her other functions, the Morrigu is an overseer of justice, for it is only right that Emer, after all, should perform the final leavetaking. And the Morrigu attends to that.

For the rest, Cuchulain's fate is in "our" hands. At the beginning of the play the Old Man explained, with the *sprezzatura* of desperation, his commitment to mythology and his contempt of "that old maid history." He used the metaphor advisedly. History, unseeded by the love and loathing that only the mythological imagination can make real, is barren. By hyperbolic implication Mr. Yeats and the "saving remnant" in his audience are the sacred keepers of the racial heritage. At the end of the play we return to the present once more, but no Old Man addresses us. It is not the connoisseurs of Milton who are commemorating the heroic dead, but a harlot. In her song to the beggar-man she tells of meeting the ancient heroes "face to face." They live in her imagination, but she does not confuse them with the flesh and blood present, which compels her loathing as well as her adoration. Art, as in the example of Oliver Sheppard's statue, does bear witness to the everliving sources of adoration, and the harlot's song testifies how deep that adoration goes.

It also shows the robust humor and rough sensuality of Yeats's late ballad style. The harlot's appreciation of "that most ancient race" of the Red Branch heroes is firmly rooted in pride of body.

> Maeve had three in an hour, they say.
> I adore those clever eyes,
> Those muscular bodies, but can get
> No grip upon their thighs.
> I meet those long pale faces,
> Hear their great horses, then
> Recall what centuries have passed
> Since they were living men.[27]

In the play we have just seen the adoration that Cuchulain could not help provoking in women, though there love and hate were entangled with past deeds and expressed in terms of a sensuality sublimated into a self-conscious if simple dignity. The harlot is franker. The legends have

[27] *Ibid.*, p. 704.

power to stir her to erotic fantasy (we note, however, that she thinks of "clever" not soulful eyes and "muscular" not sculptural bodies) but she "can get/ No grip upon their thighs." There *are* disadvantages to being dead, even for heroes. Nevertheless, the harlot is spellbound by "those long pale faces" and the sound of "their great horses." The intent conviction of those passionate riders as they thunder by on their heroic business still lives for her, even if they are (and have been) ghosts for many centuries. In comparison the lovers she has known in the flesh cannot help reminding her of her degradation even while she exults in the pleasure of interlocked thighs. So she recalls

> That there are still some living
> That do my limbs unclothe,
> But that the flesh my flesh has gripped
> I both adore and loathe.[28]

The "some" is ambiguous—we are not sure whether they too are to be classed with clever-eyed and muscular-bodied heroes who simply had the misfortune of being known in the flesh, or whether they are more ordinary fellows, perfectly capable of giving and taking virile pleasure but with no pretensions to anything grander. At any rate, fleshliness necessarily involves loathing as well as adoration.

"Adore" and "loathe" remind us of the Old Man of the prologue, who spoke of the "tragi-comedian dancer" who bore "upon the same neck love and loathing, life and death." The dancers painted by Degas offended him because they are mere "objective" reflectors of history, mindless and passionless like the "old maid" they reflect. The Old Man believes in myth because severed heads that sing

[28] *Ibid.*

prove that there is something beyond the otherwise mean-
ngless drift of history. He has said of the musicians that
'I will teach them, if I live, the music of the beggar-man,
Homer's music." The harlot's song would seem to indicate
that he had succeeded. Though his point of view identifies
him with the intellectual and artistic élite, whereas the harlot belongs to the "folk" who do not worry about art or
thinking but know what they like, both "adore" the cold
passion of heroes who give themselves fully to life just because they do not value it too highly and "loathe" what
reminds them of the stench of mortality, whether of body
or soul.

Thus Yeats binds his play together, dramatizing for us
the things which we ought to adore (Cuchulain's magnanimity, coolness, and supreme self-confidence; the
"timeless" devotion of his feminine admirers) and the
things we ought to loathe (Maeve's dirty tactics, the Blind
Man's "good sense"). Comparatively, the play is thin in
verbal imagery; it gets its resonance from our memories
of the past—specifically of the past Yeats has given us.
The Death of Cuchulain does *literally* depend on our
knowledge of "the old epics and Mr. Yeats' plays about
them." Yet we might remark on two unifying images, the
veil Aoife wraps around Cuchulain like a winding sheet
and the pillar-stone to which he attempts to tie himself.
The play shows the efforts of those around him to en-
tangle Cuchulain so that he can be caught and dispatched;
ironically, Cuchulain is only too willing to go to his death,
but he intends to go clear-eyed and unillusioned, not like
a rat caught in a trap. Unlike the Cuchulain of the earlier
plays in the series, he is not locked in combat with others
or with himself. All that is behind him. He has loved and

hated many things and people, and risked death (and life) for them, but death itself he has never feared. Now he wishes to die upright. The pillar-stone, his sacrificial stake is also the very image and symbol of his rocklike firmness and his indestructible vitality. Aoife's veil is rich with her undying love; she uses her love to help bind him more securely to himself. With the help of those who love him Cuchulain will, to borrow Auden's words, die a "vertical man." *

We see Cuchulain die his life and live his death. And Yeats has thought it fitting to return to blank verse to write this valedictory for his favorite hero. In the first part of the play, where Cuchulain is disengaging himself from the world of transitory things, he is cruel to Eithne Inguba only to be kind. But she cannot and will not understand.

> You're not the man I loved,
> That violent man forgave no treachery.
> If, thinking what you think, you can forgive,
> It is because you are about to die.[29]

Cuchulain would have her speak more softly if she would speak of his death, or at least "not in that strange voice exulting in it." But he is not angry. His strange calm only arouses her passion, and she cries out

* Let us honor if we can
The vertical man,
Though we value none
But the horizontal one.

From W. H. Auden, *Collected Shorter Poems: 1927–1957* (Random House, Inc., 1967).

[29] *Ibid.*, p. 697.

When you are gone
I shall denounce myself to all your cooks
Scullions, armourers, bed-makers, and messengers,
Until they hammer me with a ladle, cut me with a knife,
Impale me upon a spit, put me to death
By what foul way best please their fancy,
So that my shade can stand among the shades
And greet your shade and prove it is no traitor.[30]

This is a Dido indeed anxious to greet the shade of her Aeneas! All the passion is now on her side, and we see how easily Yeats's verse accommodates itself to this rising torrent of anguished protest. It is equally at ease in the quieter passages. Whether "high" or "low," it carries the intonations of the speaking voice. Nevertheless, it serves to distance the play contained between the prose of the Old Man's prologue and the harlot's song.

For Yeats, the harlot, as Wilson has reminded us, is the symbolic matrix of the civilization to come.[31] Influenced by Indian thought and the Noh tradition, Yeats connects her with attitudes opposed to Christian values, but not on that account immoral. In fact, as far back as "The Adoration of the Magi" he had thought of the harlot figure as a priestess of the new annunciation, and Blake's identification of Mary with harlotry in "The Everlasting Gospel" and in *Jerusalem* obviously had a profound effect on Yeats's symbolic picture of those radical opposites which the human imagination strives to restore to their original unity. Wilson convincingly argues that "Yeats's harlot figure . . . represents all that is cast out in this era, all that

[30] *Ibid.*, pp. 697–698.
[31] Wilson, *W. B. Yeats and Tradition*, pp. 177–180.

will be justified in the era to come." [32] I am not so sure that he is right, however, in interpreting the final song in *Death* as assuring us that divinity "will beget the heroes of a new age" on *this* harlot.[33] She is no Leda. Nevertheless, if her adoration helps keep the memory of "that most ancient race" alive, she will be contributing to those divine conjunctions when a terrible beauty is born and small men discover a greatness within—Cuchulain has "stood where they had stood." In death as in life, Cuchulain's "keeping" is a woman's work.

Whether the harlot's loathing applies to the living whom she has known in the flesh or, as Wilson thinks, to the dead who are fleshless, her imagination is completely dominated by the heroic dead. Though "an old man looking on life" may scorn any bodily image—even Cuchulain's—because it is so insignificant compared to the spirit that made it heroic (after all, a blind man can extinguish the body for twelve pennies but not the singing spirit), harlot and old man *essentially* agree in spite of their different perspectives. They adore that regenerative power that once planted in the human imagination not only refuses to die but gives the living a permanent standard by which the shortcomings of timebound life can be loathed or scorned. The act of creation—be it sexual, military, philosophic, or artistic—gains its reality by wedding blood to song, mortal impulse to an immortal tune. When motive becomes unworthy, when the ideal fails and the riderless horse becomes a rampaging centaur, eternity must rage at the products of time. Cuchulain going to his death displays his heroism in a new and icy vein. As he disappears from our view, so our view must fade for him. No wonder he exas-

[32] *Ibid.*, p. 180.   [33] *Ibid.*, p. 185.

perates Eithne with his imperturbable magnanimity and treats Aoife and the Blind Man with impartial and laconic justice. His passion is no longer directed at them, as it once was; he has successfully detached his soul from his body *before* the Blind Man separates the heroic head from the mortally wounded trunk. In this last play, Cuchulain truly succeeds in casting a cold eye on life, on death.

It will be apparent that Wilson's characterization of *Death* as "a play of rejoicing" [34] seems much nearer the mark to me than Vendler's judgment that it is spoiled by "obscurity and confusion." [35] It is a forbidding play, almost completely lacking in charm and warmth, but intentionally so. Without the prologue and the conclusion, its compacted narrative would indeed seem unsatisfying, but the fierce humor of the first and the intense conviction of the second give both motive and meaning to the rugged calm they enclose. Ure, regarding the play proper as self-contained, sees "the death of the hero . . . as the final irony of his fate." [36] And so it is, but surely we lessen the play if we disregard the irony directed at *us*. Besides, as Ure's own analysis shows, there is far more than irony involved in the kind of success Yeats achieves. I think Ure is right in pointing to the intentional irony of breaking the pattern of "what is plainly [the play's] one right ending"—that Aoife should revenge the death of her son—by abruptly bringing in the Blind Man to take over her role. [37] But both the irony and the majesty of what Ure calls "the most perfect of the fine [Cuchulain] plays" [38]

[34] *Ibid.*, p. 163.
[35] Vendler, *Yeats's Vision* (Cambridge, Mass., 1963), p. 247.
[36] Ure, p. 78.   [37] *Ibid.*, p. 81.   [38] *Ibid.*, p. 82.

would be incomplete without Emer's dance and the harlot's song. Nathan compares Cuchulain's magnanimity with Achilles' generosity in returning Hector's body to Priam (it seems to me that Achilles is just coming to realize something that Cuchulain is on the point of leaving behind, but the two heroes *do* share a kind of tragic poise) and *does* think Cuchulain achieves a kind of transfiguration: "It is the hero's triumph that he sees and accepts, and yet can prophesy a singing beyond his death." [39] Opinion of the play seems to divide on whether Yeats is still in command of his craft or has lost his grip. So Bjersby feels the play "is written by a man, in whom the need for passion is still alive, but who tries in vain to stir up this passion." [40] On the other hand, Frank Kermode says, "this superb play has a deliberate quality of personal allegory which must always dominate our interests." [41] Compared to *Purgatory*, *Death* seems to me both gayer and more personal. It lacks the remarkable unity of effect and the power of blackness in *Purgatory*, but it opens outward and upward instead of inward and downward. *Death* restores a balance.

[39] Nathan, p. 201.
[40] Birgit Bjersby, *The Interpretation of the Cuchulain Legend in the Works of W. B. Yeats* (Upsala, 1950), p. 103.
[41] Frank Kermode, *Romantic Image* (London, 1957), p. 82.

[15]

Conclusion

Yeats belongs more to the Symbolist tradition than to any other, but his kind of anti-realism is nevertheless quite distinct from the variety developed in Paris by such writers as Maeterlinck in the 1890's. Rémy de Gourmont's satirical sketch of the "ideal" Symbolist play is more telling and concise than abstract analysis can be:

Hidden in mist somewhere there is an island, and on that island there is a castle, and in that castle there is a great room lit by a little lamp. And in that room people are waiting. Waiting for what? They don't know! They're waiting for someone to knock at their door, waiting for their lamp to go out, waiting for Fear and Death. They talk. Yes, they speak words that shatter the silence of the moment. And then they listen again, leaving their sentences unfinished, their gestures uncompleted. They are listening. They are waiting. Will she come perhaps, or won't she? Yes, she will come; she always comes. But it is late, and she will not come perhaps until the morrow. The people collected under that little lamp in that great room have, nevertheless, begun to smile; they still have hope. Then there is a knock—a knock, and that is all there is; And it is Life Complete, all of Life.[1]

[1] Quoted from *Le Livre des masques* in John Gassner, *Form and Idea in Modern Drama* (New York, 1956), p. 101.

This provides an uncanny prevision of *Waiting for Godot*, a play which might fittingly be described as the end of the Symbolist line, or perhaps a parody of it. Beckett is coarser, grimmer, funnier, and more serious than is the writer this sketch adumbrates, but the portentous *waiting* characteristic of the Symbolist mode is very well caught. In Yeats's drama too there is typically a strained spiritual expectancy. The waiting, however, is always combined with activity; people move toward their destiny; nobody, or almost nobody, merely waits for it to overtake him. That is the Old Man's trouble in *At the Hawk's Well*. In fact, in proportion to their length, a great deal happens. Consider the many shifts and turns crowded into *The Death of Cuchulain*. Gourmont's description of the setting, with its emphasis on remoteness from the bustle and activity of the world and its suggestion of aristocratic isolation, is very appropriate to some of Yeats's plays, the less social ones, though his pastoral symbolism is more at home outdoors than in lamplit rooms. The idea of a group united by their waiting in common, however, won't fit Yeats at all. In his plays the crisis arises from and realizes itself in conflict, and victory—where there is victory—implies the recognition that, for better or worse, death is not final. No individual is complete in himself, neatly enclosed in the span between birth and death; in fact, Yeats's plays often suggest that the hero's true kinship is more "vertical" —closer to those before and after him, or outside time entirely—than it is "horizontal"—a sharing of the common lot of his contemporaries.

If his characters are uncertain about their goals or beliefs, what they are "listening" for, it is not because they are born sceptics but because the dialectic of action knocks one purpose against another, tests one faith against another. Life may present an immovable obstacle, but no Yeats hero or heroine is ever paralyzed by the thought of death. Nor do they ever pin their hopes on anything so insubstantial as a knock at the door. What they sacrifice is felt as a poignant loss—Emer's chance to be loved by Cuchulain is a good example—but they are convinced of the necessity for sacrifice by their vision of a more impressive demand on them than any who have not been vouchsafed such a vision will ever be able to understand. True, this vision is mysterious in the sense that its logic is absurd judged by the standards of common sense, for its principle of self-preservation assumes an immortal memory and values a life only as it connects with the greater life before and after itself, but the dramatic presentment of the vision is never obscure. It is exactly Yeats's point that any attempt to account for man's achievement as though he were a rational animal is bound to fail, and that—as the Greek discovers in *The Resurrection*—this failure will come as a dramatic shock when spiritual truth manifests itself. Nothing could be more deeply implanted in our heritage than the ideas and feelings at the core of these plays; their strangeness lies in the way a distant and savage primitivism is intertwined with an intellectually subtle and emotionally sophisticated civilization.

Their weaknesses are not a result of too great preciousness—the more *avant-garde* plays are the strongest—but of a hesitancy (which Yeats overcame the older he grew) to allow full expression to the rougher and wilder aspects of human nature. The tougher the action and the language of his plays became, the greater became his skill at formal control of structure. *Cathleen ni Houlihan* is a skillful and successful play, but once the occasion of its excitement is gone, it seems a mere literary exercise compared to *A Full Moon in March*. And *On Baile's Strand*, for all its very considerable power and charm, has an antiquated air compared with the gripping immediacy of *Purgatory*. As a Symbolist, Yeats is closer to Beckett than he is to Maeterlinck, but he is not very close to either. He resisted the rarefication of their art, preferring a well-defined action to the evocation of a state of soul and the traditional matter of Ireland to the invention of "international" fairy tales or fables. Though he shared their dislike of the didactic and argumentative theater, his characters often act out of strong moral conviction, and his plays are never empty of ideas.

When in his seventies Yeats was asked to give a broadcast for the BBC on modern poetry, he responded with an idiosyncratic address revelatory of his keen awareness of new directions and his blunt hostility to their significance. It was obvious that he preferred the poetry that had been modern when he was a young man to the work of Eliot and his successors, and yet he had to admit the "satiric intensity" of this new force. What he disliked was the poet's willing immersion in the "destructive element" his poetry was ostensibly mocking. For Yeats, even to borrow the voice and manner of a Prufrock as a dramatic strategy would seem an impossible belittling of the poet's own dignity, as though such an imaginative exercise in vulgarity could not help rubbing off on one who indulged in such practices.

The disillusion brought about by the first world war was something he could share to a degree; what he could not accept (nor of course could Eliot) was acquiescence to a whimpering world in which the artist devoted himself to an accurate projection of nervous instability and intellectual paralysis. If it was true that the best lacked all conviction and the worst were full of a passionate intensity (a statement about which Eliot in his turn would have had some qualifications), the proper response was to offer the best model of passionate intensity in the service of a conviction capable of withstanding the corrosive effects of the world's harsh weather. One could escape to the balmier climate of a poet's utopia, or one could confront the cynicism and opportunism of the age with an aggressive arrogance fortified by one's sense of superiority, and Yeats tried both. As he gained self-confidence he acquired the freedom to practice the "recklessness" he had poetically advocated in his youth, and the plaintive tone often heard in his early work was replaced by a sterner note. He expressed his scorn for what he hated with an open brutality sometimes bordering on callousness, but the strength of his feeling for friends, for beautiful things and gallant actions, for his country, and for the unconquerable spirit of humanity, and his ability to make memorable words carry that strength saved him from becoming a hard old man isolated in his inhumanity. He successfully resisted the mechanical substitute for a quick imagination, the kind of mechanism represented by rhetoric, abstraction, or rationalism that he had fought all his life.

Believing like most poets that the past is our only key to understanding the present, he differed from many of his contemporaries in England and Europe in finding usable a more primitive and distant past than they did. In spite of the high literary gloss in many of his longer poems and plays, something naive, something imaginatively closer to the fall of man, is evident under the surface. Perhaps this is a matter of the single-minded concentration on a few themes and of the childlike self-consciousness of those large-scale men and women whose happiness or misery so transparently depends on the satisfaction of clear and distinct desires. For the subtlety lies all in the allusive and evocative language, not in the complexity of character or situation. Yeats is the only complex character in his own work. The people in his plays have no nagging little worries, no concern over their appearances, no baffling problems in trying to ferret out the truth about other people's motives; only an obsession with one big question on which all their interests and energies are focussed. The suspense is as lucidly defined as in any TV Western.

The relevance of the plays to the modern theater depends on the validity of Yeats's "gamble"—that mythological truth is timeless and that its showing forth, its epiphany, is intrinsically dramatic. Lacking the sophistication of the French symbolists or the interest in period styles of a Hofmannsthal, Yeats neither abandoned all moorings in external reality nor attempted the task of authentic historical reconstruction. He used the speech and scenery and lore of Ireland to set his (usually) tragic scene in all but a few plays; but these backgrounds are highly stylized and theatrical. In the *Plays for Dancers* and in other plays both earlier and later the verse does the main job of creating the scene, and the scene is indispensable for placing character in the right relation to country and nature, but the most important effect of the setting is putting the audience at the ideal psychological distance from the action. We are to open the window of our mind on a scene that will, ideally, be like a reminiscence of something familiar, though we cannot recall ever having known it before. A knowledge of Irish history and legend will be neither a sufficient nor necessary cause of our understanding; this country of the mind is open to anyone who has the poetic habit of allowing the inchoate impulses of the soul to take on shape and sound in forms shared by many ancient mythologies.

The difficulty arises from the intellect, for in spite of Yeats's emphasis in his theory of drama on the sharing of a common emotion, these plays are not tales retold for children (though we do well not to forget their kinship with such tales). Part of their power comes from their trenchant, if oblique, commentary on ideas we must test against the experience of our adult lives. If these plays never tell us how, or whether, to vote in the next election, they nevertheless *do* tell us that the quality of our lives depends on the interior landscapes that furnish our minds, that the shock of new ideas may effect great changes in us, that the preservation of civilization may well hinge on the proper ordering of our instinctive energies in accordance with a traditional decorum. (About this last possibility Yeats seemed to grow ever more pessimistic.) The motto for all his plays might be: "How but in custom and in ceremony/ Are innocence and beauty born?" *

All very well, but we have our lives to live. Even to fellow Irishmen, or perhaps especially to them, the theater of Yeats must often have seemed an imposition: who was he to be telling them, in poetic parable, that most of them were blind men or fools? At least Synge, and later

* From "A Prayer for My Daughter," *Collected Poems*, p. 187.

O'Casey, gave them things to laugh at, and characters to hate or love. Why put up with Yeats's pet fantasies, beautiful poetry though they might be? And then there was hardly time to get a grip on the thing before the play was over anyhow. It was not surprising that Holloway could say, "Yeats spells empty houses." [2] *Our* problem with the plays is rather different. They come from a famous poet, and undoubtedly this gives them a special interest, but in a curious way it works to their disadvantage too. The great lyrics have the quality of personal utterance. In "The Second Coming," "Sailing to Byzantium," and "Among School Children," for instance, immense vistas are opened up in terms of dramatized autobiography. We need know nothing of Yeats's private, or even public, life to grasp the fact that here is a thoroughly contemporary voice speaking to the twentieth-century sensibility. In the plays, however, where the author divides himself up among a number of figures, none of which provides a mask nearly so complex or interesting as the poet himself, and where ancient story and esoteric doctrine seem to require us to be bemused and alert, intuitive and intellectual, at one and the same moment, we may well find an adequate response more difficult. Yet the plays are, I think, almost as impressive an achievement as the poems. They do not neatly fit into any genre; they are uneasy on the stage; but they are truly dramatic and truly poetic and, in the final analysis, truly modern.

Or at least they become more modern as Yeats grows older. Yeats's old-fashioned liking for characters who command authority by some grace or power of personality, who are heroes or heroines (or villains) in the old roman-

[2] Greene and Stephens, *Synge* (New York, 1959), p. 226.

tic sense, and for sentiments expressive of a concern for personal dignity and magnanimity on the part of the strong for those dependent on them is much in evidence from *Countess Cathleen* through *The Green Helmet,* nor are these predilections entirely absent in the later plays, though there is seldom leisure for their indulgence because the conflicts are further advanced or more narrowly focussed. Emer in *The Only Jealousy* can think only whether or not she will use the unwanted power she has to save Cuchulain at almost unbearable cost to herself; she is not offered Deirdre's opportunity to revenge herself on her enemy and make an open triumph of her own death. In general, the climaxes of the later plays bring a shattering enlightenment but no chance for a liberating action. The "stories" are not noticeably more modern, with one or two exceptions; the psychological tension is. From *At the Hawk's Well* to *The Death of Cuchulain* the meaning of what they are doing becomes more ambiguous for the characters themselves and has less to do with their conscious intentions. Heroic purpose may still be proclaimed with something of the old bravado and eloquence, but we are made aware of the murky depths "where all the ladders start,/ In the foul rag-and-bone shop of the heart." Unlike Strindberg in his *A Dream Play,* for instance, Yeats does not translate what might be "real life" episodes into symbols of unconscious strife; instead he suggests the aptitude of myth for throwing light on our contemporary preoccupations.

One poetic advantage of his method is that while sex and violence, alienation and madness are unmistakably *there,* so are the splendors of human achievement, those aristocratic sublimations of our natural barbarism which help us maintain our human dignity in the midst of despair. We feel the resistance to chaos and degradation all the more strongly as the danger of collapse grows more imminent. The old Cuchulain in Yeats's play refuses to accept his young mistress's confession of treachery. He will not alter his course through fear or favor of anyone. "I make the truth!" he proudly declares. And when Aoife, the mother of the son he killed on Baile's Strand, recounts how she hated Cuchulain because he had overcome and then left her, and yet she hunted him out and begot a son, Cuchulain replies, "I cannot understand." Since early boyhood Cuchulain has always had his troubles with women, and the bewildering ambivalence of the two women here, the young and the old, will be the death of him! And yet there is a further irony: Aoife retreats when the blind beggar-man comes in, to cut off the hero's head for the twelve-penny reward he has been promised. Everything and everyone conspires to bring Cuchulain down: *he* is certain that his head will sing. *The Death of Cuchulain* is not a pretty play—it has a kind of summary jaggedness. Yet its peremptory tone does not preclude an austere majesty reminiscent of the epitaph Yeats composed for himself.

At the end of his life Yeats proudly accepted what at the moment seemed like defeat. The theater had gone his way no more than history had. He wondered if he had been right in giving so much of his time to other men's work. He was shocked by a play which "displayed a series of bare actions without anything to show that its author disapproved or expected us to do so . . . The wicked should be punished, the innocent rewarded, marriage bells sound for no evil man, unless an author calls his characters

before a more private tribunal and has so much intellect
and culture that we respect it as though it were our own."
Thus Jonson does not reward the young people with marriage in *Volpone*, "and this excites us because it makes us
share in Jonson's cold implacability."[3] If Yeats was still
old-fashioned in ethical matters, he was equally so in his
insistence on the primacy of action over thought. And he
cites as examples Odysseus, Don Quixote, Hamlet, Lear,
Faust, remarking, "we are not coherent to ourselves
through thought but because our visible image changes
slowly." Hamlet's hesitations are a matter of thought;
"outside that he is a mediaeval man of action." Yeats puts
his trust in action for an interesting reason: "Our bodies
are nearer to our coherence because nearer to the 'unconscious' than our thought."[4] He is objecting to an art
where understanding depends entirely on arriving at opinions. Despite everything, however, he felt his lot had been
a fortunate one.

Then I say to myself, I have had greater luck than any other
modern English-speaking dramatist; I have aimed at tragic
ecstasy and here and there in my own work and in the work
of my friends I have seen it greatly played. What does it
matter that it belongs to a dead art and to a time when a man
spoke out of an experience and a culture that were not of his
time alone, but held his time, as it were, at arm's length, that he
might be a spectator of the ages. I am haunted by certain
moments: Miss O'Neill in the last act of Synge's "Deirdre"
"Stand a little further off with the quarrelling of fools"; Kerrigan and Miss O'Neill playing in a private house that scene
in Augusta Gregory's "Full Moon" where the young mad

3 *On the Boiler* (Dublin, [1939]), pp. 32–33.
4 *Ibid.*, p. 34.

people in their helpless joy sing "The boys of Queen Anne"; Frank Fay's entrance in the last act of "The Well of the Saints"; William Fay at the end of "On Baile's Strand"; Mrs. Patrick Campbell in my "Deirdre," passionate and solitary; and in later years that great artist Ninette de Valois in "Fighting the Waves." These things will, it may be, haunt me on my deathbed: what matter if the people prefer another art, I have had my fill.[5]

His arrogant assurance that his is a generally "dead art" firmly places him as a modern artist. And time may prove that his drama partakes of that immortality he so obviously and ardently desired for it.

[5] *Ibid.*, p. 14.

Index

(*The Collected Plays* is not included in the index.)

Masks of Love and Death

Designed by R. E. Rosenbaum.
Composed by Vail-Ballou Press, Inc.,
in 11 point linotype Janson, 3 points leaded,
with display lines in monotype Janson.
Printed letterpress from type by Vail-Ballou Press
on Warren's 1854 Text, 60 lb. basis
with the Cornell University Press watermark.
Bound by Vail-Ballou Press
in Columbia Milbank Linen
and stamped in All Purpose foil.